MODERN LEGAL

LAW, LEGITIMACY
AND THE
CONSTITUTION

Essays marking the Centenary of
Dicey's *Law of the Constitution*

AUSTRALIA AND NEW ZEALAND
The Law Book Company Ltd.
Sydney : Melbourne : Perth

CANADA AND U.S.A.
The Carswell Company Ltd.
Agincourt, Ontario

INDIA
N. M. Tripathi Private Ltd.
Bombay
and
Eastern Law House Private Ltd.
Calcutta and Delhi
M.P.P. House
Bangalore

ISRAEL
Steimatzky's Agency Ltd.
Jerusalem : Tel Aviv : Haifa

MALAYSIA : SINGAPORE : BRUNEI
Malayan Law Journal (Pte.) Ltd.
Singapore

PAKISTAN
Pakistan Law House
Karachi

MODERN LEGAL STUDIES

LAW, LEGITIMACY AND THE CONSTITUTION

Essays marking the Centenary of
Dicey's *Law of the Constitution*

Edited by

Patrick McAuslan
Professor of Law, University of Warwick

and

John F. McEldowney
Lecturer in Law, University of Warwick

LONDON
SWEET & MAXWELL
1985

Published in 1985 by
Sweet & Maxwell Limited of
11 New Fetter Lane, London
Computerset by MFK Typesetting Limited
of Saffron Walden, Essex.
Printed in Scotland.

British Library Cataloguing in Publication Data

Law, legitimacy and the constitution: essays
  marking the centenary of Dicey's Law of the
  constitution. — (Modern legal studies)
  1. Great Britain — Constitutional law
  I. McAuslan, J.P.W.B.   II. McEldowney, John F.
  III. Series
  344.102   KD3989

  ISBN 0-421-33120-8
  ISBN 0-421-33130-5 Pbk

PREFACE

1985 sees the hundredth anniversary of the publication of Dicey's *Introduction to the Study of the Law of the Constitution* and as its long title indicates, this book is intended to mark that anniversary. That is not its only purpose however; it is intended too as a contribution to the growing debate on the state and the constitution of the United Kingdom and the stresses and strains to which both are being subjected, but at a more general and theoretical level than lawyers are wont to essay. It seemed to all of us that law students—and this is pre-eminently a book for students—ought to be expected to grapple with fundamental issues of law and state in a course on constitutional law and that other students—of political science, public administration, policy studies, government—ought too to have the opportunity to get to grips with constitutional issues during the course of their studies. The book then does not set out to be a textbook but to be a book to stimulate an awareness of issues, problems and ways of analysing and approaching them in the broad field of law, state and government. It will achieve its purpose to the extent that students who read it are better able to understand and comment on the evolving British Constitution.

As editors we would like to thank all our contributors who have written for us for doing so both ably and promptly and thereafter for sticking to a tight timetable for proof-reading so that the book could come out in 1985. We would like to thank our publishers for the speed and efficiency with which they processed the manuscript, and our secretaries Margaret Wright and Sally Venables for their unflagging efforts using old and new technologies—typing, word processing and copying—to get materials ready for us and the publishers.

Patrick McAuslan
John F. McEldowney

University of Warwick
Coventry.
June 1985

CONTENTS

THE AUTHORS

Patrick McAuslan was a founder member of and has been a Professor of Law at the University of Warwick since 1972, and General Editor of Modern Legal Studies since its inception in 1969. His main fields of interest are public law, urban development and law, and law and the developing world. He has written *Public Law and Political Change in Kenya* (1970 with Professor Y. P. Ghai); *Land, Law and Planning* (1975); *The Ideologies of Planning Law* (1980) and *Urban Land and Shelter for the Poor* (1985). He has co-edited *Urban Legal Problems in Eastern Africa* (1978 with G. W. Kanyeihamba) and *Lord Denning, The Judge and the Law* (Sweet & Maxwell, 1984 with Professor J. L. Jowell). He is the co-editor of *Urban Law and Policy*. He is at present engaged in a study of the current crisis of the British Constitution.

John McEldowney is a Lecturer in Law at the University of Warwick. He has researched and written on Irish legal history, constitutional law and history. He is editing a book of essays on Irish legal history with Professor Paul O'Higgins to be published in 1986. He is currently researching the work of the Comptroller and Auditor General and the National Audit Office.

Carol Harlow is a Lecturer in Law at the London School of Economics and Political Science. Her interests are in the fields of tort and public law, with a special interest in the problems of disadvantaged groups in society.

Martin Loughlin is a Lecturer in Law at the London School of Economics and Political Science. He previously taught at the University of Warwick and Osgoode Hall Law School, York University, Toronto and in 1982/83 was Visiting Fellow at the School for Advanced Urban Studies, University of Bristol. He is a co-editor (with David Gelfand and Ken Young) of *Half a Century of Municipal Decline 1935–1985* (Allen & Unwin, 1985) and his *Local Government in the Modern State* will be published by Sweet & Maxwell in 1986.

Norman Lewis is Professor of Public Law at the University of Sheffield where he is Director of the Centre for Criminological and Socio-Legal Studies. He has engaged in broad-ranging empirical research, mainly concerning areas on the law and government interface. He has recently co-authored a book on the Rule of Law and the British Constitution and is currently engaged in research concerned with constitutional law reform.

Laurence Lustgarten is a Senior Lecturer in Law at the University of Warwick. He is author of *Legal Control of Racial Discrimination* and numerous articles concerning various aspects of public law. He is presently completing a book on *The Governance of the Police* to be published by Sweet & Maxwell in 1986. His main interests are public law, discrimination and social welfare with particular interest in their comparative dimensions.

Patrick Birkinshaw lectures at the University of Hull in public law and jurisprudence. His research interests include all aspects of public law and he has published work on central government, local government, freedom of information and prison administration. His publications include: *Grievances, Remedies and the State* (Sweet & Maxwell, 1985); *Open Government, Freedom of Information and Local Government* (Law Society, Local Government Group, 1985); and *Prisoners' Rights* (ed. with Jeremy McBridge, Legal Action Group, 1986). He is a member of the Legal Action Group's Prisoners' Rights Group and is working with Norman Lewis and Ian Harden on an E.S.R.C. funded project: *Corporatism and Accountability*.

Tony Prosser is a Lecturer in Law at the Centre for Criminological and Socio-Legal Studies, University of Sheffield. His current teaching interests are public law and law and social policy. He is currently working on *Nationalised Industries and Public Control*, to be published by Basil Blackwell in Spring 1986.

Martin Partington is Professor of Law and Dean of the Faculty of Social Sciences at Brunel University. He has written extensively on housing law and social security law. The research in which the chapter in this volume is based was undertaken during a period as Visiting Professor at the University of New South Wales, in 1983.

TABLE OF CASES

TABLE OF STATUTES

Chapter 1

LEGITIMACY AND THE CONSTITUTION: THE DISSONANCE BETWEEN THEORY AND PRACTICE

PATRICK MCAUSLAN AND JOHN F. MCELDOWNEY

Mr. Clive Ponting's acquittal by a jury in February 1985, after he had admitted to passing official Government papers to a person not authorised to receive them, the very essence of section 2 of the Official Secrets Act 1911, and despite the most explicit summing up by the trial judge that they should convict, raises the question of what motivated the jury. It would suggest that when faced with a choice between a case which rested on constitutional theories about limited government derived from a "higher law" which controlled what government could legitimately do, and a case which rested on actual practices of government bolstered by actual law, the jury preferred the theory of what the constitution ought to be to the practice of what it is.[1] Little wonder that, as one newspaper put it, Ministers were aghast at the verdict.[2] The *Concise Oxford Dictionary* defines "aghast" as meaning terrified. This essay will seek to show Ministers would indeed have good reason to be terrified if ordinary people began preferring constitutional theory to government practice and acted on their preferences in their judgment of politicians. More particularly the jury's verdict in the Ponting trial may be seen then as the response of ordinary people to trends in government practices which seem to them to be, in perhaps indefinable ways, wrong.

The essays in this book develop the theme that current government practices are a major contributory factor to what, without over-exaggeration, may be called an incipient crisis in our constitution. The origin of the essays was a desire to mark the 100th anniversary of the publication of Dicey's *Introduction to the Study of the Law of the Constitution*. The theme of the essays was to be representation and democracy and was to discuss the contribution which public lawyers could make to those issues. These particular issues were chosen as being both central to British Parliamentary democracy and as providing a link to some of the underlying issues which concerned Dicey; the fundamental principles behind a system of limited government.

[1] C. Ponting, *The Right to Know* (Sphere, London, 1985), Chaps 6 and 7.
[2] *Daily Telegraph*, February 12, 1985.

As the essays were written, the fundamental issue of limited government began to be presented in a different way. As noted above,
lawyers were becoming aware of an incipient crisis in our constitutional
arrangements, a crisis that goes beyond the usual fare of late twentieth
century constitutional debate:—devolution, redress of grievances
against the state, Bills of Rights, the effectiveness of Parliament, etc.,
to an issue underlying all these topics. This is the issue of legitimacy—
whether the Government correctly exercises power and the arrangements governing that exercise of power in the United Kingdom. The
issue of legitimacy goes to the heart of any debate on constitutions and
the exercise of power. It seems desirable that this essay, rather than
providing a commentary on all the essays which come after it,
addresses this central issue of legitimacy, and why lawyers are concerned about the issue now.[3]

---

[3] In the limited space available for an essay it is not possible both to discuss in detail
the concept of legitimacy and the current concerns about and the performance of
governments in the U.K. in the last decade. We have opted to concentrate on the
latter. A brief note on the former is in order here. According to Schaar the older
definitions of legitimacy concentrated on "the element of law or right and rest the
force of a claim . . . upon foundations external to and independent of the mere
assertion or opinion of the claimant . . . . Thus a claim to political power is
legitimate only when the claimant can invoke some source of authority beyond or
above himself" J. H. Schaar, "Legitimacy in the Modern State," in *Legitimacy
and the State* (Connolly ed., Oxford, 1984), p. 108, *i.e.* by a constitution which
prescribes how a political leader shall be selected. Legitimacy here appears to be
similar to Hart's rule of recognition and Kelson's Grundnorm and would pose few
problems in states which have a long period of constitutional stability. It is
otherwise in many new states where constitutions are overthrown or altered by
means not recognised in those constitutions. For some legal discussions of these
issues, see de Smith, "Constitutional Lawyers in Revolutionary Situations" [1968]
Western Ontario L.Rev. 93, McAuslan, "Now we are six: first steps in the Law of
African Commonwealth Revolutions," paper given at African Studies Centre
Seminar Edinburgh 1970.
   More recent definitions dissolve legitimacy into belief or opinion. If a people
holds the belief that existing institutions are "appropriate" or "morally proper"
then those institutions are legitimate (Schaar, p. 108). Popular opinion determines legitimacy and that legitimacy is "a function of the system's ability to
persuade members [of a society] of its own appropriateness" (Schaar, p. 109). We
agree with Schaar that this is not a satisfactory definition of legitimacy. We agree
with Freidrich's approach which stresses that legitimacy revolves around the
question of the right or title to rule (Schaar, p. 109) but goes beyond mere legal
rights or entitlements. These are, particularly in the U.K., which has no written
constitution, issues of moral or ethical entitlement, issues of the ends for which
power is used and issues of the means or procedures by which power is used. There
are in short political issues in legitimacy, perhaps best highlighted by Habermas in
his essay in the same volume as Schaar—"What does a Legitimation Crisis mean
today? Legitimation problems in late capitalism," pp. 134–155. We deliberately
concentrate in this essay on certain governmental practices and on relations
between the executive and other organs of government because that was Dicey's

To adapt John Stuart Mill's famous aphorism, lawyers did not wake up on a summer morning and find the issue of legitimacy sprung up.[4] To explain why it is an issue now, a necessarily brief comment on the growth of government since the first edition of Dicey's *Law of the Constitution* and of legal reaction to this growth, must be given to provide the historical context for current concerns.

In the last 100 years the activities of government have rapidly expanded. In addition to the traditional areas of defence of the realm and foreign affairs, the administration of law and order and the protection of private property, there is now a concern for or at least heavy involvement in the economic and social welfare of the nation as a whole and of individual citizens. Even the scope of the traditional areas has expanded. International trade and financial issues now dominate foreign affairs, while the police, the courts and the various programmes for dealing with those convicted by the courts have all grown. The administration of law and order is now a major industry. The protection of private property, once largely left to the police and civil and criminal action in the courts, has now been transformed out of recognition by the plethora of programmes, agencies and laws designed to protect the citizen in his or her every contact with property, both real and personal.

Increased activities of government have meant increased powers for government. In the last few years of the "Dicey" century, the impact of the technological and information revolution has begun to make its presence felt in the area of government power. Quite apart from the traditional and public means whereby governments confer power on themselves and their agencies and quangos; legislation via Act of Parliament or statutory instruments or exercise powers—via the royal prerogative—governmental power has been further and greatly increased. The acquisition of new machines has in a sense meant that governments are now in a position to know more about, do more to and interfere more with the activities of the citizen than ever before. There is correspondingly less effective controls on these hidden but enormous powers. Much of the constitutional history of the last 100 years can be seen in terms of large and often hastily formulated accretions of governmental power, followed usually some way behind by attempts to control the power. These attempts are often preceded

focus and the focus of these essays, and because we consider that it is these practices, more than the underlying problems discussed by Habermas which are causing a wide range of people to be concerned about the crisis in our Constitution.

[4] J. S. Mill, *Representative Government* (London, 1865), p. 4 quoted in W. I. Jennings, *The Law and the Constitution* (5th ed. London, 1959), p. 80.

by a committee of inquiry whose report urging a range of controls is rarely accepted in full.

So much is well known. But while the trend of developments has been in one direction only—more governmental power, proportionally less effective controls on that power—legal interest in and concern about these developments has waxed and waned both at the level of practice and at the level of comment and discussion. Dicey's concern in his 1915 article "The Development of Administrative Law in England"[5] drew attention both to the fact that:

> " . . . since the beginning of the twentieth century, the nation as represented in Parliament has undertaken to perform the [sic] large number of duties with which before the Reform Act 1832, no English Government had any concern whatever"

and to the fact that the courts were developing and

> "will always find the means for correcting the injustice, if demonstrated, of any exercise by a Government department of judicial or quasi-judicial authority."

His optimism on the effectiveness of courts—an optimism made the more necessary by his ideological position on the central role of ordinary courts in preserving "that rule of law which is fatal to the existence of true *droit administratif*"[6]—would not be shared by the contributors to this volume, but at least Dicey's prescience pointed to developments with which lawyers ought to be or to become concerned.

With some notable exceptions, this concern did not manifest itself for many years. Lawyers generally acted as if Dicey was right in his belief that the ordinary courts would always find means for correcting injustices, "if demonstrated." The reach of government—central, local and quangos—continued to grow between the two World Wars, during the Second World War, and afterwards, with the creation of the Welfare State. Yet there was no general perception on the part of lawyers that this rapid growth in governmental power called for some fundamental re-thinking about the role of law, the courts, the creation of new agencies to administer new programmes of social or economic welfare or to provide redress where administrators had made mistakes.

In the 40 years from Dicey's article on administrative law, the courts made little progress in evolving a judge-made administrative law, and the publicists and academics followed suit. Port, whose volume on

---

[5] (1915) 31 L.Q.R. 148. The essay is reprinted in the 10th ed. of Dicey, *Law of the Constitution* (E. C. S. Wade ed., London, 1959) in App. 2 at pp. 493–499. The quotations are at pp. 495 and 498.
[6] At p. 499.

administrative law published in 1931 never went to a second edition, Robson[7] and Jennings[8] in the 1930s, Carr[9] and Lord Denning[10] in the 1940s, and Griffith and Street whose first edition of *Administrative Law* was published in 1951 were virtually the only legal writers in that period who perceived that the growth of public administration was necessarily giving birth to an administrative law and bringing about changes in the balance of power and forces in our constitutional arrangements.

The turning points in judicial, official and academic legal perception of the problems of administrative and governmental power came in the period of the late Fifties and early Sixties. Three seminal events may be mentioned. First, there was the publication of the Report of the Committee on Administrative Tribunals and Enquiries,[11] the Franks Report, in 1957. It is still, almost 30 years later, the most frequently referred to guide and standard-setter for good administrative practices. Secondly, the publication in 1959 of the first edition of de Smith's *Judicial Review of Administrative Action* brought scholarship of a high order to and clarified principles in a subject which to that point lacked and needed both. Thirdly, in the courts, the decision of the House of Lords in *Ridge* v. *Baldwin* in 1963[12] heralded the start of a more active and creative phase in judicial review of administrative action.

Like all turning points, these events and this period can only now, in retrospect, be seen to be so significant. At the same time as highlighting these peaks of achievement, however, it would be misleading to suggest or imply either that there was no movement or thinking going on before the late Fifties or that in this period, these were the only notable achievements. Developments in official, judicial or academic legal thinking for the most part build on the past and make incremental rather than revolutionary steps forward. But when all allowances are made for these points, one can, quite fairly, talk of a pre- and post-Franks Report approach to tribunals, enquiries and public administration generally, and a pre- and post- *Ridge* v. *Baldwin* era in judicial review of administrative action. The same is arguable for the academic legal world's approach to public law pre- and post- de Smith as well. That is the measue of the achievement of these three events.

From the Fifties and Sixties, and over the last two decades, there has been a continuous stream of cases in the courts; official and semi-

---

[7] W. A. Robson, *Justice and Administrative Law* (1st ed., 1928).

[8] W. I. Jennings, *The Law and the Constitution* (1st ed., 1933).

[9] C. T. Carr, *Concerning English Administrative Law* (1941).

[10] See Alfred Denning, *Freedom under the Law* (Hamlyn Lectures 1st Series), especially Lectures 3 and 4 (London, 1949).

[11] Cmnd. 218.

[12] [1964] A.C. 40.

official reports on aspects of governmental power and how it might be more adequately controlled by Parliament or other specially created agencies; a growth of select committees in Parliament; legislation establishing controlling devices—Ombudsmen and the like; and publications by legal and other academics on all these matters. If, at first, academic lawyers tended to write about the activities of the courts and saw the developing area of public law too much in terms of judicial decisions abstracted from the substantive areas of law those decisions arose out of, and ignored the wider world of social science scholarship, by the beginning of the 1980s, that too was changing as these essays testify. The issues raised in the essays are for the most part discussed and discussable without reference to cases; where cases are discussed they are placed firmly in their political and social context. The authors clearly display a familiarity with a wider range of scholarship than the purely legal and many of them "move outwards" from a specific area of legal or socio-/politico-/economic-legal concern to the general issues which the specific appears to highlight.

All this might seem to suggest that the concerns displayed in these essays with the legitimacy of government and its exercise of power is no more than lawyers catching up or keeping up with intellectual fashions. As other social scientists have begun to turn their attention to questions of legitimacy in the last decade or so—of the collection of 11 papers in Connolly's *Legitimacy and the State,* published in 1984, all bar two—by Marx and Weber—are from the last two decades and four are from the 1980s—it was, it can be argued, only to be expected that eventually lawyers would turn their attention to this issue.

It would be idle to pretend that intellectual fashion does not play a part in the funding and production of academic research and writing, but that is at best only a very partial explanation of the widespread concern, in political and other social science literature, for legitimacy. More to the point is the evidence of disaffection for government and the constitutional system that sustains it apparent in many countries of Western Europe over the last two decades. This manifests itself in violence, as in Northern Ireland, and the separatist movements in Spain, France (Corsica), Belgium (between Flemish and Walloon speaking parts of the country); and urban riots as in England. Another manifestation is aggressive and sometimes violent demonstrations and campaigning against specific government policies—nuclear energy in particular, but also policies of economic retrenchment which leave whole communities without work and without hope of work—coal and steel workers in England and France are particular examples of this; and in voting patterns in elections when parties whose raison d'être is disaffection with the existing system, achieve striking results; the

Greens in Western Germany and the new Fascistic Right in France are the best examples.

In so far as there is one underlying reason for all these different manifestations of disaffection, we suggest it lies in the increasing gap between the ideology and public posturing of governments in Western Europe and their performance in practice; between on the one hand the rhetoric of democracy, of even-handed administration, and of equal opportunities for all, and on the other the increasing centralisation and insensitivity of public administration, the unevenness of the distribution of the costs and benefits of economic growth and, increasingly, contraction, and the ever faster build up of military might and the cost that that is imposing on basic health and welfare programmes.

Nowhere in Western Europe or indeed in the "West" (as opposed to the Eastern bloc or the South) is this gap between rhetoric and reality more evident now than in the United Kingdom. It is no surprise that lawyers whose main area of concern is public law and who now as a matter of course regard the world (and literature) of politics, policy-making and public administration as being part of their domain of concern, should begin to comment on this gap and the implications that it has for the future of our constitutional system. But we would claim that the matter goes more deeply than that. We would locate a specifically legal concern with questions of legitimacy to a perception by legal observers, both academic and in practice, of the increasing use of governmental power and law for partisan ends, the increasingly aggressive manner in which this power is exercised, and the increasingly casual way in which the legal framework for and legal controls on the exercise of power are being treated. This in turn is generating opposition, not merely to a particular exercise of power or a particular law or proposal for a law, while it is in the process of being enacted which is the usual role of opposition in a parliamentary democracy, but to the institutions which exercise power, make and enforce the law and to instruments of power themselves—Parliament, the courts, and Acts of Parliament. What is being perceived then is a crisis in the living constitution. The rules and principles taken so much for granted, that for many years they have not been thought worth discussing in the legal literature are being ignored, or subverted by those who claim, or are generally expected, to uphold them.

These are strong words and they must be justified. We will attempt to do so by contrasting what is implicit or explicit in the essays here and in many writings of lawyers and political scientists since Dicey produced his *Law of the Constitution*—which contained the assumed fundamentals of the constitution—with practices over the last six to ten years. It is the contention of this essay that it is the growing dissonance between these fundamental principles and political practices that is giving rise to a crisis in constitutional legitimacy. This form of legitimacy crisis is at least as serious as one which arises out of disaffection borne of contrasting the promise with the performance of government.

First then, what is or are the fundamental principle or principles of the British constitution, implicit in Dicey's and much other writing on the constitution? It is, *au fond,* the principle of limited government, government limited both in what it can do and how it can do it. In many countries, the United States is probably the best known example, limitations on governmental power are enshrined in a written constitution and enforced by a Constitutional or Supreme Court or Commission. This is not the case in the United Kingdom. Here limited government is very much auto-limitation, bolstered, it is true by conventions, but these are not enforceable by bodies external to the government of the day.

Auto-limitation means in essence that governments recognise that there are some actions either legislative or administrative they should not take, and some ways of exercising power they should not adopt. These off-limit actions and methods of exercising power would be those which would tend to detract from such political, legislative, administrative, or judicial checks as there are on government. The abolition or curtailment of elections, the abolition or drastic curtailment of the powers of one or both Houses of Parliament, the expropriation of property without either hearing before or compensation after the act of expropriation, the abolition or curtailment of access to courts and other grievance-handling devices are all examples of matters which it would be perfectly lawful to bring about by Act of Parliament but which would generally be thought to offend against the principle of limited government.

In a democracy such as the United Kingdom, any description of the operation of the concept of limited government which left out of account political actors and factors would be misleading. In addition to the self-imposed non-exercise of powers which it would be lawful to exercise, there are political checks on government. These are of various kinds; elected local governments, of which at any one time, many are controlled by the political party or parties not in power in central government; major national representative pressure groups and associations such as the CBI, the TUC, the NFU are the best examples. Virtually every matter or subject over which governments exercise or are contemplating exercising some power will have a pressure group with a point of view which even if ignored in official consultation will find other outlets through which to try and influence governments.

Then there are the multiplicity of quagos and quangos. Many of these are created by governments; they may be executive bodies, advisory bodies, bodies concerned with the redress of grievances or the amelioration of particular social or economic conditions; or bodies whose functions it is to administer on behalf of the central government certain programmes—*e.g.* the National Health Service administered by Regional and District Health Authorities—whose size and complexity make a fully centralised system of administration impractical. While the membership of quangos is predominantly appointive by central government, practice over the years, together with the perceived desirability of ensuring that they are broadly acceptable to the areas, people and institutions they are to be involved with and that continuity of policy and administration is encouraged, has tended to ensure that a mixture of people—not all of them members of, sympathisers with or contributors to the finances of the ruling political party—are appointed to these bodies. There is here a close relationship between the political and these more administrative factors, for the practice of seeking the view of representative pressure groups, local authority associations, advisory bodies and the like, before making appointments to quangos is a fairly standard one, and contributes to the continued influence of a wide variety of political, social and economic viewpoints on government. This in turn inevitably operates as an additional limitation or control on government.

A fairly standard line of justification for the maintenance of the existing constitutional arrangements in the United Kingdom is that there has in effect been substituted for a written constitution enforced by a Supreme Court, which limits what governments may do and how they may do it, a sophisticated arrangement of checks and balances, part legal through the activities of the ordinary courts, part constitutional convention, and part politico-administrative. These last are practices which while generally adhered to would not be thought of as being constitutional conventions. The system works and provides us with limited government because, so the argument runs, the actors in part perceive it to be in their own interests to work within and maintain such a system, and in part because the actors do actually believe in the system. That is, they believe in parliamentary democracy, in checks and balances, in limited government, and in Dicey's phrase, the rule of law.

Dicey's formulation of this fundamental principle of limited government was in the terms of a constitutional triptych; parliamentary sovereignty, the rule of law and constitutional conventions. Whatever the deficiencies in the details of his analysis or the political motives that drove him to produce the analysis,[13] one of its great strengths is that it

[13] As to which see McEldowney, Chap. 2, below.

immediately directs our attention to the overwhelming legal powers of a government via the actuality of parliamentary sovereignty. This overwhelming legal power is controlled, in practice, according to Dicey, by the rule of law and constitutional conventions. He gave both those controlling devices too much legal content trying thereby to show that there were effective legal checks on parliamentary sovereignty and political practices and policies of which he disapproved. Thirty years after the publication of the *Law of the Constitution* he was still urging the same point, contrasting in his article on administrative law, the "very feeble guarantee" which "so-called" ministerial responsibility provides against action which "evades the authority of the law courts" with the role "of ordinary law courts [to] deal with any actual or provable breach of the law committed by any servant of the Crown."[14] Partly because of his political beliefs and postures—fully discussed by John McEldowney in his essay—and partly because the modern administrative state was not yet fully developed when Dicey wrote, he either declined to accommodate or under-estimated the political and politico-administrative dimension to the checks on parliamentary sovereignty.

Thus too, he did not face up to the problems that might be posed if all these non-legally binding checks failed adequately to control the legal powers of government derived from a vigorous and literal use of the sovereignty of Parliament, accompanied by a claim that since the powers being exercised derived ultimately from law—either the royal prerogative or an Act of Parliament—what was being done was in accordance with the rule of law. Even the modern formulation of the requirements of limited government put forward by Norman Lewis— openness and accountability[15]—though admirable in themselves are also no more than political precepts—arguably no more than a modern formulation and expansion of the constitutional convention of ministerial responsibility derided even by Dicey 70 years ago—and depend upon the continuance of auto-limitation of power for their introduction or efficacy as the case may be.

To return to the principal matter under review here, that of the legitimacy of our constitutional arrangements, the issues at stake may now, hopefully, be better understood. An example of a clear case of an action which would be perceived as raising an issue as to the legitimacy of an institution of the constitution may be given by way of introduction. The House of Lords in its judicial capacity—the Appellate Committee of the House of Lords—consists of up to eleven Law Lords, judges appointed to their position by the Prime Minister on the advice

---

[14] *Op. cit.* p. 498.
[15] At pp. 115 *et seq., infra.*

of the Lord Chancellor. For more than 100 years the vast majority of the Law Lords have been either eminent practitioners elevated straight to that position—Lords Reid and Radcliffe are two post-Second World War examples of that—or judges who have served in the Court of Appeal and/or one of the divisions of the High Court or their Scottish equivalents and are generally considered to be good judges. The only statutory qualification for appointment is that an appointee must have held high judicial office for two years or be a barrister of 15 years standing. Thus it would be perfectly lawful, *i.e.* in accordance with the rule of law literally defined—for a Prime Minister to "pack" the House of Lords with M.P.s from his or her own party who were barristers of 15 years standing. A House of Lords so constituted could continue to hear appeals and give judgments; it too would be acting perfectly lawfully in so doing. But there would be a large question mark over the legitimacy of the House of Lords so constituted and over its judgments. It would be widely perceived as having been changed from a court, the highest court in the land, with all that that implies, or is popularly thought to imply, to a partisan arm of the government of the day, passing off political decisions as "judgments."

Legitimacy then does not deal so much with whether activities of government are lawful as whether they accord with what are generally perceived to be or what have for long been held up to be, the fundamental principles of the constitution according to which government is or ought to be conducted. Lawfulness is clearly an issue in so far as one of the fundamental principles of the British, no less than most other constitutions, is that government action should take place under the authority of, and in accordance with law—the narrow literal meaning of the rule of law—so that repeated unlawful actions or a perceived casualness towards the duty to comply with the law would in itself begin to raise doubts about the legitimacy of governmental action. The rule of law is generally thought to have a broader "political" meaning which covers the same ground as, if it is not quite synonymous with, the concept of limited government. This meaning embraces such matters as fair and equitable administrative practices; recognition of the rights of political opposition and dissent; complying with constitutional conventions; adequate means of redress of grievances about governmental action affecting one. Thus a government which while adhering to the rule of law narrowly defined, flouted all or most of the practices generally thought to be covered by the rule of law broadly defined would also give rise to doubts about its legitimacy. One of the clearest and best examples of a government on the whole scrupulous to comply with the rule of law narrowly defined yet consistently flouting it, as to the majority of its citizens, when broadly defined is the government of the Republic of South Africa, in relation to its non-white citizens.

What makes the issue of the legitimacy of our constitutional arrangements so problematic is the general open-endedness of those arrangements; that is, the difficulty of knowing whether a practice or non-practice is or is not constitutional. The example given above of "packing" the Appellate Committee of the House of Lords with overt political supporters of the ruling party was put forward as a clear example, yet 50 or 60 years ago it would not have been thought particularly remarkable for a Prime Minister to appoint known supporters of his party to the House of Lords or to do likewise with the office of Chief Justice. Scottish judicial appointments still are influenced by political considerations[16] and Northern Ireland by politico-religious.[17] Practices, in other words, change over time and may differ in different parts of the United Kingdom.

Even where practices may not differ over time, or place, there may be an inconsistency about them or a lack of knowledge about them, or a long-standing dispute about them, which could make it equally difficult to argue that following or not following a practice was or was not constitutional or legitimate. Probably the best example of this is the use of the royal prerogative, and the extent to which the courts may pass judgment on any particular use. Notwithstanding that the royal prerogative as a source of power for the government antedates Acts of Parliament, has been at the root of a civil war and a revolution in England and has been litigated about on countless major occasions in respect of its use both at home and overseas, its scope is still unclear as is the role of the courts in relation thereto. The use by the Prime Minister of powers under the royal prerogative to ban trade unions at the Government Communication Headquarters at Cheltenham in 1983 was contested both for its lawfulness—that is whether such powers could be used and if so whether they were used correctly—and also for its legitimacy—that is whether, even if the constitutional power existed, this was a proper and fair use of the power. It can be seen that questions of lawfulness and legitimacy shade into one another here though the answers do not: the lawfulness of the action taken, confirmed by the House of Lords in 1984[18] did not and does not dispose of its legitimacy.

The G.C.H.Q. case is valuable for another point. We have pointed out that lawfulness is not to be confused with legitimacy. No more is constitutionality. What the Prime Minister did was not merely lawful;

---

[16] S. A. de Smith, *Constitutional and Administrative Law* (4th ed., 1981), p. 367 n. 47.

[17] K. Boyle, T. Hadden, P. Hillyard, *Law and State; the case of Northern Ireland* (London, 1975), pp. 12–13.

[18] *Council of Civil Service Unions* v. *Minister for the Civil Service* [1984] 3 All E.R. 935.

she exercised the constitutional powers of her office in the way in which those powers had always been exercised. That is, the use of the royal prerogative as the legal backing for the management of the public service, the principle that a civil servant is a servant of the Crown and holds office at the pleasure of the Crown is one of the best known principles of constitutional law, hallowed by usage and sanctioned by the courts.[19] What is in issue from the perspective of legitimacy is whether the particular use made of that undoubted constitutional power, the manner of its use, and the justification both for the use and manner of use—that considerations of national security required both a banning of trade unions and no consultation with affected officers before the ban was announced—was a fair and reasonable use of power? Did it accord with legitimate expectations of fair and reasonable persons or was it a high-handed exercise of power of a kind more to be expected of an authoritarian government than one guided by and subscribing to principles of limited government?

In considering the issue of legitimacy in relation to our constitutional arrangements and the exercise of governmental power, what has to be done is to examine a range of practices, decisions, actions (and non-practices, -decisions and -actions) statements and policies which between them can amount to a portrait of power, so that we can form a judgment or an assessment of that power set against the principles of limited government outlined and discussed so far. It is not every failure to comply with law or every constitutional and non-constitutional short cut which adds up to an approach to powers which gives rise to questions of legitimacy. If that were so, there would scarcely be a government in the last 100 years which could be regarded as legitimate, but it is those uses of power and law which seem to betray or which can only be reasonably explained by a contempt for or at least an impatience with the principles of limited government and a belief that the rightness of the policies to be executed .xcuse or justify the methods whereby they are executed. If, as we believe to be the case, powers are being so exercised, then the issue of constitutional legitimacy which arises is quite simply: what is the value or use of a constitution based on and designed to ensure the maintenance of a system of limited government if it can, quite lawfully and even constitutionally, be set on one side? Have we not in such circumstances arrived at that "elective dictatorship" of which Lord Hailsham gave warning in 1977[20]:

> "It is only now that men and women are beginning to realize that representative institutions are not necessarily guardians of

[19] de Smith, *op. cit.* pp. 199–210.
[20] The Dimbleby Lecture 1977, expanded in *The Dilemma of Democracy* (London, 1978), especially Chap. 20.

freedom but can themselves become engines of tyranny. They can be manipulated by minorities, taken over by extremists, motivated by the self-interest of organised millions."[21]

What then of the practices? To write in full detail of the practices of government over even the last decade would require a book in itself. Within the compass of an essay therefore all that can be done is to take up some issues of administration and government[22] which have given rise to general concern in the last few years and discuss them within the context of their contribution to or detraction from the principle of limited government. The first issue is that of representative and elective government and institutions discussed both by Carol Harlow and Martin Loughlin in their essays.

Harlow discusses the theories behind representation, and highlights the radical critique of the dominant Burkeian ideas of representation, and the stress now laid by many commentators and politicians on greater participation by the people in the governing process. Elections were and are meant to be that element of participation and it may be hard for students today who take elections and the electoral process for granted to understand the passions that were roused by electoral reform in the nineteenth and early twentieth century, or that it was only in 1948 that the principle of "one person one vote" was finally enshrined in the law of the United Kingdom. Even now, as the case of *R. v. Boundary Commission for England, ex parte Foot*[23] in 1983 showed, the principle of "one person, one vote, one value" a necessary principle to prevent gerrymandering, is not part of our law. This gap in our law, exploited for many years by the Protestant majority in Northern Ireland to their advantage and by the Labour Government in 1969[24] is however of less importance than the abuse of and attacks on the electoral process that have taken place over the last decade.

---

[21] Hailsham, *op. cit.* p. 13.

[22] It may be thought that the behaviour of government and police in Northern Ireland should feature in this essay. We recognise that the issue of legitimacy of the government in Northern Ireland is a major factor in the continuing political trouble there and that "emergency" legislation raises in an acute form questions of the legitimacy of governmental power. But we deliberately leave out emergency legislation of all sorts because our concern it to show how "ordinary" government and administration is departing from traditional constitutional precepts and not how emergency legislation in an area where there is something akin to civil war is doing so. There is an obvious defence to the charge of the unconstitutional nature of governmental actions in Northern Ireland: "It is an unconstitutional situation on the ground, we are fighting terrorists." Such a defence is not available in respect of the matters discussed in this essay.

[23] [1983] Q.B. 600.

[24] de Smith, *op. cit.* pp. 248–250.

Once again we may refer to Lord Hailsham's diagnosis; talking of elective dictatorship he states:

> "All the more unfortunate does this become . . . when at least one of the parties believes that the prerogative and rights conferred by electoral victory, however narrow, not merely entitle but compel it to impose on the helpless but unorganized majority irreversible changes for which it never consciously voted and to which most of its members are opposed."[25]

Lord Hailsham was writing in the context of the Labour Government of 1974–79 which never had a majority in the House of Commons greater than three and for much of the time was in a minority and reliant on the Liberal and other parties to support it. During that period the Government expanded the scope of the Welfare State, conferred significant legal rights on trade unionists and trade unions, nationalised the shipbuilding and aircraft manufacturing industries and attempted to provide for a measure of devolution of power—a matter which Lord Hailsham elsewhere appears to support[26]—to Scotland and Wales. All these matters were spelt out in manifestoes in the two elections of 1974 and in the case of devolution there was in those elections, in terms of votes cast, an absolute majority for that in those two countries. Nonetheless it could be argued and was being so by Lord Hailsham, that a government elected by a clear minority of the voters albeit with a majority in the House of Commons would be wrong—*i.e.* it would not be legitimate—to attempt to bring about "irreversible changes" to which the majority of the voters are opposed, and to the extent to which those Labour Governments sought to do that, they were abusing the electoral process and not acting in a legitimate manner.

The performance of the Labour Governments of 1974–79 in attempting to bring about irreversible changes may be compared to the performance of the Conservative Governments that have succeeded it. Elected on a 43.4 per cent. minority of votes in 1979, and a slightly smaller percentage in 1983, the Conservative Governments, of which incidentally Lord Hailsham is a senior member, as Lord Chancellor, and with comfortable majorities in the House of Commons, have consciously set about a course of radical social and economic change. Such changes departed from the existing political consensus of successive governments since 1945 on how and in accordance with what principles the country should be governed, and when these programmes of change have been opposed by elected and appointed

---

[25] *Op. cit.* p. 21.
[26] *Op. cit.* Chap. XXV.

representatives of other parties and groups within the community, they have set about dismantling the institutions from which opposition has come and curbing their independence. In the course of doing this they have demonstrated that no irreversible changes were introduced by the Labour Governments of 1974–79 since virtually all their innovations have been reversed. They have, however, themselves via policies of privatisation, monetarism and drastic reductions in the financing of housing, in particular, brought about irreversible changes in the economy and in the opportunities of many people to work, or to live in or obtain adequate housing. It would be difficult to claim that the electorate in 1979 and 1983 "consciously voted for" these (and others yet to come) irreversible changes.

These comments may be criticised as being partisan and more political than constitutional. Governments since 1979 may be more vigorous and more effective than those that went before them in the preceding 30 years but they have not done anything which other governments did not do or try to do during their tenure. Moreover, given the electoral system that we have and have always had—first past the post—it is more than likely that a government will win a majority of seats with a minority of votes, which is why it is the majority in the House of Commons which traditionally has determined the legitimacy of what a government has undertaken during its tenure of office. Viewed from this perspective there can be no valid comparison between the situation Lord Hailsham was concerned about, where a party which obtained less than 40 per cent. of the votes of the electorate, in two successive General Elections failed to gain, then obtained and then lost a bare majority of seats in the House of Commons, yet continued to try and implement its manifesto commitments, and the current position where a party may have obtained less than 44 per cent. of the votes cast at two successive General Elections but nonetheless obtained first over 53 per cent. of the seats in the House of Commons, and then over 60 per cent. Such a large, and then larger, majority of seats in the House of Commons, it is argued, legitimises radical and irreversible change.

Put in these percentage terms, the argument for the legitimacy of the post-1979 governments or rather of their more extreme policies seems weaker rather than stronger. In 1974, in the two elections of that year, the Labour Party obtained, in the second election, marginally more votes and marginally more seats in the House of Commons than in the first election, albeit still a minority of votes cast and only a bare majority of seats in the House. In 1983, the Conservative Party obtained *fewer* votes than in 1979 yet finished up with vastly more seats in the House of Commons. A principle of legitimacy that sanctioned, in such circumstances, radical and irreversible change to be introduced into a nation's economic, social and political arrangements would seem to lack credibility. On this matter, let Lord Hailsham have the last word:

> "We should surely need our heads examined if we were to go on with the system by which members selected as candidates by existing methods of nomination, and elected as members by existing methods of voting, are entitled to vote general legislation without adequate control, legal or political, on the use of their powers."[27]

These general points are somewhat inconclusive. Less so, and arguably much more serious from a legitimacy perspective is the policy which has been pursued consistently since 1979 via legislation and administration; to whittle down, reduce or eliminate the role of local electoral institutions; local participation in the administration of services affecting local areas; and local opposition, lawfully expressed, to central government policies. All these practices, to be discussed briefly below, are good examples of that centralised democracy or elective dictatorship which is counterpoised to limited government.

Take first, the assault on local elected government. We do not pretend that local government is without faults, some of them indeed—secretiveness, denial of rights to the opposition, waste and petty abuses of power—going to the question of the legitimacy of its existence or activities, but it has three crucial features which are vital attributes in that diffusion and limitation on central government power which the concept of limited government necessarily involves. These features are: localness, the elective principle, and an independent taxing power. These characteristics are interrelated and fundamental because between them they virtually guarantee that at any time in the history of the state there will be alternative policies and spending patterns being pursued by alternative elected governments, local governments, to those being pursued or desired by central governments. And the maintenance of such alternative governments, however inconvenient, foolish or inefficient they may be is essential to the continuance of a system of limited government. Any central government, intent on increasing its own powers and decreasing opportunities for dissent from or alternative approaches to its policies, will sooner or later feel the need to attack and emasculate these alternative governments, these alternative centres of power, at their electoral and financial roots.

This is precisely what has happened over the past few years.[28] In the

---

[27] *Op. cit.* p. 130.
[28] See for more details, Loughlin's essay at in Chap. 4 and Loughlin, *Local Government, the Law and the Constitution, Local Government Legal Society Trust* (1983).

early years of the post-1979 Conservative Governments, legislation and administration concentrated on re-casting and reducing the financial grants central government made to local governments—a perfectly proper object of policy—and seeking to penalise, through diminishing grants those local governments whose spending priorities did not accord with central government's—a permissible if less laudable exercise of power. But these actions did not succeed in forcing local governments to comply with central government's spending limits, nor, when they had the opportunity, did local electorates support the central government line. The next and fateful two steps followed. The Rates Act 1984 gave the central government power to limit both the rates that could be levied by and the spending of a local government; such a local government would effectively lose its financial independence. By the same legislation, an inroad was made on the elective principle by requiring local governments to consult with representatives of business before fixing their rates. Thus a special interest group was given a privileged access to policy-making and information within a local government, so indicating to the local electorate that election results were no longer of much importance since by law, the representatives of one group within the community would always have a special opportunity to ensure that their interests were given particular attention over and above those of other electors or ratepayers.

But inroads on the elective principle did not stop at special consultative rights for special groups of ratepayers, a throw-back to the business vote abolished in 1948. The next step, duly proceeded to in legislation passed in 1985 was to abolish certain elected local governments and transfer their functions either to other existing elected local governments or to central government appointed bodies or bodies with a mixture of central and local government appointees or joint boards of local government members. The initial argument in favour of this "reorganisation," that it would be more efficient and save ratepayers money, did not stand up to independent private sector financial scrutiny.[29] Alternative arguments that abolishing upper-tier authorities would bring government closer to the people and thus be more democratic and remove a source of conflict and tension were belied by the plethora of non-directly elected bodies, especially in London, that were provided for in the legislation to replace the directly elected Greater London Council and the metropolitan counties that were being abolished.

---

[29] Coopers & Lybrand Associates produced two reports in early 1984 analysing the costs of implementing the proposals contained in the Government's White Paper, *Streamlining the Cities*. They estimated a range from an annual saving over the then current costs of the Metropolitan County Councils of ¼ per cent. to an annual *cost* of 3¼ per cent. The Government's own estimate was a saving of 7½ per cent.

At the root of the abolitionist case was the political fact that the local governments scheduled to be abolished were controlled by the Labour Party, in some cases aggressively so, and as upper-tier authorities they could both obtain funds from and influence policies in lower-tier authorities controlled by the Conservative Party, and could act, and particularly in the case of the GLC and the South Yorkshire Metropolitan County did act as focal and effective points of opposition to the Government. This the Government was not prepared to countenance, especially in London which was the seat of national government. Rather than wait for or use the democratic electoral process to try and displace their political opponents, the usual tactic in a democratic society supporting a system of limited government—the Government decided to abolish these centres of opposition—quite possibly only temporary centres—altogether.

The enormity of what was proposed may be judged by the case of London. London is universally and instinctively recognised as one city, albeit with many parts. It has had its own upper-tier local authority since 1888, when the London County Council was established, and even for 33 years before that, the Metropolitan Board of Works constituted a London-wide indirectly elected authority for many purposes. So after 130 years, London as a local government unit is being abolished to "provide a system which is simpler for the public to understand."[30] The legitimacy of the actions is not advanced by the subterfuge of reason which accompanies them.

As noted above, an inevitable corollary of the abolition of elected local governments is a considerable increase in the patronage available to central government in appointments to boards and commissions which will take over functions from the abolished local governments. In this area of power too, governments have since 1979 displayed little regard for local opinion or political consensus. Regional Water Authorities were "reorganised"—a favourite word—so as to reduce the local indirectly elected element, and permit meetings to be held in private; a private member's attempt to re-open meetings to the public failed to gain government support in 1985. The chairmanships and members of Regional Health Authorities were purged of opponents or non-sympathisers with the ruling party. The same tactic was adopted in respect of other quangos, particularly those set up to take over functions from local government.

Carol Harlow quotes Bagehot's aphorism that elections are a buckle between people and power. They provide a means for maintaining a democratic check on power, for changing those wielding power and for informing those wielding power of the reaction of people over whom

---

[30] *Streamlining the Cities,* Cmnd. 9063, para. 1.19.

power is being wielded. The democratic ethic behind the electoral process provides too the rationale for the greater involvement of people in the process of government not only through elections but through service on public bodies which are involved in the process of governing. This greater involvement in government brings a greater commitment to the whole constitutional process. For many commentators as Harlow points out, a major problem in government today is that there is, despite some gains in some areas, notably planning, still too few opportunities for participation in government and too little meaning to elections. Successive governments, prior to 1979, were at best lukewarm towards the arguments and reluctant to take action for greater participation. But only since 1979 has there been positive hostility towards greater participation in government. Specific action has been taken or planned to cut down on participation, on elections and on the institution of local government, the standard-bearer for greater participation in government. In their place, have come greater centralisation of power, greater secrecy over how decisions on rates, formerly open to local electors to see and comment on, are made; and greater efforts to appoint the "right" sort of person—"one of us"—to quangos rather than ensure a representative cross-section of the community on such bodies. In a sentence, government is withdrawing from the people—not in the sense of becoming smaller but in the sense of becoming less open to persuasion, more authoritarian—and the buckle between people and power is being loosened.

The principal objective of elections is to elect a representative assembly, either the House of Commons at the centre or local councils at the local level. At the centre, the House of Commons sustains and should exercise some sort of supervision over the executive. The research and writing is legion however that Parliament exercises little if any effective control over the Executive, and that the principle of ministerial responsibility is used not as a means of bringing Ministers to account before the House of Commons but as a justification for not creating other and more effective means of accountability.[31] As far back as 1915, Dicey was expressing considerable scepticism about "so-called ministerial responsibility" and commenting that it "is a very feeble guarantee indeed against the action which evades the authority of the law courts."[32] Time has not invalidated that comment.

What has developed over the last two decades and particularly since 1979 is a multitude of Select Committees, established to increase the effectiveness of Parliamentary control over the Executive, by increas-

---

[31] C. Turpin, "Ministerial Responsibility—Myth or Reality" in *The Changing Constitution Law* (J. Jowell and D. Oliver eds., O.U.P., 1985).

[32] Dicey, *op. cit.* p. 498.

ing the opportunities for M.P.s to question, with the aid of specialist advisers, both civil servants and Ministers, about policy and its implementation. A further step in the direction of increased financial control came with the National Audit Act of 1983 which expanded the powers of the Comptroller and Auditor-General to conduct value for money audits of government departments and other public agencies and affirmed his status as an officer of Parliament not of the Government. These steps could be regarded as off-setting trends noted earlier. Maybe there are less checks on government outside Parliament and less commitment to participation, but the checking role of M.P.s has been boosted and their participation in useful fact-finding committees increased. This is precisely the development one should be looking for in a parliamentary democracy.

The establishment of committees is one thing; taking them seriously and facilitating their work another. The latter requires that information be released to committees and that Ministers and civil servants appear before and answer questions fully and to the best of their ability. It requires in short, the co-operation of the executive and to that extent is a species of auto-limitation. Auto-limitation via Parliamentary Select Committees has then replaced or may be seen as a partial replacement for the potentially more effective checks on central governmental power which large and well financed elected local governments may ensure.

How has this species of auto-limitation worked? The committees have produced many reports, been responsible for the publication of a great deal of useful information given to them in evidence and have to that extent undoubtedly increased our general understanding and knowledge of the policy-making process and the forces and arguments that bear upon that process. But that is not their main function. In respect of that function, the checking and controlling of the Executive, we cannot give such a sanguine verdict. Ministers from both Labour and Conservative Governments have been, at best, reluctant participants in the process and have instructed civil servants likewise. There have been well publicised occasions when information has been refused to committees. As the Ponting trial brought out, misleading information has been given to committees, information which by no stretch of the imagination could be claimed, as it was in that case, as being in need of protection because of national security. Nor has the enhanced status, powers and salaries of the Comptroller and Auditor-General and his staff resulted in any dramatic improvement in controlling the way central government spends its money; waste still occurs and there remains the problem of ensuring that action is taken to meet the criticism of the Comptroller and the committee to which he reports. This is a problem which affects all the committees.

Again, it may be argued that this is carping criticism. The committees are in place and despite some inevitable tension between them and the Executive, are producing more information about what the government is doing which is a major factor in increasing accountability. Even the discovery of false and misleading information which is given to committees is evidence of their success, as, without their perseverance, such behaviour might well not have been unearthed. No government can or would hand over policy-making and implementation to the House of Commons and critics of the alleged ineffectiveness of the committees seem to assume that that is what should have happened. It is, *au fond,* a question of balance, of give and take, and overall judged on that common-sense basis, the committees are a useful adjunct to the total process of ministerial responsibility.

We come back to our point made earlier. The committees exist to do more than provide more information about the policy-making process and if that is all that can be claimed for them, then they cannot be accounted a success in the matter of controlling the executive. The issue may be put in this way. At a time when other checks are being done away with or made less effective, can we see the committees as effective replacements? Can we see any evidence that government goes about its business in a positively better way because of the presence of the committees? If on the other hand the evidence is that policy-making is more secretive, implementation is more casual in matters of complying with law and fair administrative practices, the House of Commons is treated in a more cavalier fashion then we would be forced to conclude with Ian Aitken that:

> "It should by now be obvious . . . that a system greeted with such fanfares of libertarian enthusiasm six years ago is little more than a sham unless it has full powers to demand and to get the truth from public servants paid from the public purse . . . If their [the MPs who created and believed in the committees] creation is worth keeping, it must have the powers to perform its investigative function."[33]

At best then, there is a question-mark over the usefulness of the post-1979 select committees as a partial replacement for those devices and institutions outside Parliament which can operate as a counter to central government power but which have had their existence or effectiveness reduced over the same period. But committees are not the only parliamentary mechanism over which a question-mark hangs. There is increasing evidence of government reluctance to allow the

[33] "Why Parliament should put select committes on trial" *The Guardian*, February 15, 1985, p. 9.

House of Commons to discharge its legislative function properly. The period from 1972 to the election of 1979 was one when governments of all political persuasions suffered numerous defeats on the floor of the House and in standing committees on their Bills. Even after that period, we can still point to occasions when the government has been defeated in standing committee including one case in 1985, when a Bill was effectively killed when a bipartisan majority on a standing committee voted not to proceed with it.[34] But we must set against that the fact that the governments elected since 1979 have been far more willing to use the guillotine motion on Bills in committees than other governments. One (Labour) participant notes that:

> "More bills (14) have been guillotined in Standing Committees in the five years of the Thatcher government than in the preceding 20 years."

He goes on to comment:

> " . . . we have faced so many guillotine motions because the government has brought forward much ill-thought out legislation which it has sought to beat through the Commons without change, 'brandishing the theory of the detailed mandate in the face of reasoned argument' to quote the words of Conservative MP William Waldegrave, now junior environment minister."[35]

It is not however just the use of the guillotine motion which betrays a certain indifference towards the House of Commons. The actual legislation which is being brought forward is, particularly in contentious matters, drafted in such a way that it gives away as little information as possible to Members of Parliament. When a few years ago, the then leader of the House of Commons, Mr. Short, suggested that in order to speed up business in the House and give the government of the day the necessary powers to take immediate and effective action to meet whatever problems arose, "outline" only legislation should be passed, conferring broad powers and leaving the details and safeguards to be formulated later by regulations, as with the Emergency Powers Acts, he was pilloried as wanting to confer dictatorial powers on government and downgrade the role of Parliament. It is however precisely that sort of legislation which is now being "beaten through" the House of Commons.[36] A further and equally undesirable develop-

---

[34] This was the Civil Aviation Bill, see Parliamentary Debates, House of Commons Official Report Standing Committee F. Civil Aviation Bill February 12, 1985.

[35] Jack Straw M.P. "Cut the Guillotine down to size," *The Times*, February 4, 1985.

[36] The Rates Act 1984 is a good example of this kind of legislation, compounded by the refusal of the Secretary of State for the Environment to give details to the House of Commons of how he calculated the proper rates to be levied by those authorities whose rates he was "capping" under the Act. See H.C. Deb., Vol. 55, cols. 258–299 (February 29, 1984).

ment is the bringing forward of legislation, presented publicly as being
a reform in the interests of limited government in the sense that it
appears to create a legal framework for and hence legal controls on the
exercise of government power, which on careful and close inspection
actually increases government power, either by providing legal backing for powers which previously lacked it, or by conferring additional
powers on central government as part of a package of reforms.[37]

The House of Commons is then being downgraded or by-passed as
an effective check or control on the powers of central government; a
point made by commentators of all political hues for many years. This
is quite simply because the effectiveness of the House of Commons
depends ultimately upon the co-operation of the government of the
day with the members of the House, other than in those comparatively
rare occasions when a government has no majority in the House. A
government minded to get its way, and give nothing away, can reduce
the House to comparative impotence. It will always be possible to
point to some "victories": concessions on legislation forced out of an
unwilling government running out of time in a session; admissions on
misleading information, and an apology given to a select committee;
the backing down on a policy initiative because of (government) back-
bench opposition. Examples of all of these can readily be found over
the last five or six years; but at a time when effective extra-Parliamen-
tary though lawful checks on government power are being reduced,
Parliamentary checks need to be increased and that is not happening.

Lurking behind the discussions both on elections and participation
and on the Parliamentary process is the issue of open government. In
both areas we have noted that a reluctance to disclose information or to
allow matters to be discussed in public has been one aspect of the
reduction of the effectiveness of these checking devices. The issue of
open government generally however needs a discussion in its own
right, as general trends in this area have an important bearing on
legitimacy.

Openness of government tends to be seen and discussed in terms of
the Official Secrets Act and the reform of section 2. The Ponting trial
highlighted the murky world of section 2 and the jury's verdict may
quite fairly be seen as a sharp comment on the legitimacy of the

---

[37] The Interception of Communications Bill introduced into the House of Commons
in March 1985 is an example of the first type of Bill, legalising the governmental
interception of communication but providing neither adequate ministerial
accountability for, nor normal judicial review over the exercise of the power. The
Local Government, Planning and Land Act 1980 is an example of the latter; it was
proclaimed to be "An Act to relax controls over local and certain other authorities . . . "; it sharply increased central controls over local spending, local public
land management and planning.

activities of government in withholding information from, and deliberately misleading, the House of Commons and hence the electorate about the circumstances surrounding the sinking of the *General Belgrano*. A sensitive response to that verdict would have been to accept it and its logic and be more forthcoming on the *General Belgrano* case to the House. It is, we suggest, a measure of the extent of the departure by government from the principles implicit in the concept of limited government that its reaction to the verdict was in effect to arrange for and conduct a re-trial of Mr. Ponting via a full-scale debate in the House of Commons with Ministers acting as prosecutors and their supporters acting as the jury.[38]

The Ponting trial and the Official Secrets Act may have raised in a dramatic and stark form, issues of the illegitimate use of government power, but open government as Sir Douglas Wass has realised, goes beyond the Official Secrets Act. He put the issue and summed up the problem thus:

> "Raising the quality of public debate and providing the public with the material on which to make an informed judgment on matters of public policy are two major requirements if we are to make the government process operate efficiently and responsively. . . . More important in my view, than any institutional changes is the need for a commitment on the part of all who work in the field of government positively to want an informed public. If this is lacking, little in the way of machinery will help."[39]

He makes the point too that not all relevant information is in the possession of government; academic research and the media have a role to play in "opening up government."

Can it be said that there is this positive desire for an informed public and an informed public debate on government policies? If before the 1979 election the evidence pointed in two directions—the "Croham directive"[40] on disclosure of official information and support given to

---

[38] H.C. Deb., Vol. 73, cols. 737–824 (February 18, 1985). The headline in *The Times* the day after the debate summed up the Government's approach: "Heseltine discloses secrets to discredit Ponting," February 19, 1985. It must be admitted that there was a precedent of sorts for this action See Lord Devlin *Easing the Passing: The Trial of Dr. John Bodkin Adams* (London, 1985), pp. 188–191.

[39] D. Wass, *Government and the Governed* (London, 1984), pp. 83–84, 100. The author was formerly a Permanent Secretary to the Treasury and Joint Head of the Home Civil Service.

[40] This was the directive issued in 1976 by the then head of the Civil Service, Lord Croham, to all permanent secretaries "This decreed that the background material relating to policy studies and reports would be published unless ministers explicitly decided it would not. It declared that the aim normally would be to publish as much as possible . . . . But critics have rightly noted that the control of information remains firmly in Whitehall's hands and that there is no provision for checking up on or auditing the observance of the directive." Wass, *op. cit.* pp. 88–89.

public participation in several fields of local government, on the one hand being balanced by strong government opposition to Freedom of Information legislation and support for an official information bill which finally surfaced, and shortly afterwards ignominiously sank in late 1979, since that event, the evidence points in one direction only—closed government.

It is not just the disinclination already noted to give information to select committees of the House of Commons which is the issue here. We would also refer to the cut-back on the funding of research, particularly social science research which has done so much over the last two decades to open up knowledge about society, and its underlying problems.[41] Mention may be made here too both of the closure to the public via legislative provision of meetings of the Regional Water Authorities and the advice via circulars on similar closures of Regional and District Health Authorities. An example is the "advice given" by the Department of Health and Social Security to a hospital governor that proposals for the hospital's closure should be kept secret until after the 1983 General Election. This was part of a general warning issued to all health administrators against publishing politically sensitive documents in the run-up to the election, a practice alleged to be a standard one adopted at all elections.[42] Another important piece of evidence is the use of the criminal process, other laws and straight-forward political pressure, to try and restrict the activities of the investigative journalist, in the press and in television, and to penalise those who disclose information which is politically embarrassing.[43] Few activities are more likely to alter the climate for open or closed government than legal-based attacks on the press and their informants.

There has, then, been a consistent policy since 1979 to close down

[41] A good example of this is provided by the total withdrawal of Government funding in mid-1979 from the Centre for Environmental Studies, a research centre founded with Government support in the mid sixties to provide informed policy-orientated research on urban issues. Following the withdrawal of Government funding, the Centre effectively closed.

[42] *The Guardian*, July 8, 1983.

[43] Apart from the criminal cause célèbres of Sarah Tisdall in 1984 and Clive Ponting in 1985, there is the less well-known case of Ray Williams, a Ministry of Defence official convicted of passing secrets to the *Observer*, in a trial which pilloried that newspaper without its being able effectively to reply since it was not on trial and could not comment for fear of *subjudice* rules until the trial was over. See too *Home Office* v. *Harman* [1982] 1 All E.R. 532, *Secretary of State for Defence* v. *Guardian Newspaper Ltd.* [1984] 3 All E.R. 601, and the Conservative Party's complaints about a BBC Panorama Programme on Right wing "entryism" into the Party. *The Guardian*, February 14, 1984. See too D. Trelford, "Britain's press has its back to the wall," *South China Morning Post* (March 30, 1985). See now the furore over the BBC Governor's decision at the request of the Home Secretary not to televise a programme on N. Ireland, *The Times*, July 31, 1985.

rather than open up government. That this is so, and the threat that such a policy poses for the principles of limited government was highlighted by the Ponting trial, in many respects a watershed in this matter of constitutional legitimacy as the whole saga exposed to a very wide audience the nature of the government's attitude to power and its control. The fact that the case was taken to court in the obvious expectation of a conviction, the crude and not convincingly denied government suggestion of the need for a tough judge to take the case—both indicate that the government saw the case as the best opportunity yet to deal a fatal blow to the proponents of open government. More serious however for our perspective was the aftermath. The Attorney General specifically stated in the House of Commons that he agreed with the judge's definition of the law in his summing up to the jury; *viz.* that the interests of the state meant the policies of the government of the day.[44] As commentators have almost unanimously pointed out, no proposition of law is better calculated to facilitate government of unrestricted and unrestrained power, able to do virtually what it likes—*i.e.* ban trade unions in the national interest; conceal what it likes—such as defence and economic information from the House of Commons and its select committees; act how it likes—to be discussed in the next section; and put under surveillance whom it likes in order to prevent that "informed judgment" of which Sir Douglas Wass spoke, being made on its performance.

It is this equation of national or state interest with the policies of the government of the day, an equation which would totally ignore any constitutional principle aimed at ensuring limited government, which lies at the root of many of the actions of governments since 1979. For these governments have conceived of themselves as having a mission to shake up, radically alter, or if necessary, curtail the activities or the very existence of many institutions, programmes and policies which have been for a long time an accepted part of the government and administration of the country. Such a mission makes an uneasy bedfellow for the concepts associated with limited government; checks and balances, openness and accountability, effective supervision of and control on administrative action. To revert to the traditional language of Dicey's constitutional triptych, parliamentary sovereignty, taken to mean the wishes of the government of the day, has been elevated over

---

[44] H.C. Debs., Vol. 73 *op. cit.* col. 182 (February 12, 1985). See however for an alternative legal comment on the summing up, Lord Denning's speech in the House of Lords during a debate on section 2 of the Official Secrets Act, H.L. Deb., Vol. 461, No. 61, cols. 563–566. See further however for an alternative view by Lord Denning; *R.* v. *Secretary of State for the Home Department ex parte Hosenball* [1977] W.L.R. 776.

the political and legal constraints involved in the rule of law and constitutional conventions.

Much of the discussion so far in this essay has focussed on matters which can without too much difficulty be brought under the head of constitutional conventions; we now turn to matters which come under the head of the rule of law, in the sense in which Dicey used that term.

The issue here may be simply stated. In pursuit of their mission, governments since 1979 have become increasingly careless of their obligations to comply with the law in the implementation of their policies. Indeed so general has become this abuse and excess of power, and the taking of actions of doubtful legality that observers would be forgiven for thinking that there was a studied practice of such behaviour. It is important to be clear about the nature and extent of the charge being made. We are not referring to what may be called the ordinary or typical case which arises on an application for judicial review of administrative action—a planning inspector infringing the rules of natural justice; a departmental (nominally ministerial) decision taken on the basis of what turns out to be an incorrect interpretation of a relatively minor point of law—or even the leading cases where the courts have seized the opportunity to advance the scope of fair administration in an area hitherto assumed to be off limits for such a development—prisoners' rights is the obvious example. We are referring to cases whether they come before the courts or not, where Ministers themselves have acted in a lawless fashion, or careless as to whether their actions are legal or not, or in a doubtfully legal manner which can only with difficulty be justified, where justification is attempted.

To describe and discuss all the cases in detail would unduly lengthen this essay. To give no examples would leave us open to the charge that we are making unsubstantiated and unsustainable charges of a grave nature against the government, or rather against Ministers in the government. What follows, then, is a catalogue of some of of the more noteworthy examples of this casual approach to the use of governmental power.

The catalogue is as follows:

1. Mr. Jenkins's attempt, within three months of taking office as Secretary of State for Health and Social Security in 1979, to replace the Lambeth, Southwark and Lewisham Area Health Authority with Commissioners because the A.H.A. appeared not to be willing, in his view, to cut back expenditures to the extent he required. His claim to exercise emergency powers under the Health Services Act was rejected by the Divisional

Court, but the unlawful exercise of powers by the Commissioners was validated by retrospective legislation in 1980.[45]

2.   Mr. Heseltine's refusal in 1982, when Secretary of State for the Environment, to hold proper consultations with local authorities before penalising them for alleged overspending—that is spending more than he thought they should, not spending in excess of anything the law allowed; his decision on penalties was quashed in the Divisional Court,[46] and repeated after a process of formal consultation. The next round of penal legislation, the Rates Act 1984, provided for the possibility of consultation before penalties but coupled it with a power in the Secretary of State to increase penalties after any process of consultation.

3.   The actions of Mr. Fowler as Secretary of State for Health and Social Security in using his powers under the Social Security Act 1980 to make regulations to reverse, by regulation, decisions of the Social Security Commissioners, which have gone against the arguments of the DHSS. Drafts of the regulations are required to be put before the Social Security Advisory Committee for their comments but there have been occasions when that Committee, established by the Act of 1980 has been given only one week to comment on such drafts.[47]

4.   The action, admitted to be illegal, in March 1984 by Mr. Clark, the Minister of Health, of requiring chemists to pay £10 million to the government on the grounds that they were being overpaid by the National Health Service for the drugs they dispense. Legislation was proposed "to put matters beyond doubt," *i.e.* confer retrospective power to require chemists to make the payments.[48]

5.   The actions by Mr. Clark in directing District Health Authorities to accept tenders from the private sector for cleaning and other work in National Health hospitals despite the fact that they were not the lowest tender, that being from the D.H.A. or its employees.[49]

6.   The disinclination by the Home Office Minister, Mr. Waddington, to withdraw circulars dealing with immigration acknowledged to be contrary to immigration legislation.[50]

---

[45] Health Services Act 1980 (c. 53).
[46] *R.* v. *Secretary of State for the Environment, ex p. Brent L.B.C.* [1982] Q.B. 593.
[47] A further example: *R.* v. *Secretary of State for Social Services, ex p. Cotton, The Times*, August 5, 1985.
[48] *The Guardian*, March 2, 1984. See too *R.* v. *Secretary of State for Social Services, ex p. Association of Metropolitan Authorities, The Times*, May 29, 1985. Secretary of State acted wrongly in failing to consult AMA on housing benefit regulations.
[49] *The Times* January 29, 1985.
[50] See H.C. Deb., Vol. 55, cols. 659–704 (March 5, 1984).

7. The secret deal between Mr. Parkinson, when Secretary of State for Trade and Industry, and the Stock Exchange, made in July 1983, under which Mr. Parkinson:

   "effectively quashed the case correctly brought by the Director-General of Fair Trading against the monopolistic elements of the Stock Exchange's rule book under the Restrictive Trade Practices Act . . . this is not an isolated example of the present Government overruling legal process to suit interest groups."[51]

8. Sir Gerald Vaughan's action, when Minister for consumer affairs, in seeking to cut the government grant to the Citizen Advice Bureau on the strength of unsubstantiated and in the event totally false allegations about the activities of a C.A.B. worker Mrs. Ruddock, at the time a leader of the Campaign for Nuclear Disarmament.[52]

9. The wrongful demand made by Mr. Ridley, the Secretary of State for Transport, on the Greater London Council for £50 million under the London Regional Transport Act 1984, to support the London Transport Authority set up under the Act. The demand was quashed by the Divisional Court in January 1985 which called it "unlawful, irrational and procedurally improper," but rather than appeal the decision, Mr. Ridley introduced retrospective legislation the following month to reverse the ruling and require the payment of the £50 million by the GLC. Not content with the introduction of retrospective legislation, the Government then procured the suspension of the Standing Orders of the House of Commons to enable the stages of the Bill to be taken on successive days, thereby reducing the opportunities for proper consideration of the measure.[53]

10. The action by Mr. Heseltine as Secretary of State for Defence to appoint a leading defence contractor as the Ministry of Defence's defence procurement adviser and to dismiss suggestions that there was any conflict of interest involved; the appointment violated the rules governing the appointment of civil servants which had therefore to be retrospectively altered at the Prime Minister's instigation to legalise the appointment.[54]

---

[51] *The Times*, September 29, 1983.

[52] Debate preceeding the setting up of a review by Sir Douglas Lovelock. H.C. Deb., Vol. 41, cols. 875–880 (April 27, 1983).

[53] *The Times*, Law Reports, January 14, 1985. Transport Bill 1985. Also see H.C. Deb., Vol. 72, col. 417 (January 31, 1985) and H.C. Deb., Vol. 73, cols. 192–266 (February 12, 1985).

[54] *The Guardian*, March 19, 1985, for the disclosure that the appointment was not merely unwise but illegal, and March 26, 1985 for the allegation that Sir Robert

11. Rate-capping by Mr. Jenkin, as Secretary of State for the Environment. Leaving aside the nature of the legislation which was drafted so as to minimise the possibilities of either challenge in the courts by affected local authorities or meaningful control by the House of Commons of the use of the novel powers of rate-capping, the first exercise of the powers was characterised by mistake, evasions, denial of information to affected parties[55] and the House of Commons, justified by the argument that information was held back:

"because rate-capped authorities would merely exploit any weaknesses in [the Secretary of State's] calculations to challenge him both publicly and through the courts."[56]

12. The action of Mrs. Thatcher, as Minister for the Civil Service in banning trade unions at the Government Communication Headquarters, Cheltenham. Although this action was ultimately upheld by a unanimous House of Lords,[57] on the grounds, not advanced by the Minister until she had lost at first instance, that reasons of national security necessitated both the action and the refusal to consult the trade union representatives of the affected civil servants, their lordships made it quite plain that, but for the issue of national security, the civil servants had a legitimate expectation that they would be consulted before their terms of service were altered and that "the respondent had acted unfairly in failing to consult unions or staff before making her decision."[58]

It may be urged that just as one swallow does not a summer make, so 12 ministerial peccadilloes do not a rule of law break. Given the

Armstrong, Cabinet Secretary and Head of the Home Civil Service "made it clear that if the [Civil Service] Commissioners did not go along with the appointment, then the Government would simply change the Rules to ensure that it could go ahead." Richard Norton-Taylor: A hint of bias for Whitehall's even-handedness, p. 21.

[55] *The Guardian*, March 2, 1985, for an unsuccessful attempt to obtain a Court Order to force disclosure of information.

[56] Mr. Jenkin was directly quoted in an interview in the *Sunday Times*, February 24, 1985. See too H.C. Deb., Vol. 73, cols. 19–21, on allegations that Mr. Jenkin disclosed information to Conservative opposition councillors in London that he refused to disclose to Labour governing councillors. Mr. Jenkin denied the allegations but shortly after they were made, the level of rates which Haringey L.B.C. could raise under the Rates Act 1984 was sharply lifted. H.C. Deb., Vol. 73, col. 863.

[57] *Council for Civil Service Unions* v. *Minister for the Civil Service* [1984] 3 All E.R. 935.

[58] *Per* Lord Scarman at p. 949.

thousands of decisions taken by or in the name of Ministers every year, if one can only come up with 12 examples of technical legal infractions or casual as opposed to outright abuses of power, in six years, then once again political prejudice is causing a mountain to be made out of a molehill. These examples may be embarrassing but hardly evidence of a concerted attack on the rule of law.

Several answers may be made to this argument. First, space forbids the complete catalogue of Ministerial abuses of power; one very important area left out of the catalogue is the whole matter of the security services, the police and the role of the Government in politicising and centralising these services. This subject is too big and in a sense still emerging, particularly in the context of the coal strike and its aftermath,[59] for it to be satisfactorily encapsulated in a paragraph. Many however would regard developments on those matters as more serious than all the above examples put together.

Secondly, these quoted examples and other similar unquoted ones cannot be seen in isolation from other developments discussed in this essay. Alongside the policies of whittling down the autonomy of local authorities, abolishing hostile local authorities, denying information to the House of Commons, curtailing discussion of government measures in the House of Commons, vigorous use of the law to try and suppress moves towards more open government, these examples of abuse of power do fall into place as part of a general pattern of contempt for, or if that is too strong a word, short-temperedness with the constraints on power imposed by the checks and balances, inadequate though many think them to be, necessarily involved in a constitution based upon the concept of limited government. This short-temperedness with constraints is giving rise to an arrogance in the use of power, as the above examples bear witness. This is increasingly widely remarked upon because it seems to be uncheckable. Retrospective legislation forced at break-neck speed through Parliament, pleas of national security to overcome judicial control, can see off any check under our constitution. All these factors raise increasingly insistent questions about the legitimacy of governmental power and a constitution which appears totally ineffective in the face of challenges to its fundamental principles.

Dicey's answer to this problem would have been: "the ordinary courts, can be relied upon to 'deal with any actual and provable breach of the law committed by any servant of the Crown.'"[60] He elaborated this point in the *Law and the Constitution* when seeking to explain the relationship between Parliamentary sovereignty and the rule of law:

---

[59] See on this the interesting collection of essays edited by Bob Fine and Robert Millar: *Policing the Miners' Strike* (London, 1985).

[60] *Op. cit.* p. 499.

"The fact that the most arbitrary powers of the English executive must always be exercised under Act of Parliament places the government, even when armed with the widest authority, under the supervision, so to speak, of the courts. Powers, however extraordinary, which are conferred or sanctioned by statute, are never really unlimited, for they are confined by the words of the Act itself, and, what is more, by the interpretation put upon the statute by the judges."[61]

This passage makes many assumptions and begs many questions. It ignores the techniques of drafting which as Martin Loughlin claims in his comments on *Norwich C.C.* v. *Secretary of State for the Environment*, made judicial review impossible.[62] It ignores the defence of national security which the House of Lords felt, one detects somewhat reluctantly, in *Council of Civil Service Unions* v. *Minister for the Civil Services*[63] to provide a complete answer to a claim of unfair administrative action. It ignores too the influence which the government of the day can have on the climate in which the judiciary carry out their functions and the nature of the judiciary. On this latter point, it is fair to point out that by the beginning of 1985, Lord Hailsham as Lord Chancellor had appointed more than half the judges of the Queen's Bench Division, and Mrs. Thatcher as Prime Minister had, with the advice of Lord Hailsham, appointed more than half the Law Lords, more than three-quarters of the judges of the Court of Appeal, the Master of the Rolls and the Lord Chief Justice.

We do not suggest that all these appointments are political in the sense in which that term is used by de Smith when he wrote in 1981 that:

"during the past forty years hardly any judicial appointment in England appears to have been influenced by political considerations,"[64]

meaning as the context makes clear, party political considerations. But to suggest that these most important appointments were entirely apolitical, that the broad philosophical and political views of all these appointees were ignored and their technical legal skills and knowledge alone were taken into account, stretches credulity too far. The matter may be put thus. Would there be the same apparent confidence in the judiciary shown by the current government if it were in opposition and

[61] 10th ed., *op. cit.* p. 413.
[62] At pp. 103–104 *infra*.
[63] [1984] 3 All E.R. 935.
[64] de Smith, *op. cit.* p. 367.

for six years a Prime Minister openly committed to radical social change and ensuring that key public decision-makers reflected his/her views aided and abetted by a Lord Chancellor, openly and on the record as hostile to the philosophy of the opposition and some of the major political institutions which ensure the maintenance of an open and plural society, had been appointing the higher judiciary? The answer may be given by Lord Hailsham himself; writing in 1978 during the time of the Labour Government of 1974–79, he stated:

> "Never since the latter part of the seventeenth century was it more important that the independence of the judiciary should be safeguarded from intrusion by the legislature as well as the executive."[65]

It has often been remarked that despite the best efforts of the government of the Republic of South Africa to ensure a judiciary reflecting the government's views on the organisation and management of society in South Africa, judges do quite often find against the government and for those whom the government is trying to harass or whose views it is trying to suppress. So it is in the United Kingdom. Despite the preponderance of Thatcher/Hailsham appointees on the bench, the government cannot be assured of a smooth passage through the courts for all its activities. As the examples quoted above show, the grosser and more blatant abuses of power can be and are effectively, if only momentarily, halted by the courts; notions of fair administrative practice, hallowed now by many years of precedent cannot be as easily ignored by the courts as they are by Ministers. But there are limits to what courts can do, or should feel they should do. On the first point, if Ministers exercise powers which from their nature are not questioned in court, *e.g.* Mr. (as he then was) Vaughan's action against the C.A.B.—or are strictly legal if unjust or unethical, *e.g.* the Prime Minister's banning of trade unions at G.C.H.Q., Mr. Fowler's reversal of the decisions of Social Security Commissioners by regulation—then courts have no handle by which they can intervene.

The second point is more subtle and more a question of interpretation of a range of judicial decisions. Our view is that, after a period of judicial activism in control of the administration, pursued by a House of Lords led by Lord Reid, and a Court of Appeal dominated by Lord Denning, the courts, now influenced by the very different philosophies of Lord Diplock in the House of Lords and Sir John Donaldson M.R. in the Court of Appeal have, if not gone into reverse, become less active in their willingness to advance their control of administrative action. Procedural barriers to litigants thought to be cast down by

[65] *Op. cit.* p. 105.

judicial decision and legislation are being re-erected under new names[66] and a seemingly greater tolerance of the exercise of discretion in the making of decisions by Ministers is being shown. We would argue that this is in part because the broad thrust of the philosophy of the governments elected since 1979 if not all the detailed implementation of it,[67] is more congenial to the judiciary than that of their predecessors, but in part because the governments have made it quite plain that they will not accept defeat for, or opposition to, their policies, and any decision which stops a policy being implemented is in the government's eyes a defeat and a manifestation of opposition. In these circumstances, the era of the brave spirit is over; the era of the timorous souls who hope to live to fight another day is upon us. In this connection the attempt by Lord Hailsham, to do away with the right of appeal against a judge's refusal to grant leave to apply for judicial review is symptomatic of the present government's attitude both to judicial review—that there should be less of it—and to the judges. The unprecedented rebuke by Lord Hailsham, delivered in the House of Lords when it was considering the proposal, to judges in the Court of Appeal who had expressed concern in public of the proposal, amply supports our view that the present political climate is as hostile to judicial review as to any other challenge to government action. As was said of the rebuke:

> "These are not the actions of the head of the judiciary defending its independence: these are the actions of a peeved minister voicing his anger over public criticism of a particularly compelling kind."[68]

One is tempted to ask whether this was the same Lord Hailsham who

---

[66] *O'Reilly* v. *Mackman* [1982] 3 W.L.R. 1096.

[67] The issue is too large to be discussed in this essay but many people have shown that judicial activism in control of the administration inevitably embraces both procedure and substance, that is judicial attitudes towards particular policies or institutions will influence their willingness or unwillingness to exert control over the implementation of a policy or the conduct of an institution. Judges have policies; these tend on the whole to favour a conservative individualistic rather than a non-Conservative collectivist view of society and its arrangements. The cases mentioned in the text where the courts have found against the Government and sparked off retrospective legislation or attempts to cut down the possibilities of judicial review are cases where a more collectivist style of central government intervention was occuring which in part, we think, explains the court's decisions. Government reaction to them has been in line with the trends noted in this essay. On individualist and collectivist administration and judicial reaction thereto see McAuslan, "Administrative Law, Collective Consumption and Judicial Policy" (1983) 46 M.L.R. 1. See too H. W. Arthurs, *Without the Law: Administrative Justice and Legal Pluralism in Nineteenth Century England* (Toronto, 1985).

[68] G. Zellick, *The Guardian*, February 25, 1984.

in 1978 inveighed against "direct attacks on the judiciary . . . constantly being made . . . by ministers"[69] and stated that:

> "they [the judiciary] should jealously pursue their undoubted right to invigilate the validity and fairness of administrative acts of ministers and local and subordinate authorities . . . ."[70]

We consider then that the concern for the legitimacy of the constitution raised in these essays, their general thrust that public lawyers should be concerned with the social, political and economic context of their work and that theory has a highly relevant part to play in any analysis of public law, or suggestions for its reform is amply borne out not just by the essays themselves but by the wider world of governmental power which we have attempted to portray here. What we have all observed in our respective areas of concern and from our various perspectives, is a progressive acquisition and centralisation of governmental power, a progressive arrogance and carelessness about its use and a progressive weakening of any effective opposition to or check, political, legal or societal, on that use. No wonder then that we are all concerned about the fundamental principles of the constitution, about the government's disregard of constitutionalism, about the need for a more considered and fundamental programme of reform of public law to ensure effective redress against administrative errors or worse, about, in other words, the legitimacy of our present constitutional arrangements and what may happen if present trends continue.

We must however counter one or two criticisms which may be made of the stance adopted in this essay. A general one may be to say that by abstracting the procedures or the general exercise of power from the substance of what is being done, we are failing to appreciate that something far more sinister is afoot than failure to comply with the law, namely, that there is an assault upon the substantive rights of ordinary people to a decent home, to health and to work. Thus, were the excesses detailed here to be corrected, we, as lawyers, would be forced to concede that there was nothing we could criticise in government policies. This is true as far as it goes; if the rules of public law and the principles of the constitution are being observed, we as public lawyers, could not fairly make the criticisms we have here made.

But we would argue that first, the discussion here has not concerned itself with human rights which might well have something to say about a right to a home, health and work, and secondly, that were the excesses outlined here corrected, or had they not taken place, then substantive policies which have been introduced over the last few years

[69] *Op. cit.* p. 105.
[70] *Op. cit.* p. 108.

might very well have been modified or not introduced at all. The abolition of elected local authorities is an obvious example, but the greater acceptance of inconvenient, from the government's perspective, decisions of courts and administrative tribunals might also have helped ameliorate some of the harsher elements of current policies. Procedures in other words do affect substance and public lawyers are not wholly misguided to direct attention to procedures.

A second criticism is more substantial. This essay and indeed the whole book, is implicitly based on an acceptance of the liberal democratic constitution described by Dicey 100 years ago, based furthermore on a belief that that constitution remains in existence so that it is a valid and useful exercise to criticise or comment on current policies and actions by reference to that constitution and its fundamental principles. But, this criticism would continue, that constitution no longer exists, if it ever did, outside the cloister. We have, and have had for many years, an elective dictatorship, a centralised and increasingly authoritarian democracy in which governmental power is not, and is not meant to be, controlled or checked in any effective way. All that has been happening over the last few years is that, in line with a general policy of sweeping away cant, inertia, institutional blockages and interest groups dedicated to the status quo, the barnacles encrusted on the ship of state have been removed, and it stands revealed for what it always has been; a vehicle for swift and effective action.

At this point, the argument bifurcates. On the one hand, there are those who argue that the barnacles and the centralising tendencies were, and are, broadly composed of the institutional and political mechanisms of the welfare state, so that the brusque and temporarily painful removal of much of those mechanisms is a necessary forerunner to the re-establishment of the Diceyan liberal democratic constitution which could, when once re-established, be bolstered by legal mechanisms; this broadly is Lord Hailsham's position and may be thought to provide a way of reconciling the preaching of the Seventies with the practice of the Eighties. It would also dispose of our criticisms since it would be a confession and avoidance; "Yes, we agree things aren't perfect now, though you are naive, not to appreciate the cause; but in the near future, everything will be all right."

The other strand of this argument relates back to the point about procedure and substance made earlier. This strand would argue that far from present economic and social policies leading on to a re-establishment of a Diceyan liberal democratic constitution, they can in fact only be implemented by moving further and further away from such a constitution and adopting an ever more authoritarian and centralised form of government. What has been happening in the last few years is the steady dismantling of all those accretions, justified in the name of a

Diceyan liberal democracy, on governmental power which did indeed slow it down, force it, often unwillingly, to take account of interests which it would have preferred to ignore, and generally slowly but surely increase public knowledge about, and participation in, government. The hollowness of the Diceyan liberal constitution now exposed, is that when confronted with this drive for centralised, uncheckable power, it has no answer. Elected authorities can be abolished or have their financial autonomy undermined; judicial decisions can be reversed by retrospective legislation; Ministers can mislead Parliament and the public on matters of public business; the media can be threatened and harassed for exposing government errors and illegalities, and to all this, the Diceyan liberal constitution and its proponents can point to no effective device to control or prevent these abuses of power. In such a situation, it is a refusal to face reality to continue to write in terms of a constitution which enshrines limited government, when clearly there is no such constitution in existence.

  This is not an easy argument to combat. Certainly, we find it more convincing than one that claims that a golden age of constitutionalism is around the corner, once the excesses of the Welfare State have been pruned back. It is grounded in the reality of the present and takes note of the fact that in modern bureaucracies of whatever political persuasion, powers once acquired are rarely relinquished. But we think there is an answer. What is the solution to the present incipient crisis in the constitution? Is it to argue for and assist in the establishment of an alternative government within the present centralised authoritarian framework of government? Or to argue for the overthrow of all government? Or to publicise the present dangers, argue for an alternative, and pose as the desirable model towards which society should aim, a constitutional system which limits and controls the way central government can act and behave, by legal, political and societal checks on power? If this model bears a resemblance to the model Dicey offered us 100 years ago, it is none the worse for that, for it may well be that the Diceyan model is etched more deeply in the general public consciousness than we realise and this would explain increasing general unease at centralised governmental power and its use now so prevelant. The members of the Ponting jury stood in a direct line from Dicey and these essays should be read in that context; like them they are concerned with the loss of democratic and legal controls over governmental power and we offer them as our contribution to a growing and necessary debate on that matter.

See: Gavin Drewry, "The Ponting Case—leaking in the Public Interest" [1985] *Public Law* 203–212. Also, Graham Zellick, "Government Beyond Law" [1985] *Public Law* 283–308.

Chapter 2

DICEY IN HISTORICAL PERSPECTIVE—A REVIEW ESSAY

JOHN F. MCELDOWNEY

Introduction

"My lectures," wrote Dicey to James Bryce, on September 2, 1884 "will I feel greatly disappoint you. They are simply lectures and intended to explain very elementary matters to students who seem to me in need of guidance."[1]

The lectures, so modestly described by Dicey in his letter to Bryce, probably referred to the lectures which formed *An Introduction to the Study of the Law of the Constitution.*[2] Dicey's book was written during the two years prior to its publication in 1885 and originated as a collection of his Oxford lectures. The idea for turning lectures on the Constitution into a book seemingly came from a visit Dicey and Bryce made to the United States in 1870.[3]

Dicey's *Law of the Constitution,* as the book was commonly referred to, was at once a success. The first edition of about 700 copies exceeded Dicey's expectations and was sold out within months, publication having coincided with the beginning of the Oxford term where Dicey as Vinerian Professor lectured on constitutional law. Soon Dicey asked for Bryce's help to negotiate arrangements for a second edition. Commercial success for the book (the profits for the first edition all went to the publishers), ensured Dicey's academic reputation. Financial security followed with the continued success of the second and subsequent editions with generous royalties to Dicey who edited the seven editions up to 1908.[4]

Dicey's reasons for publishing *Law of the Constitution* were expressed in the preface to the first edition. Addressed to his students,

---

[1] Ms. Bryce Papers 3, September 2, 1884 (Fol. 44). Bodleian Library, Oxford. The convention I have used is to give a full reference to a Manuscript and when appropriate where it appears in R. A. Cosgrove, *The Rule of Law: Albert Venn Dicey, Victorian Jurist* (Macmillan, 1980). Hereinafter referred to as Cosgrove. I have found Cosgrove a useful and important biography in writing this chapter.

[2] A. V. Dicey, *Introduction to the Study of the Law of the Constitution* (Macmillan, 1885). Hereinafter referred to as Dicey's *Law of the Constitution.*

[3] Ms. Bryce 3, February 12, 1907 (Fol. 52).

[4] Cosgrove, *loc. cit.* n. 1.

39

Dicey intended to provide a manual containing the two or three guiding principles which in 1885 pervaded the Constitution of England.[5] As far as it is possible to judge from Dicey's letters to Bryce such modest aspirations were genuine. Much later in his life when Dicey's book was regarded as an outright success, Dicey himself conceded that the book had been "born under a lucky star" and was far better than anything else "I ever wrote or am likely to write."[6]

The immediate attraction of a work of constitutional law as distinct from constitutional history was obvious for English lawyers who lacked a written constitution. In the absence of a written constitution lawyers had traditionally found it difficult to discover principles of constitutional law to explain the relationship between Parliament, the institutions of Government and the law. Constitutional development had been achieved through historical accident rather than in accordance with any grand plan. No revolutionary break had occasioned the complete rethinking of what was the function of a constitution or what part, if any, law performed in the constitution. No opportunity had been taken to write a completely thought out constitution.

Dicey's *Law of the Constitution* filled a gap without encroaching upon law reform or the codification movement. Its attraction was not confined to guiding students; it offered lawyers a legal framework for the British Constitution. Dicey made no claims for originality in his work nor "could it ever be seen," he wrote, "as truly novel."[7] Instead he offered lawyers a recognisable explanation of the law of the constitution of 1885 "grounded in principles." His form of presentation was made attractive by his clever arrangement in simple language of legal principles under the headings; the "Sovereignty of Parliament," the "Rule of Law" and the "Conventions of the Constitution."[8] The concept of sovereignty he owed to Austin, the term "rule of law" to W.E. Hearn[9] and his understanding of conventions to the work of the historian Edward A. Freeman.[10]

---

[5] *Loc. cit.* n. 2.

[6] Ms. Bryce 3, May 16, 1902 (Fol. 13).

[7] Ms. Bryce 2, December 9, 1884 (Fol. 55), also see Cosgrove *loc. cit.* n. 1.

[8] See Cosgrove, *loc. cit.* n. 1, pp. 23–28. Generally, Austin, *Lectures on Jurisprudence* (Campbell ed., 4th ed., 1879).

[9] William Edward Hearn (1826–1888). Educated Trinity College, Dublin, Professor of Greek at Queen's College, Galway. Irish Bar 1853, and the Bar of Victoria 1860. First Dean, Faculty of Law, University of Melbourne. See W. E. Hearn, *The Government of England, its Structure and its Development* (London, 1867). See: H. W. Arndt, "The Origin of Dicey's concept of the Rule of Law" (1957) Austl. L.J. 31 117–123.

[10] Edward Augustus Freeman (1823–1892). Historian, born Harbourne, Staffordshire. Educated Trinity College, Oxford. See E. A. Freeman, *Growth of the English Constitution* (London, 1872).

Dicey's clarity of style and economy of expression commended his writings to a wide audience both nationally and internationally. Students of constitutional law were attracted by Dicey's convenient format which encouraged certainty and precision in a subject which was vague and imprecise. British lawyers gained a legal language to discuss political institutions and issues. Although the British Constitution remained unwritten, after Dicey's book it was presentable in a written form which was recognisable to American or European lawyers who were more familiar with written constitutions. Dicey was fully aware of the desirability of allowing an identifiable constitution to emerge from his book. He went so far as to attempt to incorporate the separation of powers doctrine to explain part of the functions of the English Constitution.[11] But the doctrine he found inappropriate and he conceded to Bryce that the experience of the doctrine in France and America differed from anything really existing under the English Constitution.

Dicey's influence has endured. His critics have succeeded in pointing out limitations in his work and these shortcomings may be more clearly apparent today than when Dicey first wrote. Dicey was content to find main principles rather than to produce a work which would survive as an historical document. Often it is unclear how flexible or susceptible to change Dicey regarded his principles or the extent to which our understanding them has been derived from his critics rather than from Dicey himself.[12]

Much is written about Dicey's work but little is known about the man or how understanding the man might help to understand his work. The recent publication of Richard Cosgrove's *The Rule of Law, Albert Venn Dicey, Victorian Jurist*[13] written by an historian helps to highlight aspects of Dicey's career which help to explain his ideas. Lawyers have tended to neglect the study of Dicey in the context of his period. Undoubtedly lawyers are tempted, when brought up in the common law tradition, to read Dicey as if his book were a constitutional statute and offered interpretations as binding as once were House of Lords decisions.

It is true that for lawyers, history is difficult. There have been exceptions to the general neglect of Dicey in his historical context such as the Jennings critique. Jennings pointed out that Dicey should be viewed as a politician as well as a lawyer and that *Law of the Constitution* was influenced by Whig principles. Another exception, but more in defence of Dicey, was Lawson's article in 1959 which

---

[11] Ms. Bryce 2, May 6, 1887 (Fol. 103).
[12] Cosgrove, *loc. cit.* n. 1, pp. 66–68.
[13] *Ibid.* See D. Sugarman, "The Legal Boundaries of Liberty: Dicey, Liberalism and Legal Science" (1983) 46 M.L.R. 102–111.

pointed out how Dicey was influenced by the continuing changes in the French *Droit Administratif.*

Since Lawson[14] and Jennings[15] recent legal writers such as Craig[16] have paid deferential homage to Dicey's influence. Shades of Dicey are still in evidence casting an influence over present day constitutional and administrative law.[17] Further historical work on Dicey's political views as well as the publication of Cosgrove's biography have added to Dicey scholarship and allow an historical perspective on Dicey.[18]

The centenary of *Law of the Constitution* is an appropriate moment to think about the state of public law and aspects of the present state of public law are variously examined in the contributions to this book of essays. It is also an appropriate time to reflect on our understanding of Dicey, his influence and the contribution made by Cosgrove's biography. This essay is intended to assess Dicey in an historical perspective and picture the man as well as the ideas which may have influenced him.

Dicey and His Times

Cosgrove's apt description of Dicey as a "mid Victorian," a term Dicey approved himself, reminds us of the period in which Dicey lived.[19] He was born three years after the Great Reform Act 1832.[20] During his life he witnessed the extension of the parliamentary franchise in 1867, 1884 and 1918.[21] Major political changes included the development of the political party system and a growth in Government activity. Many economic and social changes were brought about by industrialisation, the concentration and mobility of population, new transportation systems and the progress of scientific discovery and economic growth. The resultant growth of organised labour was recognised in The Trade Disputes Acts 1906–1913[22] which permitted peaceful pickets and granted civil immunity to trade unions.

[14] F. H. Lawson, "Dicey Revisited" (June and October 1959) 7 *Political Studies* 109–126, 207–221.

[15] Sir W. Ivor Jennings, *The Law and the Constitution* (5th ed., London, 1959) also "In Praise of Dicey" (April 1985) 13 *Public Administration* 123–134.

[16] P. Craig, *Administrative law* (London, 1983), p. 28.

[17] For example: Harry Arthurs, "Rethinking Administrative Law" (1979) 17 *Osgoode Hall Law Journal* 1–45, and Harry Arthurs, *Without the Law Administrative Justice and Legal Pluralism in Nineteenth Century England* (Toronto, 1985).

[18] For example, Trowbridge Ford, "Dicey as a Political Journalist" (1970) 18 *Political Studies* 220–235.

[19] Cosgrove, *loc. cit.* n. 1.

[20] Representation of the People Act 1832 (2 & 3 Will. 4, c. 45).

[21] Representation of the People Acts 1867 (30 & 31 Vict. c. 102), 1884 (48 & 49 Vict. c. 3) and 1918 (7 & 8 Geo. 5, c. 64).

[22] Trade Dispute Act 1906 (Edw. 7, c. 47).

Major constitutional changes also occurred during his life time. The United Kingdom of Great Britain and Ireland was altered by the Government of Ireland Act 1920[23] and Dicey lived to see the creation of Northern Ireland with a local parliament but remaining part of the United Kingdom. The creation of the Irish Free State by the provision of a parliament for Southern Ireland was also achieved. But what Dicey did not live to see, by a matter of months, was the ratification of Northern Ireland's exclusion from the jurisdiction of the Parliament of the Irish Free State. Dicey, the elder statesman of Unionism regarded the 1920 Act unsympathetically; "England has been degraded and Ireland corrupted."[24]

When Dicey died in 1922, the system of modern government had already taken a form which is recognisable today. The Northcote-Trevelyan Report on the Civil Service in 1854[25] had set out the aims and responsibilities of a permanent Civil Service and set the standards of entry. Patronage was replaced by open competition. The Exchequer and Audit Department Act 1866[26] had established the office of Comptroller and Auditor General and parliamentary accountability of public expenditure. The Official Secrets Acts 1911 and 1920[27] provided Government with a framework of secrecy which endures today. The function of the Cabinet in the co-ordination of Government activities was considered by the Haldane Committee on the Machinery of Government in 1918 after[28] the experience of the War Cabinet set up during the First World War. Major reforms in Local Government had been achieved in 1888 and 1894 by legislation which set up a unified local authority system.[29] The Parliament Act 1911 had regulated the powers of the House of Lords and the authority of the House of Commons.[30]

During Dicey's life time, the courts also had contributed principles towards the development of constitutional law. Leading cases such as *Edinburgh and Dalkeith Railway Co.* v. *Wauchope*[31] on parliamentary sovereignty, *Dimes* v. *Grand Junction Canal*[32] on bias in natural

---

[23] Government of Ireland Act 1920 (10 & 11 Geo. 5, c. 67).
[24] Quoted in Cosgrove, *loc. cit.* n. 1, p. 284.
[25] Report of Sir Stafford Northcote and Charles Trevelyan on the Organisation of the Permanent Civil Service (1854) Parl. Pap. XXVII. 1.
[26] 29 & 30 Vict. c. 39. and also 11 & 12 Geo. 5, c. 52.
[27] 1 & 2 Geo. 5, c. 28.
[28] Report of the Committee on the Machinery of Government, Cd. 9230 (1918).
[29] Local Government Act 1888 (51 & 52 Vict. c. 41), 1894 (56 & 57 Vict. c. 73).
[30] 1 & 2 Geo. 5, c. 13.
[31] (1842) 8 Cl. & F. 710; 8 E.R. 279.
[32] (1852) 3 H.L.C. 759.

justice and *Bradlaugh* v. *Gossett*,[33] *Stockdale* v. *Hansard*[34] were decided during his lifetime.

Principles of administrative law were considered in *Cooper* v. *Wandsworth Board of Works*,[35] *Local Government Board* v. *Arlidge*[36] and *Board of Education* v. *Rice*[37] and raised the question of whether administrative law was being developed in English courts. The latter two cases caused Dicey to question his own ideas on English administrative law compared to *Droit Administratif* and eventually led him to recognise the existence of administrative law in England.

Major reforms in the court system, public health, and workmen's compensation reflected the diversity of law reform and statutory consolidation. Dicey himself referred to the period 1865 or 1870 to about 1905 as the period of Collectivism. As Harold Perkin described it, it was a period "dominated it seems by no great thinker of powerful mind and principle, but merely by the pragmatic need to propitiate the emerging and increasingly powerful working-class voter."[38] Whether Dicey was correct in this view is debatable but it is accepted that he lived during a period of unparalleled growth in prosperity and change.

Dicey belonged to that "aristocracy of intellect"[39] which began to form at the beginning of the nineteenth century. Cosgrove's biography[40] provides a glimpse of how Dicey's middle class family background, through marriage, brought him within the new intelligentsia. Dicey's mother was Anne Mary Stephen, daughter of James Stephen the Evangelical and a Master in Chancery, and this brought Dicey within the evangelical movement known as the Clapham Sect. Dicey was brought up in the evangelical tradition, which greatly influenced his later work.

Dicey's father, himself a proprietor of *The Mercury*, came from a family whose background was in newspaper publishing. His father was devoted to social reform, free trade and he epitomised the political liberalism of his times.

This combination of Whig principles and evangelicalism took hold of Dicey. A mixture of intellectual curiosity and belief in rationality dominated his thinking rather than membership of any established Church and throughout his life his interest in religion remained.

---

[33] (1884) 12 Q.B.D. 271.
[34] (1839) 9 Ad. & E.1.
[35] (1863) 14 C.B. (N.S.) 182.
[36] [1915] A.C. 120.
[37] [1911] A.C. 179.
[38] Harold Perkin, "Individualism versus Collectivism in Nineteenth Century Britain: A False Antithesis" (1977) 17 *Journal of British Studies* 105–118.
[39] Lord Annan, "The Intellectual Aristocracy" in *Studies in Social History: a Tribute to G. M. Trevelyan* (J.H. Plumb ed., London, 1955), pp. 243–287.
[40] Cosgrove, *loc. cit.* n. 1. See C. Harvie, *The Lights of Liberalism* (London, 1976).

Dicey, time and again, in his letters reveals his evangelical child-hood. He constantly reiterated the work or "labour" he had devoted to any problem or writing and believed that honest labour and toil produced good work.[41] Through work, he believed happiness was possible, although one was not the guarantee of the other.

At home, politics and current affairs dominated discussion and this strong influence remained with Dicey. He received tuition from his mother to the age of 17 and this included formal instruction in the Classics, French and German. He visited the Continent after attending Kings College School, London, two years before matriculating at Balliol College, Oxford in 1854.

Dicey flourished at Oxford under the tutorship of Benjamin Jowett.[42] Cosgrove believes Dicey later formed his own style of teaching from Jowett, such was Jowett's energy and personality and the impression it made on the young Dicey. The Old Mortality Society, founded by Oxford undergraduates in 1856, was also an important influence on Dicey for the friends he made and the ideas discussed. Bryce was also a member and in later life in a letter to Dicey, he reflected on the wide issues discussed at meetings of the society and the debates over papers read before the Society. Religion and politics dominated discussions. Bryce believed that then he and Dicey and their friends believed in individualism:

> " . . . We all assumed individualism as obviously and absolutely right. We were not indifferent to the misfortunes of the past but looked upon them as inevitable misfortunes and did not feel the restless anxiety to remove them in defiance of economic laws which burn in the breasts of the modern youth."[43]

The membership of Old Mortality went on to achieve remarkable success notably Bryce[44] as a Professor and Cabinet Minister, and Dicey himself as Vinerian Professor. Such achievements reflected the newly found influence of academic ability and worth over status through birthright.

Dicey graduated at Oxford in 1858 with first class honours. Sadly his father died before his graduation. The subsequent two years were spent attempting to obtain a fellowship. Success was achieved when he was permitted to dictate rather than write his papers. For Dicey, according to Cosgrove, was not physically strong and suffered

---

[41] Ms. Bryce 2, December 9, 1884 (Fol. 55).
[42] Benjamin Jowett (1817–1893). Master Balliol College, Regius Professor of Greek, Oxford University.
[43] Ms. Bryce, 4, April 6, 1915 (Fol. 83) (Bryce to Dicey).
[44] James Bryce (1838–1922). Jurist, historian and politician. Born Belfast, educated Glasgow University.

throughout his life from a muscular weakness which made physical exercise and writing legibly and rapidly very difficult without exhausting himself.

In 1861, Dicey left Oxford and moved to London to reside with his mother, where he read for the Bar. After call, his ambition was to build up a good practice and if possible to enter politics. Both ambitions were denied him. Evidently he did not make sufficient of a mark at the Bar for him to become a prominent candidate for politics. Although he joined the Northern Circuit he made little impression and the work was hard and laborious.

It may be unkind to suggest that Dicey was a failed barrister; after all, in 1876 he became Junior Counsel to the Inland Revenue. Nevertheless a career at the Bar lost many of its attractions as Dicey struggled in the face of competition based not on merit but on patronage and class.

Dicey's ambitions were aimed at gaining influence and thereby prestige. In later life he confided in Bryce his frustrated plans for a career which might have attained for him judicial office:

> "I have had many pieces of good fortune in life, but I sometimes feel that it would have been a comfort to have known that one had obtained the place which I have often longed for after I knew it was to be unattainable, of a judgeship. . . . "[45]

Dicey's disappointments remained. Whether due to lack of physical stamina or his personality, both a career in politics and the Bar evaded him. Dicey looked to academic life. Since leaving Oxford, Dicey's close relationship with Bryce had flourished. They both made frequent visits to the Continent together. Also Bryce seems to have encouraged Dicey to take an interest in law teaching. In 1871 Dicey assisted Bryce in founding the law schools at Manchester and Liverpool. Dicey continued for two years to commute between London and Manchester to give lectures at Owen's College. Through Bryce's influence, Dicey had been an examiner at Oxford from 1874 to 1876.[46]

Undoubtedly academic life offered better prospects. But Dicey's candidature for the Vinerian Chair at Oxford took two years. Eventually in 1882 he took up the Chair. His appointment imposed on him the discipline of writing through the necessity to provide lectures for his students and the opportunity to enjoy an audience for his ideas. Dicey's achievement had been won through severe competition from Anson and Pollock for the Chair. Teaching was a challenge to Dicey as

[45] Ms. Bryce 3, October 16, 1921 (Fol. 280).
[46] See Cosgrove, *loc. cit.* n. 1.

the state of law teaching in Oxford was unsatisfactory and Dicey wished to improve its reputation.

On taking up the Vinerian Chair in 1882, what was noteworthy about Dicey's belief and times? Two features of Dicey's personality and career are present. The first is the strongly held beliefs in laissez-faire and liberalism arising from Dicey's evangelical family. The second feature is Dicey's deep frustration at not finding success at the Bar or in a career in politics. Strong willed and determined, Dicey showed frustration at not being able to shape events and influence Government decisions; perhaps also a frustration over not being able to share in the influence of his friend, Bryce. Above all, Dicey seemed anxious to be caught up in current affairs, an involvement without any real determination at self discipline. Later in life he was to regret that his energy was devoted to so many "causes" with no foreseen end results.[47]

Dicey, Beliefs and Causes

Dicey devoted as much energy to political causes as he had to his legal writing. Especially during the time he wrote *Law of the Constitution*, Dicey was greatly preoccupied with political matters. In fact one of his major obsessions throughout his life was an interest in Ireland and he wrote more on the Irish question than on any other single issue.

The historians Trowbridge Ford[48] and Christopher Harvie[49] have shown how early in his writing Dicey became sympathetic to Irish Nationalism out of his belief that much of Ireland's suffering resulted from English rule. Although Ford and Harvie differ on the evidence and its interpretation they generally agree Dicey's original position. Cosgrove suggests that whatever sympathy Dicey had with Nationalism, he had an overriding principle which led him to reject the Nationalist viewpoint. According to Cosgrove between 1880 and 1885, Dicey's main principle was to reject "any proposal that smacked of fundamental constitutional change in relations with Ireland."[50] This was typical of Dicey's approach to any controversy. Select general principles and resist any changes which might fundamentally alter them. In that sense Dicey believed in maintaining intact the constitutional arrangements in Britain through the strict maintenance of the ordinary law.

However Ireland posed major problems for Dicey's tidy principles

---

[47] See n. 45, above.
[48] See n. 18, above.
[49] Christopher Harvie, "Ideology and Home Rule: James Bryce, A. V. Dicey, and Ireland, 1880–1887" (April 1976) 91 *English Historical Review* 298–314.
[50] Cosgrove, *loc. cit.* n. 1, p. 115.

and finely balanced view of English law and standards of justice. The
Irish were in conflict with the English common law mainly because, as
John Morley was to point out, they did not accept the law as their
own.[51] Dicey went so far as to accept that the lack of sympathy with
English law and its institutions in Ireland was the basic problem when
attempting to enforce the law in Ireland. Specifically Dicey attributed
the failure of law to the failure of Irish juries to convict. Yet he did not
see that even when Irish juries did convict the law was not necessarily
made more acceptable.[52]

In an effort to obtain a more efficient system of law enforcement in
Ireland, Dicey was prepared to advocate the partial suspension of jury
trial. He supported Coercion Acts which often allowed summary trial
of indictable offences and stronger powers of detention or arrest
because juries would not return verdicts for the Crown. Dicey's support for the suspension of jury trial for a limited time in prescribed
circumstances was because he hoped this would help to achieve the
maintenance of the law in Ireland. The maintenance of the law was one
of Dicey's fundamental principles.

Dicey attempted to reconcile this partial abolition of jury trial with
his Whig principles. Here Dicey is aware of a potential conflict of
principle and he is at his intellectual best in resolving any potential
conflict. Dicey was never convinced of the civil libertarian claims
attributed to the English jury system by writers such as Blackstone.
Even in *Law of the Constitution,* Dicey only makes a passing reference
to the jury believing that its success in England was due to the good
sense and independence of the judges. In situations like Ireland or in
times of "revolutionary passions" Dicey believed jury trial "could not
secure respect for justice,"[53] Dicey placed trust in the judges to maintain the rule of law and regarded their independence as a more reliable
guarantee than the impartiality of juries. Thus Dicey found it easy to
reconcile the abandonment of the jury in Ireland with his Whig
principles.

Dicey also attempted to reconcile the need for modification of the
ordinary law in Ireland with his view that the regular process of law
should govern all of the United Kingdom including Ireland. Here
Dicey fared less well. In his 1881 article on "How is the Law to be
enforced in Ireland?"[54] Dicey found it difficult to reconcile what

---

[51] John Morley, "Conciliation with Ireland" (1881) 30 *Fortnightly Review* 407–425.
Also see H. Tulloch, "A. V. Dicey and the Irish Question 1870–1922" (1980) 15
Irish Jurist 137–165.

[52] A. V. Dicey, "How is the Law to be Enforced In Ireland?" (November 1881) 36
Fortnightly Review 537–552.

[53] Ms. Bryce 3, July 30, 1907 (Fol. 59).

[54] Dicey, *loc. cit.* n. 52.

Nationalists regarded as the apparent contradiction that Ireland required special laws but if viewed as part of the United Kingdom was subject only to the ordinary law.

In fairness to Dicey, it should be stated that he argued in favour of suspending jury trial rather than the alternative of stronger Coercion Acts. He hoped that the ordinary law would become the norm through better law enforcement and that the suspension of the jury was only for a temporary period. Dicey's critics could, on the other hand, point out that temporary pressures in the past had become permanent and he failed to recognise a weakness in the view that politically Ireland could be ruled just like any other part of the United Kingdom.

Dicey's treatment of the issue conformed to his approach of applying general principles to a specific problem. Inevitably this led him to consider the Irish demand for Home Rule and Unionist opposition.

Cosgrove's analysis[55] which is supported with historical evidence is that Dicey saw the choice between the maintenance of the Union or national independence. His aim was the same whatever the choice, namely, the maintenance of law in Ireland. Home Rule as a compromise arrangement would not, according to Dicey, work. When, late in 1885, Gladstone was converted to Home Rule, Dicey's hostility to Home Rule made him a convinced Unionist. Dicey, a liberal from his earliest days, entered a prolonged and bitter dispute between himself, Home Rulers, and Gladstone's Irish policy. The debate was dominated by Dicey publishing political tracts often at the request of the Ulster Unionists. His passion for Unionism arose because the maintenance of the United Kingdom was to Dicey a more fundamental principle than any Whig sympathy or sympathy with Irish distress.

Dicey, the lawyer attempted to combine history and politics to present a dispassionate view of an issue which at heart Dicey believed was a constitutional dispute. In essence he applied a legal method to a question which many saw as purely political. Dicey's reputation after *Law of the Constitution* established him as a constitutional expert, made him attempt to influence the outcome of the Irish question. It is doubtful if the effect was what Dicey had intended it to be. His critics could claim that the Irish question had exposed severe limitations in the English common law *and* in the application of Dicey's legal instincts to a sensitive political issue. Irrespective of political viewpoint, Dicey's reputation was certainly not enhanced by his Irish writing. Even his critics, however, could not deny he had brought lucid thought to a complex problem. But as Cosgrove has pointed out, Dicey's obsession with the case against Home Rule obscured his judgment on many issues.

[55] Cosgrove, *loc. cit.* n. 1, pp. 158–169.

Aside from Home Rule, Dicey was attracted to other causes which often revealed another of his more obvious character traits. A passionate critic for one cause or other in his early life he often becomes as equally a passionate supporter in later life. Rarely does Dicey attempt to reconcile earlier views with later ones again concentrating on principles rather than substance.

The referendum issue is a good example of Dicey's approach. In his early life, and certainly before 1886, he was entirely sceptical of the referendum and a passionate defender of the electoral system without recourse to a plebiscite which he identified as an entirely Swiss system unsuited to England. Later he just as passionately argued for the use of referenda. In a letter to Bryce, who was less convinced of the merits of a referendum, Dicey argued its virtues:

> " . . . it is the best remedy in my judgment for the evils of our party system which are rampant."[56]

(March 23, 1911)

What was unclear from Dicey however, was the answer to the practical questions of who should decide what were the issues suitable for referendum and on whose initiative might it be sought? Critics might see the referendum as a crude attempt by Dicey to use what he believed was popular opinion against any measure for Home Rule. Dicey's great facility was to be able to turn all the arguments of "democracy being a check on party tyranny"[57] to advance the referendum cause when in reality what he disliked was Home Rule.

Another example of a change of heart was the vote for women. Dicey was a supporter of female suffrage in his early days but later became unsympathetic. In letters to Bryce he doubted whether the majority of women greatly desired the vote or whether it would benefit women. He feared the influence women would have in Parliament, perhaps fearing their influence on Home Rule. He thought that granting the demand for female suffrage would also intensify other demands for greater changes in political institutions again fearing that the constitutional arrangements would suffer. But Dicey was a realist to the extent that in 1907 he was convinced that the vote would be granted not because of acceptance of any major principle but due to the "calculation of party interest."[58] The latter, Dicey feared would unduly influence the British Constitution.

Dicey's opposition to the franchise for women came from his fears for the Union and an increase in party political influences in Parlia-

---

[56] Ms. Bryce 3, December 23, 1907 (Fol. 64).
[57] Ms. Bryce 3, March 23, 1911 (Fol. 82).
[58] See n. 56, above.

ment. In a letter to Bryce in 1907, Dicey readily conceded the rights of women but considered their rights could be achieved by different means than the vote:

> "The same result [from the vote for women] may possibly be attained in what I consider by far the best way if the change is to be made at all, that is by the gradual extension of womens' political rights or powers in this sphere after another 'till there is a genuine conviction which may then be justified by experience that absolute equality of political rights will be beneficial to the State."[59]

Dicey exhibits a characteristic naiviety over the practical application of his views. Once it was accepted that women had rights it was hard to believe they would be satisfied by anything less than the right to vote; this was a point Dicey seemed unwilling to accept in his finely balanced legal judgment of the entire issue.

Dicey's estimation that the majority of women were against the vote was based on his view of public opinion. As with Home Rule, Dicey rested his case against on his assumption that the majority of votes in the United Kingdom would be against. However, in both cases of Home Rule and the women's suffragette movement, he misjudged popular opinion. But more critically, the use of a referendum as a device to measure popular opinion of which Dicey approved could potentially lead to a clash with Dicey's own principles. Indeed, Dicey's own judgment of public opinion was unreliable and the referendum would inexorably have led Dicey to accept changes to which ordinarily he would not have given support.

Despite any possible inconsistencies over policy, Dicey still adhered to his own views and supported the referendum even though it might have conflicted with his case against the women's vote and Home Rule. Dicey relied on the principle which he explained to Bryce but without any apparent understanding of the problems it involved in practice. A referendum avoided:

> " . . . The possibility at any rate which no one can dispute of a fundamental change passing into law which the mass of the nation do not desire . . . "[60]

What were the issues of "fundamental change" and how might any conflict between Government policy and recourse to referendum be resolved? Again, Dicey's answer speaks from principle—not on the effects. As far as could be judged, Dicey argued, a referendum would

---

[59] *Ibid.*
[60] *Ibid.*

be " . . . an effective check on rash legislation as regards fundamental institutions such as the poor law. . . . "[61]

Many reforms enacted during Dicey's life time and which, given his liberal background and evangelical beliefs, he might be expected to have supported conflicted with some of Dicey's legal ideas on principle. When this occurred it caused Dicey great distress.

Some examples may be taken from the other causes which interested him. Dicey disapproved of the Trade Disputes Act 1906 which recognised trade unions and afforded them protection from tortious liability.[62] He saw the creation for trade unions of a special exception to the general law as conflicting with his views on the rule of law which did not allow special protection to a specific group in society.

Dicey opposed the Parliament Bill of 1911. The bill, he considered, restricted the veto power of the House of Lords, a matter which given Dicey's liberal background he ought to have approved as the bill asserted the will of an elected Chamber over the unelected House of Lords. Cosgrove believes Dicey's opposition to the bill, was due to his fear that the House of Lords would lose the absolute veto "over Home Rule." This was surely an example of political dogma overruling Dicey's own principles of democracy. Perhaps Dicey's passionate belief in Unionism prevailed over his belief in representative democracy in the Commons? Dicey feared that the House of Commons was too dominated by party politics to be a reliable champion of democracy, and in fairness this might be an alternative explanation[63] for his stand on this issue.

But there were causes that were entirely influenced by Dicey's Unionism, such as free trade. A passionate free trader, like his father, Dicey shifted his position in 1903 over the threat offered by tariff reform. The strength of his passion for Unionism is well explained in Cosgrove's consideration of Dicey's position on free trade.

Aside from Unionism, Dicey was sympathetic to law reform. On codification he was at least in sympathy—"A short and not unintelligible Criminal Code would work a real benefit for ordinary Englishmen."[64] Perhaps unsympathetic to the ideas of Fitzjames Stephens, Dicey nevertheless praised the merits of his work but stressed that the Code should have the authority of an Act of Parliament. Dicey it seemed did not envisage the successful introduction of a Constitutional Code.

Dicey complained towards the end of his life of how " . . . there

---

[61] *Ibid.*
[62] Cosgrove, *loc. cit.* n. 1, pp. 207–210.
[63] *Ibid.* pp. 215–216.
[64] Ms. Bryce 3, March 23, 1921 (Fol. 253).

were an infinite number of decisive causes which practically made success for me impossible. . . . "[65]

As we have seen, such causes were dominated by Dicey's Unionism and the application of legal principles to political issues. Dicey saw himself as a public figure and his interest in Unionism gave him a convenient platform to speak out. But he bitterly complained that constitutional law which made him an expert, was not seen by the public as a major issue of sufficient importance to allow him to influence events.

Dicey's academic success at Oxford placed him as a foremost legal authority but he lacked the status of a professional career in politics or success in legal practice or judicial office. In fact either one he believed would have allowed him greater influence than academic life. It is important not to dismiss the impact of these disappointments on the approach Dicey used when examining legal problems.

In contrast to Dicey's public causes and beliefs there was an intensely private side to Dicey's character. Dicey, the man, enjoyed public speaking but desired a private life. In 1911 in a note to Bryce he admitted that he was unsure how far "the morality of private life can be or ought to be always the morality of public life."[66]

In his own life he answered the question by maintaining a strict control over his private thought. In an attempt to resolve his private and public image, Dicey wished to be remembered by his published writing rather than his private thoughts in his private correspondence. Curiously, for a mid-Victorian, he destroyed many of his own letters and the drafts of his own writing and that of correspondents. Occasionally he asked friends to destroy his letters or return them to him. He twice declined a knighthood with characteristic modesty.

Dicey's letters to Bryce reveal his diffidence over his own worth and that of his writings. Plagued by self criticism and doubt he relied heavily on Bryce for advice and was greatly influenced by Bryce's opinion on the value of his ideas.

Law of the Constitution: Dicey's Analytical Method

Dicey's evaluation of his own work placed *Law of the Constitution* as "for effectiveness the best thing I have ever done and which cost me less labour than any other book." *Law of the Constitution* remains even today a useful beginning to explain the British Constitution and the book's great influence especially among lawyers endures.

We turn to consider how Dicey's work might best be interpreted by

[65] Ms. Bryce 3, October 16, 1921 (Fol. 280).
[66] Cosgrove, *loc. cit.* n. 1, pp. 66–69 and Ms. Bryce 3, March 23, 1911 (Fol. 85).

examining first his analytical method. Generally speaking, lawyers have been slow to discover how much care should be used when interpreting Dicey. Cosgrove's biography suggests that Dicey's writing was a complex application of legal principles to political issues. Dicey's own background, beliefs and obsession with Home Rule are an intrinisic part of his writing. But which belief has a bearing on which issue is difficult to assess.

Dicey intended the book to be an introduction for students and in the preparation of his lectures he was conscious of the need to enhance the reputation of the Oxford Law School and live up to the reputation of Jowett who as his tutor he greatly respected. Dicey wrote, not as an historian but as a lawyer. He was unattracted to the purely historical approach, he claimed it lacked precision and examined unimportant subjects.

As a lawyer, Dicey complained of the difficulties he experienced in attempting to write a good law book. His personal difficulties were he claimed because "I have not a good memory for cases; no one has read so many and remembers so few. . . . "[67] His need to dictate what he wanted to write caused him delay but he also complained of a difficulty with "ordinary legal composition." He confided in Bryce a problem with statutes " . . . but the reproduction of statutes is, I have found even more difficult than the giving the results of cases and I suspect the existence of fundamental headings."[68] Admittedly, these concerns were voiced 10 years after *Law of the Constitution* was written but it showed Dicey's concerns about his own work. Perhaps the most surprising admission was his belief that he lacked "general knowledge of principles."

> "A writer like myself is at every point hindered by his want of a good general knowledge of the principles which govern all the different branches of the law. . . . "[69]

Such admissions must encourage rather than discourage future generations of lawyers who might share Dicey's concerns over cases, statutes and general principles. But it is Dicey's obsession with principles that provides the clue to understanding his approach. Like Wade, Cosgrove believes Dicey was attracted to Austin "Dicey followed in the footsteps of Austin by subjecting Constitutional Law to scientific study."[70] The analytical method of inquiry favoured abstracting basic principles from legal material and this was the main method he followed when he wrote *Law of the Constitution.*

---

[67] Ms. Bryce 2, September 28, 1895 (Fol. 218).
[68] *Ibid.*
[69] *Ibid.*
[70] Cosgrove, *loc. cit.* n. 1, p. 70.

Basic principles were encouraged by the lawyer's technical skill learnt by Dicey and which he found attractive. But Dicey's strength was to examine political institutions to determine legal principles. For this task he owed a debt to historical scholarship such as Hallam, Hearn, Gardiner and Freeman. His hope was to encourage his students to study Blackstone and Bagehot with the advantage of an explanation of constitutional legal principles.

Dicey greatly admired Blackstone, especially his clarity of style and purpose but was unattracted to many of his ideas. Freeman he had been friendly with at Oxford and admired his historical writing. Hearn and Gardiner he followed admittedly through their writing rather than their political views.

But Dicey's admiration of Blackstone was almost equal to his admiration of Bentham who was highly critical of Blackstone. Nevertheless Dicey conceded that "many of the changes he [Bentham] and his school advocated . . . would have taken place whether Bentham had lived or not."[71]

Dicey also admired the great work of MacAulay's *History* and of Maitland on whose death Dicey commented "He is more loss to the world than most men would be. . . . "[72] Given Dicey's admiration of such different writers, many of whom accepted different approaches and beliefs from one and another, how does Dicey's method compare to his contemporaries? What makes Dicey's work distinctive?

Dr. Clive Dewey has pointed out that jurisprudence in England as an academic discipline was greatly influenced by Maine's historical approach allied to Austin's analytical legal positivism. Dewey claims that the influence of the Law Schools in Oxford, Cambridge, Dublin and London was towards historical jurisprudence. During the latter part of the nineteenth century;

" . . . the great legal discoveries of the time were made on the frontiers of historical research; and the leading law teachers— Maine, Pollock, Vinogradoff, Bryce, Maitland, Hancock and Richey—were all historical jurists."[73]

The historicists influenced not only university teaching and learned societies but also select committees and legal textbooks. They reacted against the utilitarian vision of universally valid assumptions achieved through a deductive logic which created simplified models of universal

---

[71] *Ibid.* p. 182.
[72] Ms. Bryce 3, December 23, 1906 (Fol. 49). See G. R. Elton, *F. W. Maitland* (Weidenfeld, 1985).
[73] C. Dewey, "Celtic Agrarian Legislation and the Celtic Realm: Historical Implications of Gladstone's Irish and Scottish Land Acts 1870–1886" (1974) 64 *Past and Present* 30–70.

application. Instead historicists tended to make generalisations from observed data by inductive means.

Dicey does not appear to fit conveniently into either the utilitarian or historicist schools. It is safer to see him as a distinctive figure with his own method, certainly influenced by both schools but not fitting entirely within either. It is arguable that he fits the definition of an historicist or at least had tendencies in that direction. But the extent of Dicey's obedience to Austin's thinking and his dissatisfaction with some of Bentham's ideas, although he favoured his reforming zeal and individualism, makes the job of assessment very difficult.

The question of Dicey's distinctive approach and how it compared to his contemporaries must be one of the most important questions which require further research and analysis than is possible in this short survey. What is required is further research on the intellectual history of public law.

Dicey applied his analytical method which sought legal principles from the available historical and political evidence in *Law of the Constitution*. Jennings has argued that Dicey when writing the book was influenced by Whig political beliefs. Given the evidence from Cosgrove's biography it is difficult not to see the evidence as sustaining Jennings's view. But as Cosgrove points out, it is unclear how much the Constitution of 1885 was also influenced by Whig principles and Dicey represented the situation as he found it.[74] The difficulty of assessing claims for Dicey's influence is that rarely does Dicey make clear the evidence for the reasons he gives to support the principles he so clearly expresses.

Lawson has pointed out that Dicey looked to France to find part of this analysis for *Droit Administratif*. It is equally clear from Cosgrove's biography that Dicey looked to the United States, Italy and Belgium. Dicey claimed the American visit of Bryce and himself in 1870 helped to inspire the writing of the book, and American law is mentioned as an influence in the preface to the first edition.

But the influence of the Constitution of Belgium and Italy has not been fully considered by Lawson. Dicey wrote to Bryce and compared the differences between a written and unwritten constitution by comparing the Belgian and Italian Constitutions in the sense that Dicey viewed the Belgian written constitution as not unlike the English Constitution. Dicey concluded:

> "if it were possible to repeal an article thereby enabling parliament to change every article of the Constitution you would in

[74] Cosgrove, *loc. cit.* n. 1, pp. 69–70.

short have a fair codification of the existing English Constitution."[75]

Dicey's skill in borrowing ideas from other countries was equal to his skill at developing his method of sifting legal and political material to provide general principles. In assessing Dicey's methods, the crucial question is to determine the extent to which Dicey desired *Law of the Constitution* to be descriptive or prescriptive?

Wade, in his preface to the tenth edition argues that "Dicey never claimed that the constitutional ideas which he expanded were principles which must abide for all time."[76] Indeed, Dicey himself amended his text up to the seventh edition in 1908 with the main purpose of including "any change" which was relevant to the constitution.[77] Dicey's method was to update the text rather than rewrite the entire work. Partly this was to avoid spending the very great time which an entirely revised work would require. Possibly he saw no point in revising the basic principles as he may have felt they were still a valid description of the constitution. It is difficult to know whether if Dicey applied his analytical method to his final edition he would still find valid the original principles he began with.

Great care should be taken before a truly prescriptive approach is adopted when examining Dicey. On many of his basic principles Dicey's assumptions are no longer valid today. During his lifetime, sometimes Dicey's reluctance to shift his principles was borne out of his own stubbornness rather than his belief in the principles. There were exceptions to this such as any threat to the English constitutional framework which he resisted on principle. But even here his friend Bryce gently reminded him that "Freeman in 1868 had called the British Constitution 'the paragon of the world.' Nobody would say that now; indeed few people know there is such a thing."[78]

The safer descriptive approach, at least from the historical evidence, is that Dicey provides a good description of the constitution when he wrote. Treated as an historical document more effort should be made towards understanding Dicey and those he influenced. The fault of attributing to Dicey ideas which he did not have or attitudes to law for which there is little evidence, lies not so much with Dicey, but with his critics who apply Dicey's principles to recent constitutional developments to test the validity of Dicey's analysis.

The way forward is to concentrate more on the analytical method

---

[75] Ms. Bryce 2, December 9, 1884 (Fol. 55).
[76] E. C. S. Wade's preface to the Tenth Edition *An Introduction to the Study of the Law of the Constitution* (10th ed., London, 1973), p. x.
[77] *Ibid.*
[78] Ms. Bryce 4, April 16, 1916 (Fol. 100). Bryce to Dicey.

Dicey employed when writing his book, and undertake more research on the intellectual history of public law.

Law of the Constitution: Dicey's Principles of Constitutional Law

Dicey's postulations of the sovereignty of Parliament, the rule of law and conventions of the constitution may briefly be considered. Dicey's analytical method when applied to constitutional law had obvious shortcomings. The principles which may have determined how existing institutions worked were subject to change and differing influences. So even if the basic principles were obtained through a valid process of reasoning it did not mean the principles would work for the future. It was unclear why Dicey selected one area for consideration but not another. The reasoning behind the conclusions was often made obscure because of his preoccupation to find the principles. Dicey was not a good historian and his knowledge of other legal systems was, he admitted, at times superficial.

The complexity of Dicey's analytical method and its shortcomings has been overlooked by most lawyers when considering Dicey's principles. Lawyers have favoured a prescriptive approach reading Dicey in the same manner as a statute and ignoring political influences when Dicey wrote. The critics are as much to blame as Dicey was himself for mistaken impressions. A few examples will suffice.

Dicey's denial in 1885 that there existed in England a true *Droit Administratif* has been largely held responsible for the slow development of English administrative law and the lack of firm theoretical considerations once that development began. To what extent was Dicey in error in failing to see the significance of English administrative law?

Cosgrove provides an attractive explanation. Dicey's analytical method "of abstracting fundamental concepts from the evidence then drawing his conclusions from an elaboration of those ideas"[79] was flawed. He had failed to understand developments already in existence in the process of administration when he wrote. His understanding of the French system was possibly just as imprecise.[80] Dicey's sheer obsession with the rule of law caused him to concentrate on its relationship with the omnipotence of Parliament rather than to consider the function of Government. The rule of law emphasised the theoretical possibility that all officials were amenable to the law. But this over simplified the practical difficulty of enforcing the law against officials and ignored the facts of Crown immunity.

---

[79] Cosgrove, *op. cit.* n. 1, pp. 91–101. See Harlow, pp. 72–74.
[80] *Ibid.*

Dicey's concentration on fundamental principles led him to underestimate the evidence which could have shown him flaws in the principle itself. In 1915, *Local Government Board* v. *Arlidge*[81] caused Dicey to reconsider administrative law and Cosgrove rightly asserts that Dicey's writing on *Arlidge* exonerates him of the charge that he had failed to recognise English administrative law. But Dicey did not reconsider *the effects* of recognising administrative law on his fundamental principles which indicates Dicey's lack of flexibility in his thinking. His critics are also guilty in not pointing out that Dicey's acceptance of administrative law called into question his ideas on the rule of law.

Dicey's rigid outlook is also shown by his attitude to parliamentary sovereignty. Even when he first wrote, Dicey never fully appreciated the difficulty of reconciling the power of Parliament, which at a whim could destroy it, with the rule of law. Once he devised fundamental principles he felt obliged to rely on them even when they conflicted with other fundamental principles.

His critics were slow to point out Dicey's difficulties. That Parliament could make or unmake any law did not account for the political reality of legislation which in practice would not be repealed or laws that were unenforceable. Dicey failed to provide historical evidence to support his claims. But what if Parliament introduced Home Rule or the vote for women? Dicey's use of the referendum was an attempt to curtail Parliaments' unlimited powers over causes which Dicey did not support.

Similarly, Dicey's concern over the growth of political parties was because he saw them as a threat to his finely balanced constitution. His reliance on a referendum was an attempt to place a check on political power but this did not cause him to reconsider the principles of parliamentary sovereignty. Had he done so it would have been a valuable contribution to constitutional law. At the heart of Dicey's faith in parliamentary sovereignty was his belief that English gentlemen would only pass morally acceptable laws.

Nevertheless English courts follow the Dicey approach by appearing to obey without question all acts of Parliament. Occasionally the courts adopt an interpretation which seeks to understand parliamentary intention but never will they question the enforcement of all acts of Parliament.

Parliamentary sovereignty is one area of Dicey's writing which has continued to influence the judiciary although it has not found acceptance among all academic lawyers. Yet the possible validity of Dicey's theory has obscured Dicey's method of analysis. Dicey failed

[81] See n. 36.

to consider what Professor Heuston has pointed out as the difference between rules of procedure and sovereign power itself. Today the difference might be considered as important as Dicey's view of sovereignty itself.

Finally Dicey considered conventions of the constitution. Dicey's formulation has also provoked criticism from Jennings who has pointed out a flaw in Dicey's analytical method. Jennings showed that Dicey's distinction between legal and non-legal rules rested on the enforceability of the rules by the court. But courts according to Jennings never enforced a law but made a decision or an order.[82]

Dicey's view of conventions was at best a good description of "constitutional or political ethics," which were not "laws" in the proper sense of that term.[83] Dicey's careful distinction between law, politics and conventions has facilitated discussion of an important area. But the question of enforceability was a more difficult problem for Dicey. In essence he believed that, as Cosgrove puts it, "Constitutional Conventions assured the permanent political sovereignty of the electorate."[84] Violation of a convention might ultimately lead to a breach of the law. But Dicey did not consider the effect once a convention was no longer followed. Did the convention lapse and if so was it replaced by a new convention? How could any obligation arising from a convention be enforceable?

It is here Cosgrove believes Dicey's doctrine is not "erroneous but incomplete."[85]

Conclusions

Dicey in a letter to Bryce considered he had found a mathematical evaluation which worked in order to assess the influence or contribution of great men. He suggested that the assessment was made on the length of entry in the *Dictionary of National Biography*.[86] He thought Bryce would gain one or one-and-a-half columns whereas he would gain "half a column." In fact Dicey received over three columns and Bryce fifteen.

Dicey suffered greatly because of frustrations over his lack of a career in politics and the Bar. Yet his self-assessment has proved of dubious value as the influence of *Law of the Constitution* is far greater than his entry in the D.N.B. would suggest and far greater than Bryce's writings.

[82] Cosgrove, *op. cit.* n. 1, pp. 87–90.
[83] *Op. cit.* n. 2, p. 417.
[84] *Ibid.*
[85] *Op. cit.* n. 82.
[86] Ms. Bryce 2, September 17, 1893 (Fol. 159).

The theme of this essay may be shortly stated. Dicey's analytical method deserves as much attention as his actual writing before assessing his worth. Care should be exercised before using Dicey as a prescriptive analysis of the constitution. Considerations such as Dicey's obsession with Unionism and evangelical beliefs are relevant in assessing his work.

Dicey is not easy to categorise and fits no stereotype description. It is a mistake as some of his critics would have us believe, to see him as providing us with a formal legal framework devoid of political consideration. The abstraction of simple principles from complex problems was the work of a lawyer but under the influence of a politician.

Dicey has presented us with a picture of the British Constitution but if it has any validity today we should consider how Dicey's scholarship compared to his contemporaries in the intellectual history of public law. As well as attempting to reform what we already have, we should understand Dicey's contribution. Cosgrove's biography[86a] is an aid to the interpretation of the man and his ideas. Dicey in his own way asked himself the question of how far a constitution reflects the people it serves? We ought to consider more carefully what it is that Dicey means:

> "How far does a Constitution affect the character of a people? I have no doubt that the effect of Constitutions was much exaggerated 100 years ago and later and no one I suppose now questions that, in general, a Constitution is, in the main the outcome of the character and history of the people on whom it exists. But then do people not too readily assume, when all this is granted that a Constitution does not in its turn effect the character of a people and the history of a country?"[87]

[86a] A forthcoming and critical biography of Dicey, and one which takes issue with Cosgrove's views is Trowbridge Ford, *A. V. Dicey: The Man and his Times* (Barry Rise, Chichester).

[87] Ms. Bryce 3, December 15, 1901 (Fol. 6).

I am grateful to Professors Paul O'Higgins and Patrick McAuslan for reading a draft of this article. Errors are my own responsibility. I am also grateful to the Bodleian Library for permission to consult and quote from the Bryce Papers. The research was assisted by a small grant from the Nuffield Foundation.

Chapter 3

POWER FROM THE PEOPLE? REPRESENTATION AND
CONSTITUTIONAL THEORY

CAROL HARLOW*

Lawyers might be described as "flat-earthers" who have created for
themsleves a narrow, legal universe of "rules" and "rights" which they
are reluctant to abandon.[1] They prefer to seal off the world of political
scientists, economists and sociologists, drawing arbitrary lines between
matters political and matters legal. I will argue that this discordance
between the science of law and the other social sciences is disturbing
because it leads lawyers to misinterpret legal rules and to mistake
political ideology for legal fact.

We can illustrate this if we think for a moment about the concept of
sovereignty. For more than a century, this notion has been of central
importance to constitutional law. The subject has dominated the
discourse of political scientists for much longer; they have been debat-
ing the nature of sovereignty since the seventeenth century or earlier.
Yet, by the simple expedient of distinguishing "legal" from "political"
sovereignty, lawyers have managed to shut themselves off from this
debate. Every first year law student knows that Parliament is
"sovereign" but s/he is not taught to ask why this ought to be. The
answer we should give is that Parliament represents the nation or,
more accurately, that it contains a representative component. This
answer would take us outside the usual boundaries of legal discourse
into the worlds of politics and science. We should need to think about
the concept of "representation." Immediately there would be a problem of communication. Political scientists today are more likely to
want to talk about "majoritarianism," "representation" or "democratic government" than "sovereignty." Lawyers, on the other hand,
show little interest in this terminology, an omission which for one

* My thanks are due to Richard Rawlings and Professor Kenneth Minogue for help
with this essay.

[1] The reasons why this should be so are examined by David Kairys "Legal Reason-
ing" and Elizabeth Mensch "The History of Mainstream Legal Thought" in *The
Politics of Law* (Kairys ed., Pantheon 1982), pp. 11–17, 18–39. J.A.G. Griffith
"The Law of Property (Land)" makes a similar point in *Law and Opinion in
England in the 20th Century* (M. Ginsberg ed., 1959).

distinguished constitutional lawyer has disturbing implications. "In Britain," said Professor H.W.R. Wade in a prestigious Hamlyn lecture devoted to the subject of representation, "we are so short of constitutional rights and our notion of the judicial function is so restricted, that electoral fairness is hardly thought to be the concern of lawyers. In the United States, on the other hand, it can be enforced as one of the legal essentials of democracy."[2] Of course, we may think that electoral fairness is not the concern of judges; that lawyers would be wrong to discard their limited definition of sovereignty; or, more fundamentally, that democracy has no "legal essentials." But before jumping to conclusions we need to extend our legal vocabulary a little.

The "Tyranny of the Majority"

It is possible for lawyers to forget that they do not have a monopoly of the freedom of contract idea; after all, they have been taught to see it as the fundamental principle of contract law. The revelation that freedom of contract was historically no more than the legal manifestation of classical liberal economic theory[3] was not entirely welcome to lawyers. They tend to ignore, too, that political scientists have an interest in the principle. Since the late seventeenth century the contract idea has provided one philosophical basis for modern political systems. Revolutions swept away the divine right of kings, to be replaced by the idea of the "social contract." The "social contract" is a fictional bargain whereby man, in a state of nature, is said to agree to a partial surrender of his individual liberty in exchange for the protective security of the state. In this way, the freedom of contract principle became the fundamental premiss of liberal political philosophies.

Clearly the social contract is relevant to the problem of "sovereignty." In the first place it involves a notional transfer of political authority from the ruler to the people. Secondly, limitations are imposed on the authority of the ruler. The exact terms of the hypothetical bargain by which power was conveyed from the people to the ruler were a matter for philosophical debate. For Thomas Hobbes (1588–1679),[4] the surrender by the people of the rights which they possessed in a state of nature was once-and-for-all and conditional only on the ruler's obligation to secure their protection and safety. To the

---

[2] H.W.R. Wade, *Constitutional Fundamentals* (1980), p. 8.

[3] P. Gabel and J.M. Feinman "Contract Law as Ideology" in Kairys ed., *op. cit.*; Grant Gilmore, *The Death of Contract* (1974); Atiyah, *The Rise and Fall of Freedom of Contract* (1979).

[4] For a further explanation of Hobbes' theory of the social contract, see C.B. MacPherson's Introduction to Hobbes' *Leviathan,* first published in 1651, (Pelican, 1961), pp. 39 *et seq.*

French philosopher Jean Jacques Rousseau (1712–1778), sovereignty could never be finally surrendered. The people "remains sovereign and can at any moment recall the grants it has made. Government, therefore, exists only at the sovereign's pleasure, and is always revocable by the sovereign's will."[5] For John Locke (1632–1704) the social contract was specific and limited; the very concept of sovereignty

> "[is not] as Hobbes made it, the resignation of power into the hands of some single man or group. On the contrary, it is a contract with the community as a whole, which then becomes that common political superior—the State.... Nor is Locke's state a sovereign State: the very word 'sovereignty' does not occur, significantly enough, throughout [Locke's] treatise."[6]

All these writers *derive* sovereignty from "the people" though in different ways. They differ greatly about whether "Sovereignty" "rests with" "the people" (each term raising problems). They agree however that governmental authority derives from *the consent* of the people. Thus, from the social contract is derived not only the principle of representative government but also that of universal suffrage: man, in Rousseau's phrase, born free and equal, alienates his own liberty only for his own advantage. Laski links Locke's social contract with majoritarianism; "such a contract in Locke's view involves the preeminent necessity of majority rule."[7] And we find that James Madison (1751–1836) whose ideas, expressed with those of John Jay and Alexander Hamilton in *The Federalist Papers* (1787–1783), were influential in shaping the American Constitution, accepted this. He thought it "essential to [representative] government that it is derived from the great body of society, not from an unconsiderable proportion, or a favoured class of it."[8] He went on to emphasis the popular character of the electorate. It was to be "Not the rich, more than the poor; not the learned, more than the ignorant; not the haughty heirs of distinguished names, more than the humble sons of obscurity and unpropitious fortune,"[9] who elected the Congress of the United States.

But the social contract, itself a protection against the tyranny of absolute rulers, contains the threat of a new tyranny. The twentieth century has long ago realised that popularly elected governments are

---

[5] G.D.H. Cole in his Introduction to Rousseau's *Social Contract* (Everyman, 1973), p. xxvii. Compare the views of Robespierre explained by A. Cobban, "The Fundamental Ideas of Robespierre" in *Aspects of the French Revolution* (Paladin, 1971), pp. 137–158.

[6] Laski, *Political Thought in England* (1920), p. 36.

[7] *Ibid.*

[8] *Federalist Papers* No. 39.

[9] *Ibid.* No. 57.

not necessarily "democratic"; the eighteenth century, experienced in revolution though not in universal suffrage, knew this too.[10] Thomas Paine, whose views were in their day considered dangerously populist,[11] admitted that representative government could be despotic: "It is not because a part of the government is elective, that makes it less a despotism, if the persons so elected possess afterwards, as a parliament, unlimited powers. Election, in this case, becomes separated from representation, and the candidates are candidates for despotism."[12] And Hamilton captured the essence of the dilemma when he said,[13] "Give all the power to the many and they will oppress the few. Give all the power to the few and they will oppress the many." How was the dilemma to be resolved?

One way to protect the minority against the majority—or, which is not necessarily the same thing, individual citizens against the state—is that which lawyers have come to appropriate as peculiarly their own. Locke had drawn from his vision of man in a state of nature the three primary or natural "rights" of life, liberty and estate or property. Blackstone extrapolated these into his *Commentaries* as principles of common law.[14] Starting with the Amendments of the American Constitution (1787) and the Declaration of the Rights of Man in 1789, modern constitutions one by one proclaimed the sanctity of human liberty, which they attempted to guarantee by a Bill of Rights against the arbitrary actions of the state.[15] We need not digress to discuss a subject which has become a legal obsession; it is healthy now and again to redress the balance. Our subject is that of the majority, whose claims are sometimes neglected by lawyers. Rousseau was afraid that legal systems would be used to justify that poverty and inequality which he saw as the legacy of bad government. For laws, Rousseau observed percipiently, "are always of use to those who possess and harmful to those who possess nothing."[16] We would not want to take his aphorism

---

[10] See, for example, Christopher Hill, *The World Turned Upside Down* (Penguin, 1975), Chaps. 4 and 7. See also Edmund Burke's *Reflections on the Revolution in France* (1790).

[11] For Paine's influence, see E.P. Thompson, *The Making of the English Working Class* (Pelican, 1968), pp. 95–107. But note that Isaac Kramnick, *The Rage of Edmund Burke* (1977), p. 19 describes Paine as "the perfect expression of the liberal-bourgeois theory of the state."

[12] Thomas Paine, *Rights of Man* (1791) (Pelican, 1977), p. 215.

[13] Hamilton, *Congress Debates,* Vol. v, p. 203.

[14] *Commentaries* (1765–69) pp. 129–138. See further E.S. Corwin "The 'Higher Law' Background of American Constitution Law" (1928) 42 Harv. L.Rev. 149, 365, 383.

[15] Léon Duguit, "The Law and the State" (1917–18) 31 Harv. L.Rev. 1.

[16] Rousseau, *op. cit.* p. 166.

literally. But we ought to remember it as we traverse the familiar arguments for and against Bills of Rights.[17]

Madison's expression of apparent confidence in popular democracy introduces arguments more relevant here. Robert Dahl, a modern American political theorist, defends "Madisonian democracy" as a relatively successful compromise between "the political equality of all adult citizens on the one side, and the desire to limit their sovereignty on the other."[18] Later, however, he is more outspoken about its elitist character, describing it as "a satisfying, persuasive and protective ideology for the minorities of wealth status and power" against the "popular majority" which they distrusted.[19] Why does he say this?

For Madison, the principle of representative government was satisfied as soon as the members of the government were "appointed, either directly or indirectly by the people."[20] The power of actual decision-taking, the reality of political power, belonged to the government; what was left to the people was the right to choose the decision-makers. Madison defended this theory on the ground that delegation of governmental power would "refine and enlarge the public views by passing them through the medium of a chosen body of citizens, whose wisdom may best discern the true interest of their country and whose patriotism and love of justice will be least likely to sacrifice it to temporary or partial considerations."[21] (We will meet this idea again in the later work of John Stuart Mill).

It is well to pause at this point when ambiguities in the idea of representation are beginning to emerge, and ask ourselves what we mean by the term. A.H. Birch, in a useful study of the subject, identifies three meanings of the word "representative": first, it may mean an agent or *delegate* (an ambassador or barrister would be an example); secondly it may mean an *elected* person or body; thirdly, it may imply that a person is *typical* of a class of people.[22] Madison is concerned about the second but not the third sense. A government is only representative for Madison if it is elected; but the representatives of the people need not be—indeed, probably ought not to be—typical of the electorate which they represent. This definition serves as one limitation on popular democracy. Another limitation is latent in the

---

[17] See J.A.G. Griffith, "The Political Constitution" (1979) 42 M.L.R. 1.
[18] *A Preface to Democratic Theory* (1956), p. 4. Dahl's own theory is criticised as elitist by Carole Pateman, *Participation and Democratic Theory* (1970), pp. 14–16. See also C.B. MacPherson, *Democratic Theory* (1973), pp. 78–80.
[19] *Op. cit.* p. 30.
[20] *Federalist Papers* No. 39. Madison speaks of "republican," not "representative" government.
[21] *Federalist Papers* No. 10.
[22] *Representative and Responsible Government, An Essay on the British Constitution* (1964), pp. 13–17.

term "delegate." Barristers and ambassadors have limited freedom of action, being bound by instructions which may not be exceeded and must frequently be renewed. Such is not always the case, however; agents may sometimes bind their principals even when they are acting outside the terms of the power delegated to them.

However this may be (and we shall try to resolve the ambiguity later), in Madison's constitution, the bond between electors and elected was not a sufficient restriction on the misuse of power. "A dependence on the people is, no doubt, the primary control on the government; but experience has taught mankind the necessity of auxiliary precautions."[23] The constitutional device to which Madison unhesitatingly turned is normally today associated with the writings of the French philosopher Montesquieu (1689–1755). In his great book, *De l'Esprit des Lois* (1748), Montesquieu argued[24] that the control of power depends on its fragmentation. State power therefore ought to be divided between different governmental institutions—Montesquieu classified state power as legislative, executive and judicial in character[25]—who would thus each be in a position to prevent abuses by the other organs of government. (Although we in the common law would tend to talk of "checks and balances," it is important to note that there are various models of separation of powers, of which this is only one.)

Professor Vile, in his superlative historical study, where every possible variant on the theme is carefully analysed, describes Separation of Powers as the most significant constitutional device of the modern era for the limitation of power, and declares that it "stands alongside that great pillar of western political thought—the concept of representative government—as the major support for the systems of government which are labelled 'constitutional'."[26] The inference is that the twin pillars invariably support each other. Madison, however, intended separation of powers as a foil to popular, majoritarian government. In the American Constitution as it has developed we can see how this can work. An unelected judiciary may, for example, strike down laws passed by representative legislatures. John Hart Ely tells us how dismayed the exponents of judicial activism are when they hear judicial power attacked as "undemocractic." "Majoritarian democracy is, they know, the core of our entire system, and they hear

---

[23] *Federalist Papers* No. 51. See also Nos. 49, 50.

[24] Book XI, Chap. 6.

[25] Montesquieu borrowed and refined the ideas of Locke in Books IX–XII of the Second Treatise on Government. But Locke used a binary division into "legislative" and "executive," with judicial power subsumed in the latter. Montesquieu devised the familiar threefold classification, which Paine (*op. cit.* pp. 219–221) disliked.

[26] *Constitutionalism and Separation of Powers* (1967), pp. 1–2.

in the charge that there is in their philosophy a fundamental inconsistency therewith something they are not sure they can deny."[27] Perhaps Tom Paine shared this sense of unease about separation of powers[28] for, after a tepid discussion of the subject, he suddenly burst out

> "But in whatever manner the separate parts of the constitution may be arranged, there is *one* general principle that distinguishes freedom from slavery, which is, that all *hereditary government over a people is to them a species of slavery and representative government is freedom.*"[29]

The English Constitution

What have the classic theorists of the English Constitution to say about these matters? One might describe Walter Bagehot's great work, *The English Constitution* (1867) as an analysis of *power*. Bagehot does not deal explicitly with representation and the constitutional problems which it poses. But he finds himself dealing by implication with both the second and third meanings of the representation concept. We must remember that his book was written just as a Second Reform Bill (1867) was extending the suffrage for the second time, although long before universal suffrage had arrived.[30] Bagehot thought these reforms dangerous. His views on representation were unashamedly anti-populist and he liked the "dignified" aspects of English governmental institutions. Therefore, on the one hand, he dismissed the dangers inherent in domination of the legislature by the aristocracy and landed gentry on the ground that the landed interest was too "stupid" to be despotic; on the other, he dismissed any claim of the working classes to political equality on the ground that "they contribute almost nothing to our corporate public opinion."[31] Bagehot did not stop to consider whether the absence of political rights and of a platform from which to speak

---

[27] *Democracy and Distrust* (1980), p. 7. For the answer to the charge see W. Berns, "The Least Dangerous Branch, But Only If . . ." in *The Judiciary in a Democratic Society* (Theberge ed., 1979).

[28] But not about judicial review. The power to review legislation for constitutionality is itself a judge-made power, first exercised in *Marbury* v. *Madison* I *Cranch* 137 (1803) and not entrenched in the U.S. Constitution. Paine strongly advocated a written constitution.

[29] *Op. cit.* n. 12, p. 221.

[30] The three Reform Acts of 1832, 1867 and 1885 extended the franchise to a majority of adult males with property interests. In 1918, adult male suffrage was finally conceded and the franchise extended to women over 30; universal adult suffrage arrived in 1928 when women were finally enfranchised on the same basis as men.

[31] *The English Constitution* (1867) (Fontana, 1963), p. 176.

had anything to do with this. He feared the tyranny of the majority. In the Introduction to the second edition of his work, he wrote:

> "[A] permanent combination of the [working classes] would make them (now that so many of them have the suffrage) supreme in the country; [and] their supremacy, in the state they now are, means the supremacy of ignorance over instruction and of numbers over knowledge."[32]

It is worth digressing here to contrast the views of Bagehot's contemporary John Stuart Mill. Mill castigated Parliament for its failure ever to consider the views of working men. Not only did he think that these views should be listened to respectfully; his belief that every man was his own best representative led him to concede a need for working class representation inside Parliament. In a passage which strikes a modern note, he insisted:

> "On the question of strikes, for instance, it is doubtful if there is so much as one among the leading members of either House who is not firmly convinced that the reason of the matter is unqualifiedly on the side of the masters, and the men's view of it is simply absurd. Those who have studied the question will know well how far this is from being the case; and in how different, and how infinitely less superficial a manner the point would have to be argued if the classes who strike were able to make themselves heard in Parliament."[33]

Unlike Mill, Bagehot showed no interest in devising modifications of the electoral system which, while providing for a greater degree of representation, could protect minorities against majorities. Nor was he an advocate of separation of powers. He expressly rejected the idea which he thought Montesquieu had misconstrued. In sharp contrast to de Tocqueville, who had been struck in the 1830s by the dominant position of lawyers and of the legal process in American public life,[34] Bagehot wholly ignored the contribution made by the legal profession to public affairs; there are chapters on the House of Lords and the Monarchy but not the Judiciary. Thus Bagehot may be partly responsible for fostering the illusion that the judiciary is in some way "independent" of, and not part of, the State (as opposed to the

---

[32] *Ibid.* p. 277.

[33] *Considerations on Representative Government* (Everyman, 1977), pp. 209–210.

[34] Alexis de Tocqueville, *Democracy in America* (1835). In the light of what has been said, it is noteworthy that Tocqueville describes America as egalitarian but, himself a French aristocrat, seems to find unsympathetic the uniformity of opinion and behaviour in American society.

government).[35] But Bagehot concentrated his attention on *government* and his outstanding contribution to the study of the constitution was his discovery that cabinet government is "fused" or unitary in character. (Bagehot invented the well-known metaphor of the Cabinet as a "buckle" or "hinge" between Government and Parliament). And in contrast to most of his contemporaries who described Parliament's functions in terms first, of control—Maitland, for example, spoke of the "constant supervision of all governmental affairs"[36]—and second, of legislation, Bagehot viewed the House of Commons primarily as an "electoral college." In other words, the House of Commons was a representative body into whose hands was given over the right to choose a government.[37] Once the Government—or more properly the Prime Minister—had been chosen, the Government became, for all practical purposes, the decision-maker and the lawmaker. Such a view of the constitution is likely to find favour with the ambitious politician. Perhaps this is why Bagehot has found such spirited defenders in R.H.S. Crossman and his biographer, Norman St. John Stevas.

Just how realistic is Bagehot's description of cabinet government, allowing, of course, for changes brought about by universal suffrage and the growth of the party system? Vile argues that Bagehot deliberately exaggerated the fusion of power in, and the unitary character of, the English constitution. His book was partly a nursery tale, designed to warn of the disasters which might arise from constant, unthinking extensions of the suffrage. There is room, even in the unwritten English constitution, for a theory of "checks and balances." For Vile, this is the gap filled by A.V. Dicey[38] (1835–1922), jurist and constitutional lawyer.

Bagehot rejects separation of powers, deals only indirectly with representation, makes no mention of sovereignty and focusses on cabinet government as a method for the channelling of political power into the hands of a governmental elite. By way of contrast, Dicey makes Parliamentary Sovereignty the centrepiece of his constitutional theory. Sovereignty is a slippery idea which so far we have deliberately avoided defining. John Stuart Mill defined "representative govern-

---

[35] See also Lord Hailsham, *The Dilemma of Democracy: Diagnosis and Prescription* (1978) Chap. XIII. The opposite position is trenchantly argued by Ralph Miliband, *The State in Capitalist Society* (Quartet, 1973), pp. 124–130.

[36] *The Constitutional History of England* (1908), p. 380; Mill, *op. cit.* pp. 239–241, takes a similar view.

[37] *Op.cit.* pp. 157–158. See also Sir Ivor Jennings, *Parliament* (2nd ed., 1957), pp. 519–520.

[38] *Op. cit.* pp. 213–215, 224–232. Note however, that Vile credits two lawyers, writing somewhat earlier, with similar ideas: J.J. Park, *The Dogmas of the Constitution* (1831); John Austin, *The Province of Jurisprudence Determined* (1832).

ment" to mean that "... the whole people, or some numerous portion of them, exercise through deputies periodically elected by themselves *the ultimate controlling power, which, in every constitution, must reside somewhere.*"[39] There we have a working definition of "popular sovereignty," the ultimate control being, in a democracy, that of the electorate. A definition more familiar to English lawyers, however, is that of John Austin, for whom the characteristics of the sovereign were, that

> "the generality of the given society must render habitual obedience to that certain individual or body: whilst that individual or body must not be habitually obedient to a determinate human superior."[40]

In this definition, it is less than certain that the "electorate" or "people" are sovereign, and Austin equivocates. He suggests an uneasy compromise: sovereignty is shared between the Monarch, the Lords and "the Commons," acting through their representatives for the time being in the House of Commons. In order to fit the people into the equation, he goes on to suggest that their representatives might be subject to a "trust." This might be of two kinds. Either "the representative body... might be bound to use [its] powers consistently with specific ends pointed out by the electorate: or it might be bound, more generally and vaguely, not to annihilate or alter essentially, the actual constitution of the Supreme government."[41] In the case of England, Austin comes down in favour of the second. In other words, the power delegated to the rulers by the people in terms of the social contract, must be exercised within the parameters of the existing constitution.

Austin is clearly disturbed by the relationship between the electorate and the House of Commons for which his definition of sovereignty leaves little space. We must remember, however, that the orthodox explanation of the relationship between the elector and his Member of Parliament was—and remains today—that of Edmund Burke. In a celebrated address to his electors,[42] Burke maintained that the Member is totally free at all times to exercise his own "judgment and conscience," independent of all "*authoritative* instructions, *mandates* issued, which a member is bound blindly and implicitly to obey." Austin's hesitancy is easily explained if "representative government"

---

[39] *Op. cit.* n. 33, p. 228, (emphasis mine).
[40] *Province* (Weidenfeld, 1955), p. 214.
[41] *Ibid.* p. 230.
[42] *To the Electors of Bristol* (1774), reprinted in *Burke's Political Writings* (Nelson Classics), p. 29. See also Mill, *op. cit.* pp. 315–324. David Judge "British Representative Theories and Parliamentary Specialisation" (1980) 33 Parl. Affairs 40 provides a good modern discussion.

and "popular sovereignty" amount to no more than the right to select once in a while one from a limited list of candidates; this relationship between the Commons and the electorate can hardly be described as one of "habitual obedience" by the former to the latter.

In his famous exposition of sovereignty, Dicey sweeps these difficulties to one side by defining *legal* sovereignty to mean "simply the power of lawmaking unrestricted by any legal limit."[43] He can then dispose of Austin's doubts on the grounds that they spring from a confusion between "legal" and "political" sovereignty and that "no English judge ever conceded, or, under the present constitution, can concede, that Parliament is in any legal sense a 'trustee for the electors'."[44] He uses the example of the Septennial Acts, which had extended the duration of parliamentary sessions, to show that Parliament is free from any legal restriction on its legislative power. As every law student knows, "Parliament can make and unmake any law whatsoever and no Parliament can bind future Parliaments."

Dicey's critics usually attack at the legal level, trying to show that Parliament might in certain circumstances be bound by procedural requirements.[45] It makes better sense to concentrate on the political. For Dicey, like Bagehot, has constructed a powerful machine for those who occupy the political driving seat with an unconditional licence to drive. Unlike Bagehot, he shows no concern with the realities of political power,[46] hence provides no adequate basis for its control. Perhaps the real attraction of Dicey for lawyers lies in the fact that his theory effectively insulates them from the political consequences of their legal actions.

Harold Laski once argued[47] that "it would be of lasting benefit to political science if the whole concept of sovereignty were surrendered. That, in fact, with which we are dealing is power; and what is important in the nature of power is the end it seeks to serve and the way in which it serves that end." But power was not Dicey's subject; indeed, a common criticism of his work is that he has little of pertinence to say on the subject. He has, for example, been accused of unconscious political bias in that his confusion of "arbitrary" with "discretionary" power renders the extended regulatory powers of a modern socialist state at

---

[43] *Introduction to the Laws of the Constitution* (9th ed. by E.C.S. Wade 1939), p. 72.
[44] *Ibid.* p. 75.
[45] *e.g.* R.V. Heuston, *Essays in Constitutional Law* (2nd ed., 1964), Chap. 1; G. Marshall, *Constitutional Theory* (1971), pp. 35–72. See also H.W.R. Wade "The Basis of Legal Sovereignty" [1955] Cam. L.J. 172.
[46] Dicey was actually fervently interested in politics. See T.H. Ford "Dicey as a Political Journalist" (1970) 18 Pol. Studies 220; R.A. Cosgrove *The Rule of Law* (1980) Chap. 5. See also McEldowney, Chap. 2.
[47] *Grammar of Politics* (1925), Chap. 2, p. 41.

least presumptively unconstitutional,[48] a hidden assumption said to exert its influence over judges in cases of judicial review. On the other hand, he has been accused of complacency about the arbitrary nature and extent of the Crown prerogative powers which he discounts as "residual."[49] Yet modern caselaw shows how often and in what disparate circumstances the prerogative can be invoked by government as a source of power unauthorised by the legislature.[50]

The problem with Dicey's distinction between "political" and "legal" sovereignty is that it leads the reader to infer that Parliament, the legal sovereign, is also the political master. Bagehot of course knew better. In reality, power is diffused in the English constitution, a preponderance being vested in Prime Minister and Cabinet, the rest being shared between other governmental institutions, and local government. Non-governmental bodies, such as trade unions, and powerful corporations which we vaguely think of as "the City," also have an input. Thus, many modern political scientists analyse political power in terms of competing interest-groups.[51] As Laski implied, the concept of sovereignty sits uneasily in such a frame. By fixing our attention on Parliament as the place where law is "made," Dicey encourages us to shut our minds to the realities of the long process whereby the Government introduces and drafts legislation over which Parliament generally possesses no more than rights of assent, scrutiny and, occasionally, of amendment. Today, when the proliferation of legislation, of regulations made by government departments, and the dominance of political parties have transformed the lawmaking process,[52] an interest-group analysis is probably more revealing than an analysis in terms of sovereignty. To put this differently, modern legal theory sees lawmaking as a dynamic and fluid process, involving contributions at different stages from different actors, rather than a static act centred in Parliament.

Now, Dicey's is often characterised as a "balanced" constitution—a version of separation of powers according to which powers allocated to one organ of government "check and balance" those of the others.[53] In

---

[48] W.I. Jennings, "In Praise of Dicey (1885–1935)" (1935) 13 Pub. Admin. 123, 132.

[49] H.W.R. Wade, *Constitutional Fundamentals* (1980), pp. 46–53.

[50] See, for example, *Burmah Oil* v. *Lord Advocate* [1965] A.C. 75; *Gouriet* v. *U.P.W.* [1970] 3 W.L.R. 300; *Laker Airways* v. *Board of Trade* [1977] Q.B. 643; *Council of Civil Service Unions* v. *Minister for the Civil Service* [1984] 3 W.L.R. 117.

[51] Birch, *op. cit.* pp. 83–93, 105–113 provides a helpful introduction to these ideas. See also S.H. Beer "Pressure Groups and Parties in Britain" (1956) 50 AM.Pol.Sci.Rev. 1.

[52] See M. Zander, *The Law Making Process* (1980); J.A.G. Griffith, *Parliamentary Scrutiny of Government Bills* (1974) and "The Place of Parliament in the Legislative Process" (1951) 14 M.L.R. 279 and 425.

[53] See further Harlow and Rawlings, *Law and Administration* (1984), pp. 19–22.

one sense this is true, if only because Dicey wrongly suggests a separation of the lawmaking and governmental power. But in a more real sense it is not. By down-playing the scrutinizing and supervisory function of Parliament and dwelling on its legislative role, Dicey weakens the checks and balances of the Constitution. And by fixing on *Parliament* as the sovereign, he closes the door left ajar by Austin, ruling out the possibility of any constitutional doctrine of mandate. It was not that Dicey favoured authoritarian government; on the contrary, he saw as the essential property of representative government, typified in his view by the English House of Commons, that it should produce "coincidence between the wishes of the sovereign and the subjects."[54] In other words, representative government operates to ensure the fusion of political and legal sovereignty. Yet Dicey felt that he could see in England no machinery by which the marriage could be enforced. Perhaps he was complacent, dismissing the idea of incompatibility in Leslie Stephen's celebrated metaphor of the "mad" Parliament which could pass a law to murder blue-eyed babies to which only "idiotic" subjects could assent.[55] But Dicey dealt cursorily with the relationship between Members of Parliament and constituents, assuring the reader that "the arrangements of the constitution are now such as to ensure that the will of the electors shall by regular and constitutional means always assert itself as the predominant influence of the country."[56] The truth is that, in demolishing Austin's mandate theory, Dicey is tacitly subscribing to Burke's view of the Member of Parliament as *independent*: free at any time to place his individual conscience and judgment above the expressed wishes of his electorate. Later his passionate opposition to Gladstone's Irish policies and his distaste for Home Rule, changed his view of parliamentary sovereignty drastically. In 1890, Dicey explored in an article the Swiss machinery for constitutional referenda, a device designed to ensure that representatives should not depart radically from the wishes of the electorate.[57] What is this but a theory of "limited trust"?

Dicey's conclusions were by no means inevitable. In the late Victorian age, Lord Salisbury was beginning to define the role of the House of Lords in terms of mandate.[58] At a later date, contemplating

---

[54] *Op. cit.* p. 84. This enabled Dicey to argue (p. 414) that parliamentary sovereignty was compatible with the rule of law. See Neil MacCormick "Jurisprudence and the Constitution" [1983] *Current Legal Problems* 13.

[55] *Op. cit.* p. 81. The metaphor is borrowed from Leslie Stephen's *Science of Ethics* (1882), p. 143.

[56] *Op. cit.* p. 73.

[57] "Ought the Referendum to be Introduced into England?" (1890) 57 *Contemporary Review* 489. And see Cosgrove, *op. cit.* Chaps. 6 and 7 and McEldowney pp. 50–51.

[58] G.H.L. Lemay, *The Victorian Constitution* (1979), pp. 127–151, 189–219.

the political events of the years 1908–1911, which resulted in the passage of the first Parliament Act after a general election in which the Prime Minister had put his policy to the electorate, another great constitutional lawyer, Sir Ivor Jennings, thought he could discern a constitutional convention according to which "fundamental changes of policy must not be effected unless they have been issue at a general election."[59] Perhaps the wish was father to the thought. Or perhaps we can find support here for Austin's doctrine of limited trust since the Parliament Act, in Austin's own phrase, "changed the actual constitution" of Parliament.

If, in the main, judicial attitudes to parliamentary sovereignty have reflected Dicey's views, we should not be surprised. True, judges have consistently refused to investigate parliamentary procedure[60] and have refused to circumscribe the subject matter of legislation[61]; but then generations of law students have been trained to accept Dicey's own claim that he wrote neither as critic nor apologist nor eulogist but simply as an expounder of legal fact.[62] Judges do not by and large deal in the terminology of mandate. In *Education Secretary* v. *Tameside M.B.C.*,[63] however, the doctrine did intrude. A Labour-controlled local authority had developed plans to introduce comprehensive schooling. At a local election, the Conservatives were returned having declared an intention in their manifesto to revert to selection, which they duly did. The Labour Education Minister intervened, using statutory powers to disallow local authority action which seemed to him "unreasonable." His case was that insufficient time remained for a sensible selection policy to operate and he applied for a court order to compel compliance with his view. Lord Wilberforce thought it relevant that the matter had featured in the election manifesto; in overriding the council's wishes the Labour Education Secretary "was operating under a misconception as to what would be reasonable for a newly elected council to do [and] had... failed to take into account that it was entitled—indeed in a sense bound—to carry out the policy on which it was elected."

In the later case of *Bromley L.B.C.* v. *Greater London Council*,[64] the question was whether the GLC had acted inside its statutory powers in agreeing to a policy of consistent subsidy for London Transport, for the running of which they shared responsibility with the

---

[59] *The Law and the Constitution* (5th ed., 1958), pp. 176–179.
[60] *Pickin* v. *British Railways Board* [1974] 2 W.L.R. 208.
[61] *Blackburn* v. *Attorney-General* [1971] 1 W.L.R. 1037.
[62] *Op. cit.* pp. 3–4.
[63] [1977] A.C. 1014. The citation is at p. 1051.
[64] [1982] 2 W.L.R. 62. The citation is from p. 107. And see S. Lee, "Mandate and Manifesto" (1983/4) 33 *King's Counsel* 39.

London Transport Executive. The GLC argued that its subsidisation policy had been approved by the electorate at a recent election. Lord Wilberforce was unmoved, holding that an electoral mandate might be relevant to the question of "reasonableness" but could never affect the "legality" of administrative action. In the same case, Lord Diplock spoke in strictly Burkeian language when he said that "a council member once elected is not the delegate of those who voted in his favour only: he is the representative of all the electors." This exactly mirrors Burke's own reasoning. The independence of the representative is based on the need to transcend local and sectional interests:

> "Parliament is not a congress of ambassadors from different and hostile interests; which interests each must maintain as an agent and advocate, against other agents and advocates; but parliament is a *deliberative* assembly of *one* nation with *one* interest, that of the whole."[65]

Here we find the classic liberal theory of the state as impartial and placed above sectional interests.[66] Lord Diplock deduced from this that council members must act impartially in weighing the interests of various groups of their constituents, *e.g.* electors, ratepayers, transport users, rather than blindly apply party policy. Lord Diplock now introduces a strictly legal concept borrowed from the law of charitable trusts; the council he argues, owes a "fiduciary duty" to its ratepayers to use their money thriftily. This legal trust triumphs over the (Austinian) political "trust" owed by the representative to his electors. No doubt this is true though it casts little light on the nature of the various interests and relationships.

I have called Burke's theory orthodox and so it seems, partly perhaps, because there has been so little discussion of the topic by lawyers. Some of the gaps left by Dicey and Bagehot are filled in a classic essay by John Stuart Mill (1806–1873).[67] Mill is often portrayed as a pseudo-liberal, afraid of the logical consequences of his naïve brand of philosophical radicalism.[68] This is not entirely fair. Mill, who thought that working men's views should be heard in the House of Commons, also believed in universal suffrage and introduced a Female Suffrage Bill in the House in 1867. Against this, however, we must set Mill's respect for learning, educated opinion and rationality. Fear lest the educated minority would be swamped by the "numerical majority"

---

[65] *Op. cit.* n. 42, pp. 29–30.
[66] Explained by Birch *op. cit.* pp. 65–83.
[67] *Op. cit.* n. 33.
[68] For a spirited defence of Bagehot versus Mill see R.H.S. Crossman Introduction to Bagehot, *op. cit.* pp. 5–10. A more sympathetic description of Mill is L.W. Lancaster, *Masters of Political Thought* (1959) Vol. 3, pp. 101–159.

whose "class legislation" would inevitably reflect their own parochial interests led Mill towards Madisonian compromise. In his essay, Mill presented a Utilitarian variant of separation of powers in which the legislature would retain only a basic right to assent to legislative proposals which would be drafted by an expert Commission. And he sought to ensure minority representation through the electoral system, advocating proportional representation and plural voting. Mill's views also led him naturally to espouse Burke's theory of the representative as independent and not accountable to his electorate for his views. Perhaps Mill saw this elitist solution merely as a short term expedient. His faith that education together with the opportunity to participate in political affairs would transform the political consciousness of the populace seems to have been genuine.

Mandated Delegates and Participatory Democracy

The common factor in these theories is their oligarchic nature. Each allows government by an elite, albeit a "representative" elite. The only decision left to the citizen is the power to choose representatives who will, in turn, choose the government. While state power was relatively limited, this may have been acceptable. Three developments in the nature of modern society come together to render the classic liberal constitution increasingly inadequate.

First, we must bear in mind the climate of modern opinion. There has been a gradual change by which democracy and representative government are increasingly equated with "popular" control.[69] Secondly, we have seen an accretion of power to central government, today in the grasp of the Prime Minister rather than the Cabinet. Even those governments which do not in principle subscribe to centralist theories have in practice allowed the trend to continue. Post-war administrations have fostered nationalised industry and encouraged the proliferation of semi-autonomous government agencies. The Thatcher government, publicly dedicated to quangocide and local control of local affairs, is in practice responsible for ratecapping legislation which curtails the policy choices of local authorities. Some "quangos" have been strangled but many continue to thrive. Underpinning the political elites is a sprawling Weberian bureaucracy, in the view of many observers answerable to nobody.[70] Thirdly, we have witnessed the growth of a party system which has reduced the power of

[69] C.B. MacPherson, *op. cit.* n. 18.
[70] Tony Benn "Manifestos and Mandarins" in *Policy and Practice: the Experience of Government* (1980, Royal Institute of Public Administration), pp. 57–58; compare, however, Douglas Wass, "The Privileged Adviser" in *Government and Governed* (1983), pp. 41–60.

the House of Commons. To one ex-Labour Cabinet Minister, Richard Marsh, "one of the least important parts of the British political system is the chamber of the House of Commons, and it is in very real danger of becoming a near irrelevance."[71] The power of the Member of Parliament is today transferred to party whips, the power of the House to the party. Some might argue that Burke's "independent Member" is nearly extinct. To summarise in the words of Crossman discussing the relevance of Bagehot to modern British government, "in a period when effective power in all spheres of life—economic, social, political—is being concentrated in fewer and fewer hands, parliamentary control of the executive has been steadily decreasing, without being replaced by other methods of democractic control."[72]

We find in response three types of solution. First are those which prescribe Madisonian constitutional remedies for a constitutional disease. Some favour the institutional protections of a Bill of Rights.[73] Others prefer to strengthen the latent "checks and balances" of the unwritten constitution: on one side, we find those who have concentrated their efforts on parliamentary reform[74]; on the other, those to whom extended powers of judicial review seem preferable.[75] In a sense, all these solutions are variants of the separation of powers theme. But Mill's case for proportional representation—said to favour moderate political opinion—has also found new advocates[76] and today forms the central plank in the election manifesto of a major political party.[77]

A second and more radical set of solutions aims to bypass the

---

[71] *Off the Rails* (1978).

[72] Introduction, *op. cit.* p. 46. For similar analyses see Nevil Johnson, *In Search of the Constitution* (1977), Chap. 4; Philip Norton, *The Constitution in Flux* (1982), Chap. 1. And compare G.W. Jones "The Prime Minister's Powers" (1965) 18 Parl. Affairs 167 with Tony Benn "The Case for a Constitutional Premiership" (1980) 33 Parl. Affairs 7.

[73] The arguments and the voluminous literature are conveniently summarised by Philip Norton, *op. cit.* pp. 244–260.

[74] See *e.g.* Walkland and Ryle (eds.) *the Commons Today* (1981); Bernard Crick, *The Reform of Parliament* (1964). And see Pring, "The New Select Committee System at Westminster" (1983) 64 *Parliamentarian* 57; Pitblado, "Proposals for Expanded Scrutiny of Public Spending in the U.K." (1981) 62 *Parliamentarian* 209. J.A.G. Griffith, "The Constitution and the Commons" in *Parliament and the Executive*, (1982, Royal Institute of Public Administration) 7; Harlow "Ombudsmen in Search of A Role" (1978) 41 M.L.R. 446; Beith "Prayers Unanswered: A Jaundiced View of the Parliamentary Scrutiny of Statutory Instruments" (1981) 32 Parl. Affairs. 165.

[75] Especially H.W.R. Wade, *Constitutional Fundamentals, op. cit.* n. 3.

[76] *e.g.* Enid Lakeman, *Power to Elect* (1982) *Ellis* v. *Hughes and Whitehead* "Electoral Reform," Fabian Tract No. 83 (1982); Vernon Bogdanor, *The People and the Party System* (1981).

[77] "Working Together for Britain" SDP/Liberal Alliance (1983) pp. 23–28.

problems of "representative oligarchy" or "elective dictatorship" by demolishing the centralised and secret structure of decision-making from which the government derives its monopoly of power. As Sir Douglas Wass has put it, "the choice of representative is no substitute for the choice of policy."[78] Voting is not the only nor even the best form of decision-taking and one answer to the problems of representation is not to delegate. A perpetual and inherent tension between centralism and localism fuels a movement for "participatory democracy." Nelson catches its peculiarly local flavour when he says[79] that it is "not based on the ideas of popular will and the common good, but rather on the procedures of the town meeting. It asserts that 'public policy should result from extensive, informed discussion and debate.... Public officials, acting as agents of the public at large, would then carry out the broad policies decided upon by majority vote in popular assemblies'." For Pateman, participatory democracy is a root-and-branch-affair[80]:

> "[P]articipation refers to (equal) participation in the making of decisions, and 'political equality' refers to equality of powers in determining the outcome of decisions.... One might characterise the participatory model as one where maximum input (participation) is required and where output includes not just policies (decisions) but also the development of the social and political capacities of each individual, so that there is 'feedback' from output to input."

Like Mill, whose work she admires, Pateman sees participation as a means rather than an end. The goal is education: a populace educated to run their own affairs will, in the long run, make more effective and more consensual decisions. In the limited field of land-use planning, participation has had a certain success[81]; in Pateman's chosen field of industrial democracy it has, in the West, scarcely been tried. But "development of one's social and political capacities" can prove a time-consuming luxury. If the experience of local government, where about one-third of the electorate normally troubles to turn out at elections, is anything to go by, participation may once more lead in practice to government by a dedicated minority. The question becomes once

---

[78] *Government and Governed* (1983), p. 105. But see also Barry Hindness, "Limitations to Parliamentary Democracy" 1 *Politics and Power* 103.
[79] *On Justifying Democracy* (1980), p. 37. The quotation is from Walker, "Normative Consequences of Democratic Theory" in *Frontiers of Democractic Theory* (Kariel ed., 1970), p. 227.
[80] *Participation and Democratic Theory* (1970), p. 43.
[81] P. McAuslan, *The Ideologies of Planning Law* (1980); Harlow and Rawlings, *op. cit.* pp. 437–456. The Skeffington Report, *People and Planning* (1969) is to date the high-water mark of participatory theory in the English planning system.

more, dedicated to what? To power (sovereignty) or service (representation)?

Belief in participatory democracy and decentralised decision-making is not the exclusive property of any political party. For the left of the political spectrum, decentralised decision-taking is a partial road to reform; for example, it allows inroads into corporate power via worker-participation. Inside the Labour Party we find today, as there always have been, radical thinkers deeply committed to an ideal of genuine popular democracy. But only a centralised government with untrammelled legal power can hope to carry through a substantial programme of social change by constitutional means. Parliamentary sovereignty is an old constitutional broom with which radical reformers can make clean sweeps. The problem then is to devise machinery which will ensure that governments elected with a radical mandate to implement radical manifestoes will not become "infirm of purpose." Disillusion with post-war governments, which have generally suffered from an overdose of Burkeian independence, leads Miliband[82] to argue that "parliamentarism," by which he means support for reform through constitutional means and faith in parliamentary democracy, has become yet another weapon for the containment of "popular democracy." Tony Benn describes "a break down in the social contract on which parliamentary democracy by universal suffrage was based." He feels that the "contract now needs to be renegotiated on a basis that shares power much more widely, before it can win general assent again."[83]

For Raymond Williams,[84] renegotiation must be based on a critical evaluation of the representation idea. He concludes that Parliament today is representative only in the sense that it is *elected*. It has long ceased to *typify* the electorate; indeed, women and ethnic minorities are scarcely represented. Nor do the Members act—as he thinks they should—like *delegates* of the people.

For a central tenet of this radical creed is an attack on the ideas of Burke, an attack which has triumphed to the extent that Labour Members of Parliament now have to submit periodically to "reselection" by the constituency party, which renders them more accountable to some at least of their constituents. There are parallel proposals to make the Parliamentary Labour Party more accountable to the party as a whole by allowing an electoral college of the Annual Conference to elect the Labour Shadow Cabinet.[85] This opens a controversial

---

[82] *Capitalist Democracy in Britain* (1984), pp. 20–53.
[83] *Arguments for Socialism* (1979) pp. 110–111.
[84] "Democracy and Parliament" *The Socialist Society* (1983), pp. 10–16.
[85] "Parliamentary Democracy and the Labour Movement" *Campaign Group of Labour MPs* (1983). See generally, Donald Shell, "The British Constitution in 1980" (1981) 32 Parl. Affairs 149, 160–164.

theoretical debate. Who, exactly, does a Member of Parliament "represent"? The whole constituency, as Burke insisted, or only those who worked for his election? Which is to take preference, loyalty to the nation as classic liberal democractic theory insists, or to the constituency? And where, if at all, do people mesh with party?

This particular version of popular democracy might end by substituting for government by an elected party elite, control by a different kind of party oligarchy, not necessarily more representative of popular opinion. But wider versions of popular democracy are still more problematic. Electoral manifestoes are a clumsy way to test public opinion; psephology is an imprecise science and nobody really knows how voters decide. Elections regularly prove the opinion pollsters wrong. Referenda are expensive, cumbersome and depend too heavily on the way in which questions are formulated. Technological progress may make popular participation in governmental decision-taking a possibility. Until then, we shall have to continue to struggle towards solutions for the problems of representation.

In modern democracies, the right of universal suffrage has been conceded and is no longer an issue. We have the right to *select* representatives but the extent to which we can *control* them is more doubtful. Dicey's theory of Parliamentary Sovereignty has a certain metaphorical relevance to this issue in that it reminds us that those who command a parliamentary majority are temporarily in possession of a considerable law making power. But it removes from the legal agenda the more significant questions of how that power is to be used and who is to determine this by affixing to them the label "political." Borrowing Bagehot's metaphor, we might describe representation as the buckle between power and people. How tightly the belt should be buckled is a difficult question but not one which constitutional lawyers can afford to ignore.

Chapter 4

MUNICIPAL SOCIALISM IN A UNITARY STATE

MARTIN LOUGHLIN

"The welfare state in crisis" is a theme which has been thoroughly examined in the 1980s and the economic, social and political aspects of the crisis have been investigated from a variety of disciplinary perspectives. Most public lawyers, however, have either ignored or been oblivious to the type of issues raised by themes of this nature. Public law, so the orthodoxy has it, is a practical discipline and a sharp distinction may be drawn between law and politics. The roots of this approach may be traced to Dicey, who was "the first to apply the juridical method to English public law."[1] Dicey took the view that the role of the academic public lawyer "is to state what are the laws which form part of the constitution, to arrange them in their order, to explain their meaning, and to exhibit where possible their logical connection."[2]

This approach may be acceptable in a stable and ordered system. But when the basic norms of the system are widely questioned it seems quite indefensible; silence seems the appropriate response. But public lawyers are called on to teach, to advise and to comment. It is therefore incumbent upon them, even when engaging in legal analysis, to seek to understand the forces which are shaping legal developments. Even Dicey, who lived during a period of great social change, understood this point. His *Law and Opinion*,[3] although much criticised recently, was nevertheless "a pioneering attempt to establish the relationship between law, economic thought and the origins of the modern democratic state."[4]

In this essay, therefore, I shall examine some of these broader issues in order to try to explain the nature and significance of one institutional aspect of the current crisis in the welfare state; *viz.* the recent conflicts between central and local government. My aim is to show that legal

---

[1] W.I. Jennings, *The Law and the Constitution* (Univ. of London Press, 1933), p. x.
[2] A.V. Dicey, *Introduction to the Study of the Law of the Constitution* (Macmillan, 1885), p. 31.
[3] A.V. Dicey, *Law and Opinion in England in the Nineteenth Century* (Macmillan, 1905).
[4] D. Sugarman, "The Legal Boundaries of Liberty: Dicey, "Liberalism and Legal Science" (1983) 46 M.L.R. 102, 111.

developments and legal disputes in this area of public law can be fully understood only by considering longer-term and more basic changes in economic, social, spatial and governmental structures. These changes set the scene for central-local government conflicts. They also demonstrate why the particular dimension to these conflicts on which I focus provides the key to understanding the significance of political and legal disputes in this area of government.

The dimension emphasised in this essay is the conflict between central government, who are pursuing neo-liberal economic and social policies, and the local authorities based on the major industrial cities where a distinctive "municipal socialism" is flourishing. It is along this axis that the conflict is most severe and disputatious. In this essay I shall attempt to show why.

Industrialisation, Urbanisation and Collectivism

Dicey, in *Law and Opinion*, examined nineteenth-century legal developments through a division of the century into three distinct periods; Old Toryism or legislative quiescence (1800–1835), Benthamism or individualism (1825–1870), and collectivism (1865–1900). Although many significant local government measures, such as the Municipal Corporations Act 1835 or the Public Health Act 1846, were enacted earlier it was during the period of collectivism that most local government growth occurred. During this period local authorities were charged with such functions as public health and slum clearance, the provision of education, the relief of the poor and the administration of police forces. Of particular significance was the growth in municipal trading services, including markets, slaughterhouses, bathing establishments, waterworks, gasworks, electricity works and tramways. For many, including Dicey, it was an era of municipal socialism.

But Dicey, in attempting to explain the growth of collectivism in terms of a combination of Tory humanitarianism, Benthamite ambivalence, the growth of trade unionism and the introduction of household suffrage,[5] failed to examine the key factors leading to collectivism at the local level. These factors are *population growth, industrialisation* and *urbanisation*.

During the nineteenth century, the population of England and Wales increased more than threefold, an unprecedented rate. This growth in population was accompanied by a distinct urban-rural shift: in 1801 almost 70 per cent. of the population was rural, whereas by 1901 nearly 80 per cent. of the population lived in towns.[6] This

---

[5] Above, n. 3, pp. 210–257.
[6] E. Hosbawm, *Industry and Empire* (Penguin, 1969), Fig. 13.

phenomenon of urbanisation was closely associated with the process of industrialisation. It is largely in terms of these developments that the growth in municipal services in the late nineteenth century may be explained.

Collective action was needed for several reasons. First, on simple nuisance grounds: "it is unpleasant when a town of 2000 inhabitants dumps raw sewage into the streets or local river; it is a major social and economic problem if this happens in a city of one million."[7] Secondly, the social conditions produced by urbanisation were breeding grounds for disease. This had tax consequences: "Filth caused epidemics, epidemics brought pauperisation of widows and orphans, and paupers meant increased taxation for poor relief."[8] It also had an effect on labour productivity.[9] Thirdly, the social conditions were such that they caused concern about the dangers of social unrest: "Some such measures are urgently called for," reported the Select Committee on the Health of Towns in 1840, "not less for the welfare of the poor than the safety of property and the security of the rich."[10]

It was as a result of a combination of these reasons that urban public services were provided by local authorities. Many of these services constituted local "public goods." That is, they were services which, although needed, either could not be provided by private bodies or could only be provided inefficiently. Thus, this growth in municipal service provision was hardly evidence of municipal socialism since the services were provided largely within a capitalist logic of collective action. And it is only with the establishment of this logic of collective action that the local government system is reformed; commencing with the Municipal Corporations Act of 1835 and leading to the extension of the principle of representative democracy to county councils in 1888, the establishment of district councils in 1894 and the London boroughs in 1899.

Consequently, it was only when the private sector had failed adequately to provide services that collective action occurred. Initially, Parliament passed *permissive* legislation enabling local authorities to plug the gaps left by the failures of the market. Generally these powers were given to ad hoc local bodies. The use of these permissive powers was pioneered in the major cities where the problems were greatest.

---

[7] D. Dawson, "Economic Change and the Changing Role of Local Authorities" in *Half A Century of Municipal Decline 1935–1985* (M. Loughlin, D. Gelfand and K. Young eds., Allen & Unwin, 1985), pp. 27–28.

[8] S. Merrett, *State Housing in Britain* (Routledge & Kegan Paul, 1979), p. 7.

[9] E. Gauldie, *Cruel Habitations: A History of Working Class Housing 1780–1918* (Allen & Unwin, 1974), pp. 187–188.

[10] Quoted in W. Ashworth, *The Genesis of Modern British Town Planning* (Routledge & Kegan Paul, 1954), p. 40.

Eventually, once experience in the use of these powers had been acquired, the powers were extended (*e.g.* from public health to housing to town planning) and permissive legislation was replaced by *compulsory* legislation requiring all local authorities to act. Also the need for consistency and co-ordination of activities led to the transfer of responsibilities from ad hoc bodies to local government.

In 1905, Dicey recognised rightly that collectivism was hardly a spent force; "it is not, to all appearance, even on the decline."[11] Nor were industrialisation and urbanisation. The major cities were the locus both of innovation in public service provision and of economic growth. Consequently, when 30 years later Laski, Jennings and Robson co-edited a volume celebrating the centenary of the Municipal Corporations Act they took a positive view, not only of the achievements of local government to 1935, but also of the future prospects[12]:

> "Whatever the future may hold for our economic system, local government is likely to remain firmly established as the most effective instrument of social welfare in our national life."

The Modernisation and Centralisation of Local Government

Robson's prognostication has turned out not to be accurate. Today, not only is local government not "the most effective instrument of social welfare" but some would say that it is quite peripheral. Since the 1930s, the range of government responsibilities has increased. But the 1930s marks the highpoint of *local* government's functional range and since then the trend has been towards nationalisation rather than municipalisation of functions and to the centralisation of political power generally. The key features in the development of local government over this period have been the restructuring of local government functions and the issue of local government reorganisation.

The restructuring of local government functions

During the 1930s, local government services were largely production-orientated and could be classified either as trading services or local public goods. Since then local government has been stripped of many of these responsibilities: responsibility for trunk roads (1936), electricity (1947), gas (1948) and water and sewage (1974). In addition, local authority responsibility for public assistance was lost (1934, 1940,

---

11 Above, n. 3, p. 300.
12 W.A. Robson, "The Outlook" in *A Century of Municipal Progress 1835–1935*, (H.J. Laski, W.I. Jennings and W.A. Robson, Allen & Unwin, 1935), p. 464.

1948) and the hospital services transferred to central government (1946) with the establishment of the national health service.

This has not necessarily resulted in a reduced status for local government. Local authorities have both retained and assumed responsibility for many services which have grown in importance with the establishment of the welfare state; especially education, housing and the social services. But what has occurred is the loss of production-orientated trading services, and the increased importance of consumption-orientated welfare services, which are in the nature of redistributive goods.

Why did this restructuring occur? One reason was because of the assumption by postwar governments of responsibility for the management of the economy. As a result, certain key sectors of the economy, such as transport and energy, were nationalised. Another was the pursuit of perceived economies of scale which arose because of technological changes. Finally, as with the establishment of the national health service, these reforms materialised partly because of a desire to achieve uniformity of service provision.

A further related feature of post-war developments affecting local government is the increasing central government influence over the policies of local authorities. There are political, economic and legal dimensions to this trend. First, in terms of political culture, government tends to be viewed as a single entity. This is reinforced by the fact that politicians make statements about policy goals which can be implemented only with the co-operation of local authorities and is highlighted, for example, in the field of public expenditure planning where local authority expenditure appears in the annual Public Expenditure White Paper as an undifferentiated part of public expenditure. The legal dimension focuses on constitutional structure. Britain has no key constitutive document allocating spheres of responsibility to particular institutions. Consequently, given central government's effective control of Parliament, the *capacity* of central government to influence local authority action is great. Finally, the nature of the restructuring of local government functions has provided its own impetus for centralisation. Most local authority services are now redistributive in nature; and, as economic orthodoxy demonstrates, there are critical limitations to a local authority's ability independently to undertake policies of income redistribution.[13] The impetus and the practice has therefore been for centralisation of policy in respect of key aspects of local government functions.

Local government reorganisation

The failure to reorganise local government along functionally effec-

13 C. Foster, R. Jackman and M. Perlman, *Local Government Finance in a Unitary State* (Allen & Unwin, 1980), pp. 42–45.

tive lines has been another factor which has contributed to the process of centralisation. Nineteenth-century reform was incremental and established a system of local government which was divided along urban-rural lines. With continuing urban growth in the twentieth century conflicts were thus created between urban and rural authorities as towns and cities grew beyond their administrative boundaries[14]:

> "Boundary extensions were always opposed by the county coun-
> cils for they realised that they were engaged in a zero-sum game
> with the county boroughs over territory, taxbase and . . .
> status. . . . Thus the conflict that was built into the local govern-
> ment system in the nineteenth century created *immobilisme* in the
> twentieth. . . . "

Thus, the nature of the system ensured that there would never be unanimity amongst the various groups of local authorities over the need for, and certainly the form of, any reorganisation. But if central government attempted to intervene and impose reorganisation, that itself would reaffirm the sense of hierarchy in the central-local relationship. Consequently, although the need for reorganisation was widely recognised in the 1930s and 1940s it was not until the 1960s and 1970s that local government reforms were enacted.

The structural reforms that were proposed in the 1960s were part of a broader technocratic movement which viewed institutional modernisation as the key to the reversal of Britain's economic decline. During this period reports on staffing,[15] management[16] and structure[17] of local government were commissioned. The Redcliffe-Maud Commission recognised that the failure of the existing local government structure to recognise "the interdependence of town and country" was its "most fatal defect"[18] and recommended the reform of the existing structure through the establishment of larger, unitary authorities. The structure was reorganised in the Local Government Act 1972 but the Conservative government opted for a modified two-tier system. Given the Conservatives' attachment to tradition, and the fact that their

[14] A. Alexander, "Structure, centralisation and the position of local government" in M. Loughlin *et al* (eds.) above n. 7, p. 52.
[15] *Report of the Committee on the Staffing of Local Government* (Chmn: Sir G. Mallaby) (HMSO, 1967).
[16] *Report of the Committee on the Management of Local Government* (Chmn: Sir J. Maud) (HMSO, 1967); *The New Local Authorities: Management and Structure* (Chmn: M. Bains) (HMSO, 1972).
[17] *Report of the Royal Commission on Local Government in Greater London*, (Chmn: Sir E. Herbert) Cmnd. 1164 (1960); *Report of the Royal Commission on Local Government in England* (Chmn: Redcliffe-Maud) (Cmnd. 4040. HMSO, 1969).
[18] *Ibid.* Vol. 1, para. 85.

power base lay in the counties, it is hardly surprising that the reforms were built around the existing system. But, as Alexander points out[19]:

> "By creating two-tier structures everywhere the reorganisation ensured that the 'most fatal defect' . . . of the old system, the division of town and country, would be replaced by an equally debilitating defect—the failure to recognise the predominance and the particular problems, at least outside those conurban areas that became metropolitan counties, of major urban centres. And by ensuring that the new classes of authority would be as mutually antagonistic as the old ones had been, it ensured that local government would be ill-equipped to resist the rapid increase in the pressure for centralisation."

Indeed one could go further and suggest that the reforms which were enacted were not part of a programme of creating functionally effective units through which the trend towards centralisation could be reversed,[20] but part of the centralisation process itself. This argument is based on the fact that the trends towards centralisation had placed a premium on reducing the number of local government units, since there were limits to the number of units the centre could co-ordinate in order to achieve its aims. This would suggest that, just as in the nineteenth century, the political will to reform local government structures arose only once the centre accepted that structural reform was a necessary precondition of efficient governmental action. But whereas the need in the nineteenth century was for local action, in the twentieth the impetus has moved to the centre.

Economic Crisis and Central-Local Government Relationships

The structural reforms which were implemented in 1974 came at the tail end of a period of unprecedented growth in local government expenditure[21]:

> "From little more than 8 per cent. of the Gross Domestic Product in 1955, the call on real resources had grown to 14.5 per cent. by 1975, while the volume of locally-administered transfers (subsidies, grants, debt interest etc.) had more than doubled its share of the national income. At the same time the number of employees in the local authority sector had nearly doubled, as had the proportion of the total labour force employed in the sector."

[19] Above, n. 14, p. 64.
[20] *Cf.* Ministry of Housing and Local Government, *Reform of Local Government in England*, Cmnd. 4276 (1970).
[21] R.M. Kirwan, "The Fiscal Context" in G.C. Cameron (ed), *The Future of the British Conurbations* (Longmans, 1980) p. 72.

This growth in local expenditure was largely the result of the growing importance of the social welfare services provided by local authorities. The growth in demand for these services resulted from various developments such as the nature of population changes (especially the increase in the numbers of elderly); rising relative costs (due primarily to the labour-intensive nature of these services); the impact of social change (indicated by such factors as structural unemployment and the growth in the numbers of one-parent families); and the fact that improvements in welfare generate their own dynamic for further improvements (*e.g.* improvements in secondary education result in a demand for the expansion of higher educational opportunities).[22] As a result, real increases in expenditure for local services, such as personal social services, were required merely to maintain existing standards.

However, this pattern of expenditure growth came to an abrupt halt with the economic crisis of the mid-Seventies. "The party's over" announced Anthony Crosland, the Secretary of State for the Environment, in 1976. "And so indeed it proved, even for those for whom it had never begun," as Nicholas Deakin wryly commented.[23] The Layfield Committee,[24] which was set up to examine the system of local government finance, is therefore not to be viewed as the final stage in the process of institutional modernisation but rather as a response to the financial strains caused by the costs of reorganisation and public expenditure cutbacks consequent upon economic crisis.

Local authorities receive income from three main sources; central government grants (approximately 50 per cent.), rates (30 per cent.) and fees and charges for the services they provide (20 per cent.). Governments' primary objective since 1976 has been to encourage local expenditure restraint. The Labour government 1974–1979 did so within the existing legal framework, through the combination of exhortation together with steady reductions in the proportion of local expenditure which the centre would finance. In 1975 the Consultative Council on Local Government Finance was established to act as a forum within which central and local government could meet to discuss financial matters.[25] In 1977/78 cash limits were applied to grants.[26] And

[22] I. Gough, *The Political Economy of the Welfare State* (Macmillan, 1979), Chap. 5.
[23] N. Deakin, "Local Government and Social Policy" in M. Loughlin *et al* (eds.), above, n. 7, p. 221.
[24] *Report of the Committee of Enquiry into Local Government Finance* (Chmn: Sir F. Layfield) (Cmnd. 6453. HMSO, 1976).
[25] J.A. Taylor, "The Consultative Council on Local Government Finance—A Critical Analysis of its Origins and Development" (1979) Vol. 5, No. 3 *Local Government Studies* 7; B.J.A. Binder, "Relations between central and local government since 1975—are the associations failing?" (1982) Vol. 8, No. 1. *Local Government Studies* 35.
[26] R.G. Bevan, "Cash Limits" Vol. 1 No. 4 *Fiscal Studies*, p. 26 (1980).

from 1975/76 the proportion of local expenditure which would be supported by central grant was steadily reduced. The result was that by 1979/80 the volume of grant support had fallen by 15 per cent. from the 1975/76 level and local government had largely complied with central government guidelines on expenditure.[27]

This strategy was therefore quite successful in encouraging restraint. In 1979, however, matters reached a new stage. The newly elected Conservative government took the view that Britain's economic problems largely resulted from the level and nature of public expenditure and the lack of innovation and responsiveness of public bodies. The policies of the Conservative government therefore had profound implications for local government.

Since local government expenditure constitutes about one-quarter of total public expenditure a simple pro rata reduction might have been expected. But the reordering of expenditure policies and priorities compounded this situation. The Conservative government's policies are based on attempts to reduce public sector employment, to shift expenditure priorities away from social welfare services and to reconstruct social policy on the principle of individualism rather than collectivism. Consequently they have had a severe impact of local government: partly this is because local government, as a result of the restructuring of functions, is heavily social welfare orientated; partly it is because of the fact that, owing to the labour-intensive nature of their services and central government's lack of executant responsibility, local authorities employ more people than central government; and partly it is because local government traditionally represents a commitment to the collective provision of services.

The result has been a period of serious conflict between central and local government, with many local authorities resisting pressure to comply with central government policies and the centre seeking to reinforce the hierarchical relationship which earlier trends towards centralisation had established. Conflicts over finance have been critical. The Government's immediate objective was to restructure the system of local government finance. The Local Government, Planning and Land Act (L.G.P.L.A.) 1980 introduced a new system for controlling local authority capital expenditure and a new method of distributing rate support grants. These reforms were designed to reverse expenditure growth trends by (in the case of capital) giving central government power to designate for each local authority its total

---

[27] R. Greenwood, "Fiscal Pressure and Local Government in England and Wales" in C. Hood and M. Wright (eds.), *Big Government in Hard Times* (M. Robertson, 1981); "The Politics of Central-Local Relations in England and Wales 1974–1981" (1982) 5. *West European Politics* 253.

allocation and (in the case of revenue) introducing through the block grant mechanism incentives for expenditure restraint.

The block grant mechanism, however, was not well suited to achieving expediture reductions since it was designed for achieving a different purpose—the equalisation of rate poundages. The mechanism was therefore strengthened by section 8(8) of the Local Government Finance Act (L.G.F.A.) 1982 which effectively empowers the Secretary of State to reduce the grant of local authorities not complying with the Government's volume expenditure targets.[28] For various reasons[29] the system still was incapable of giving the government the control it desired and therefore "more out of exasperation than with a conscious sense of direction"[30] it switched attention from control of expenditure through grant manipulation to direct control of the rates. This proposal, enacted in the Rates Act 1984, amounted to "a measure of last resort, a desperate expedient by a Government determined to restore control in the short run while completely oblivious to the long run damage such measures can do to the system of government in this country."[31]

The other element in the Conservative government's approach has been to seek to improve "economy, efficiency and effectiveness"[32] in local government. This approach stems from the view that public bodies are wasteful, inefficient and unresponsive and require the disciplines of economic pricing policies or other market surrogates and the stimulus of competition to ensure continuous innovation.

A host of legislative and policy initiatives covering all major areas of local government have been promoted to achieve these objectives. A variety of legal constraints have been placed over aspects of local authority decision-making which require them to consider the economic implications of their decisions. This may be seen in the context of direct labour organisations,[33] public land registers,[34] audit arrangements,[35] the requirement that local authorities consult representatives of business before making their rate[36] and the planning framework imposed on the payment of public transport revenue sub-

---

[28] M. Loughlin, "Recent developments in central-local government fiscal relations" (1982) 9 J. of Law and Society 253.
[29] J. Gibson, "Local Government 'Overspending'—Who is Responsible?" in *The Fight for Local Government* (J. Raine ed., INLOGOV. Univ. of Birmingham, 1983), p. 6.
[30] R. Jackman, "The Rates Bill" (1984) Vol. 55, No. 2. *Political Quarterly* 161, 170.
[31] *Ibid.*
[32] Local Government Finance Act 1982, s. 26.
[33] L.G.P.L.A. 1980, Pt. III.
[34] L.G.P.L.A. 1980, Pt. X.
[35] L.G.F.A. 1982, Pt. III.
[36] Rates Act 1984, s.13.

sidies by metropolitan authorites.[37] Also, the Government has encouraged local authorites to obtain a greater proportion of their income from increasing fees and charges[38]; this has been particularly controversial in such areas of housing rents[39] and school meals.[40] In the field of land-use planning, the Government have encouraged local authorities to adopt a more pro-development approach[41] and have utilised streamlined procedures[42] and corporate structures[43] to tackle urban problems. Finally, various privatisation measures have been promoted through the encouragement of the contracting out of such local services as street cleaning, refuse collection and adoption services and through asset sales, especially sales of council houses.[44]

Although promoted in the guise of achieving efficiency in local government many of these measures have the effect of undermining the original redistributive objectives of local services and also directly challenge the principle of collective action.

Urban Decline and the Rise of Municipal Socialism

The impact of Government policy has been felt by all local authorities. Nevertheless the consequences of Government policy for the local authorities based on the major industrial cities are particularly severe. These cities grew with industrialisation and urbanisation in the nineteenth century. These authorities traditionally have been in the vanguard of public service provision. Today these cities are faced with similar problems to those which they confronted in the nineteenth century; urban poverty, substandard housing and the need to modernise the infrastructure of the city. What is different, however, is that today the major cities are no longer seen as the locus of economic growth. Consequently local government expenditure in these areas cannot be justified on the ground of underwriting the process of production or, to put it another way, as part of a capitalist logic of collective action.

The major cities are no longer the focal points of economic growth essentially because of changes in the industrial structure. Since the 1960s the cities have been losing population (see 1(c) in the table on p. 94). Initially this was felt to be part of a process of suburbanisation.

---

[37] Transport Act 1983.
[38] See Coopers and Lybrand Assocs., *Service Provision and Pricing in Local Government* (HMSO, 1981).
[39] Housing Act 1980, Pt. VI.
[40] Education Act 1980, ss.22, 23.
[41] DoE Circs. 22/80; 9/80; 14/84.
[42] Enterprise zones: L.G.P.L.A. 1980, Sched. 32.
[43] Urban Development Corporations; L.G.P.L.A. 1980, Pt. XVI.
[44] Housing Act 1980, Pt. I, Chap. I.

More recently, however, studies have shown that the decline in employment opportunities has been greater than the rate of population decline. Consequently a process of *deindustrialisation*[45] is reinforcing a process of *deurbanisation*.[46] As a result, the urban-rural shift today is in the opposite direction to that which occurred in the nineteenth century.

These structural changes have had a profound effect on the local authorities based on the major cities. In particular the historic links between industrialisation, urbanisation and collectivism have been subject to challenge. Alongside deindustrialisation and deurbanisation has been the re-assertion of the principle of individualism[47]:

"For the present generation the achievement of lower mortality rates, better transport and housing, greater protection from crime etc., are increasingly viewed as requiring individual rather than collective action. The private car has released a large proportion of the population from dependence on public transport. The medical profession seems agreed that any further significant reduction in mortality rates depends on individuals deciding to change their diets and smoke less. Individuals who dislike their environment, housing conditions and crime of the cities can move to smaller towns and are doing so at an increasing rate."

Furthermore, many of the reforms promoted by the Conservative government to achieve economy, efficiency and effectiveness in local government have reinforced this trend from collectivistic to individualistic principles of action. This may be seen most clearly in relation to housing policy. Council housing is entering a new era of residualisation, marked by "a reduction in the actual size of the council stock, a minimal rate of new building, a decline in the quality of new and existing council dwellings and a reduction in subsidy for council housing (but not for owner-occupation). . . . It involves a clear rejection of ideas of optimal public service provision and a reassertion of the role of the market backed by a minimal poor law service."[48] One consequence is that *individual* means-tested housing benefit is replacing *collective* rent-pooling arrangements as the primary means of subsidising the rents of council tenants.

---

[45] D.B. Massey and R.A. Meegan, "Industrial Restructuring versus the Cities" (1978) 15 *Urban Studies* 273; S. Fothergill and G. Gudgin, *Unequal Growth* (Heinemann, 1982); A.J. Scott, "Locational patterns and dynamics of industrial activity in the modern metropolis" (1982) 19 *Urban Studies* 111.

[46] K. Young and L. Mills, "The decline of urban economies" in *Fiscal Stress in Cities* (R. Rose and E. Page eds., Camb.Univ.Press, 1982).

[47] D. Dawson, above, n. 7, p. 30.

[48] A. Murie, "A new era for council housing?" in *The Future of Council Housing* (J. English ed., Croom Helm, 1982).

Key Indicators – Core Cities and Other Areas

Percentages

	Manchester	Liverpool	Birmingham	Sheffield	Leeds	Newcastle	Other Mets.	Non. Met. Counties	Inner London	Outer London
1. *Population*										
(a) population aged:										
0–4	5.9	5.8	6.4	5.1	5.8	5.6	6.2	6.0	5.6	5.9
5–15	15.7	15.8	16.7	15.7	16.4	14.6	17.1	16.4	12.7	14.7
(b) over pensionable age (60/65)	18.9	18.5	17.4	19.9	18.0	19.5	16.5	17.9	17.8	18.1
75 or over	5.9	5.9	5.4	6.3	5.8	6.4	5.1	5.9	9.9	5.9
(c) percentage change 1971–81	−18.0	−16.0	−8.0	−6.0	−5.0	−11.0	−2.0	+6.0	−8.0	−5.0
(d) change in school population 1977–81	−13.2	−16.5	−10.9	−10.2	−7.1	−9.5	−7.4	−4.0	−17.5	−9.5
(e) change in primary school population 1977–81	−21.0	−18.4	−16.2	−18.4	−14.1	−16.6	−14.0	−10.4	−22.1	−16.2

Table contd.

Percentages

	Manchester	Liverpool	Birmingham	Sheffield	Leeds	Newcastle	Other Mets.	Non. Met. Counties	Inner London	Outer London
2. Economic and Employment										
(a) male unemployment (16–64)*	20.9	24.4	18.5	14.0	12.5	18.4	14.8	11.4	14.4	8.0
(b) female unemployment (16–59)*	11.8	14.2	11.0	7.1	7.6	8.8	9.1	6.6	9.4	5.5
(c) children in households in receipt of supp. benefit**	27.5	29.1	22.0	13.4	16.4	18.8	13.9	9.5	20.7	9.9
(d) households with no car	60.4	61.8	49.5	51.8	48.0	58.8	45.8	33.0	58.7	36.0
3. Social and Housing										
(a) elderly people living alone (as percentage of all households)	16.8	15.7	14.6	17.1	15.7	16.8	14.5	13.8	15.8	13.6
(b) children in one adult households	10.1	8.3	7.7	5.5	7.3	8.0	6.1	5.2	12.7	6.5
(c) children in care (per 1000 aged 0–18)	19.3	13.5	12.8	9.0	11.1	17.3	N/A	6.7	19.6	7.5
(d) people in households with head born in New Commonwealth or Pakistan	7.8	1.7	15.0	3.2	4.0	2.4	4.0	2.3	18.8	11.7
(e) households overcrowded (over 1.0 per room)	5.7	5.6	6.0	3.3	3.3	4.6	4.1	2.5	7.1	4.2

* = proportion of economically active below retirement age seeking work.

** = per 100 population aged 0–15.

Source: *Rate Support Grant*. A submission to the Secretary of State for the Environment by the Cities of Liverpool, Manchester, Newcastle upon Tyne and Sheffield (July 1982).

But what about those individuals who, because of their social and economic circumstances, cannot "choose" to move out of the cities, or purchase a car, or take the benefits of the subsidies available to owner-occupiers, or educate their children at independent schools? That is, what about those people who are dependent on the services provided by local authorities? As the social indicators in the table on pp. 94–95 demonstrate, these groups are significantly overrepresented in the major cities. That is, in the major cities there are higher than average numbers of unemployed, people dependent on public transport, dependent elderly, single parent families, children in care and people in substandard housing.

Consequently, these structural and political changes have imposed a very heavy fiscal burden on the local authorities based on the major cities. In part, this is because of the difficulty of adjusting expenditures downward in association with population decline or business loss; the cost of maintaining the physical fabric of the city, for example, will remain largely unchanged. But mainly this has been because the major cities contain higher than average proportions of groups dependent on local authority services. And, since most local authority services are in the nature of redistributive services, this has led to fundamental conflicts with central government which has been based on the relative merits of individualistic or collectivistic action and which has resulted in the policitisation of the entire question of spending need.

Since the late 1960s, central government has expressed concern about the social and economic conditions of cities. The major response has been a series of area-based initiatives: educational priority areas (E.P.A.s), general improvement areas (G.I.A.s), housing action areas (H.A.A.s) and community development projects (C.D.P.s). These initiatives were based on the assumption that the poverty of people in these pockets of deprivation could be eradicated by positive action, area-based action and the more effective delivery of local authority services. Many of these assumptions were challenged by the teams set up under the community development project who argued that the cause of poverty lay in much more basic changes in the economies of these areas.[49] Their conclusions embarrassed the Government which wound up the C.D.P. experiment in the late 1970s, although the Urban Programme, of which the C.D.P. was part, remained, essentially as a mechanism for "topping up" the funds of inner-city authorities.[50] In the late 1970s, however, the Government recognised that the key issue was economic rather than social and a switch in approach occurred after the

---

[49] C.D.P., *Gilding the Ghetto* (Home Office, 1977); *The Costs of Industrial Change* (Home Office, 1977).
[50] J. Higgins *et al.*, *Government and Urban Poverty* (Basil Blackwell, 1983).

White Paper, *Policy for the Inner Cities*[51] and the Inner Urban Areas Act 1978. The Conservative government has maintained an economic approach but the emphasis has switched from public to private sector initiatives, albeit underwritten by public sector funding and action.[52]

Nevertheless these initiatives have been hardly sufficient to bolster, let alone reverse the decline of, the economies of the major industrial cities. Take Liverpool for example. Since 1971 it has experimented with E.P.A.s, G.I.A.s, H.A.A.s, Industrial Improvement Areas (under the I.U.A.A. 1978); was the subject of the Shelter Neighbourhood Action Project; was one of three areas selected for the Department of the Environment's Inner Area Studies; is one of seven authorities with Partnership status under the Urban Programme; and more recently has obtained an enterprise zone at Speke, an urban development corporation to regenerate the docklands area, and, since 1981, a special Merseyside Task Force. Despite this intensive action Liverpool between 1971 and 1981 lost 25 per cent. of its jobs (compared to the national average loss of 2 per cent.), of which half were lost in the period 1978–1981. Unemployment amounts to 1 in 4 and youth (16–24 year olds) unemployment constituted almost 1 in 2 in 1981. Liverpool has some of the worst housing conditions in Europe and has 20,000 council houses in need of urgent attention. However, its housing investment allocation in 1980 was, at £47m., only half of what it received in 1974. Nevertheless, it has since declined in real terms to £28m in 1984/85.[53]

The response of the local authorities based on the major industrial cities to trends of this nature has been significant. These areas traditionally are Labour party strongholds. And generally they have remained so. Nevertheless within the last decade or so a new form of local politics has emerged within the Labour party and is most strongly represented within the major urban areas. This new politics has challenged the tradition of strong local leaders who provide the political input into a local government machine they largely did not question.[54] Consequently, within the major urban areas there has emerged a new political class and a new type of urban politics.

---

[51] Department of the Environment, *Policy for the Inner Cities*, Cmnd. 6845 (1977).
[52] Through the use of such devices as enterprise zones, urban development grants and urban development corporations.
[53] Liverpool City Council, *Liverpool's Budget Crisis 1984: The Story of the Campaign* (Liverpool City Council, 1984).
[54] H. Elcock, "Tradition and Change in Labour Party Politics: the decline and Fall of the City Boss" (1981) 29 *Political Studies* 439.

The new political class is made up of Labour councillors who are younger, were weaned on community politics in the 1970s, are most likely to be employed in the public sector in a professional capacity and are generally prepared to work almost full-time as councillors.[55] The new type of urban politics challenges the assumption that the State is a neutral instrument of power—the nature of the State is itself a problematic. Consequently, this form of politics is concerned, first, to examine the role of local government in the local economy and its relationship with the communities it exists to serve, and secondly to challenge the traditional role assigned to local government within the system of government. These are the characteristic features of the emerging municipal socialism.

A crucial element within municipal socialism is the attempt to devise local economic and social strategies which complement one another. The starting point for such strategies is the fact that, as a result of deindustrialisation, local authorities are now *the* major employers and *the* largest investors in Britain's provincial cities. With unemployment levels running at very high levels (see 2(a) and (b) in the Table on p. 95) it is hardly surprising that local authorities have resisted attempts to reduce the size of their workforces. More positively, local authorities are beginning to use their power of procurement to achieve socio-economic objectives. Sheffield City Council, for example, which spends around £20m. annually on goods and services from over 900 local firms, has tightened up tendering conditions to ensure minimum health and safety regulations, a standard ratio of apprentices to skilled people and the elimination of "lump" labour.[56]

Another feature of these authorities' economic strategy has been their economic development and employment policies. These policies are intended not merely to subsidise existing firms, but to obtain a greater understanding of the nature of the local economy, to make planned interventions and to provide aid to firms adopting user-centred and human-centred design approaches. The leaders in this field are the West Midlands County Council and the Greater London Council which have established enterprise boards operating at "arms length" from the authority and financed by local authority income derived under section 137 of the Local Government Act 1972.[57]

[55] C. Skelcher "Towards salaried councillors?: the special responsibility allowances" (1983) 9 No. 3 *Local Government Studies* 30; D. Walker, "Local interest and representation: the case of the 'class' interest among Labour representatives in inner London" (1983) 1 *Government and Policy* 341; J. Gyford, "Our Changing Local Councillors" *New Society*, May 3, 1984, p. 181.

[56] D. Blunkett and G. Green, *Building from the Bottom* (Fabian Tract 491, 1983), pp. 11, 16.

[57] M. Boddy, "Local economic and employment strategies" in *Local Socialism?* (M. Boddy and C Fudge eds., Macmillan, 1984).

The new urban politics also challenges the traditional hierarchical and professionalised structures of the provision of local services[58]:

> "our services have to be improved before they can be supported by their users and defended against our opponents. No one will easily defend a socialist principle (like, for example, direct labour) if it is encapsulated in a service (like council house repairs) which is paternalistic, authoritarian or plain inefficient."

Methods of providing services in co-operation with people (and not just for people) have been examined. The most widely publicised aspect of this initiative is the Walsall scheme for decentralising local authority services to neighbourhood offices, an initiative which is also being explored by various London boroughs.[59] Another aspect of this objective is the establishment of special local authority committees to deal with such issues as the pursuit of racial equality,[60] women's issues[61] and (in London) the monitoring of the police.[62]

Given these types of policy initiatives, conflict with central government was inevitable. Central government's objectives are to reduce aggregate local expenditure and to reduce the redistributive aspect of local services by transforming such services as council housing, school meals provision, public transport and local authority direct labour services into trading services. This challenges the logic of collective provision since, if they are provided on market terms, these services might just as well be provided by the private sector. This appears to be the government's long-term objective. If realised, the function of the local authority would be essentially to monitor a range of services provided by the private sector with any subsidy issue being dealt with through national income transfer schemes.

The rise of municipal socialism is, in part, a political response to the changes in the economic and social structures of the major urban areas. The objectives of municipal socialism are to protect the welfare of the residents who are dependent on public services; to resurrect the traditional local authority concern with production issues; to challenge the bureaucratic structures which have distanced people from their local councils; and to rekindle a sense of community in adversity. Accord-

---

[58] D. Blunkett and G. Green, above, n. 56, p. 2.

[59] C. Fudge, "Decentralisation: Socialism goes local?" in M. Boddy and C. Fudge (eds.), above, n. 57; *Socialism and Decentralisation* (A. Wright ed., Fabian Tract 496, 1984).

[60] H. Ouseley, "Local authority race initiatives" in M. Boddy and C. Fudge (eds.), above, n. 57.

[61] S. Goss, "Women's initiatives in local government" in M. Boddy and C. Fudge (eds.), above, n. 57.

[62] S. Bundred, "Accountability and the Metropolitan Police: a suitable case for treatment" in *Policing the Riots* (D. Bowell *et al.* eds., Junction Books, 1982).

ingly, municipal socialism stands for increases in local expenditure to cater for unmet needs and for the reassertion of the principle of collective action.

As a result, in a constitutional system which places few real constraints on central government's capacity to act, and in which local authorities, as statutory corporations, are dependent on statutory grants of power for their ability to act, the legal dimension to these political conflicts has become increasingly important.

Legal Relations

The analysis so far has been based on the view that legal developments can be understood only by examining broader social, economic and political developments. Nevertheless, law has its own tradition and its peculiar procedures, concepts and doctrines. Consequently, it is a dimension which cannot be ignored if we are to understand recent developments in central-local government relations.

Local government law is primarily concerned with *powers* rather than *duties*. Local government law essentially establishes a legal framework within which local authorities are given discretionary powers to act. Many of these powers are subjectively formulated so that, subject to judicial review, the local authority is effectively free to determine the limits of the power. Central government possess a variety of powers enabling them to influence and restrain local authorities. However what is most significant is that the law was never intended to establish *norms* governing relations between central departments and local authorities. That is, local government law primarily performs a facilitative role; central-local relations are conducted through an administrative process of structured bargaining and the courts are of marginal importance.

This legal framework was established during the post-War period of economic growth and expansion of services. In the period of retrenchment, the Conservative government found that the framework was inappropriate. As a result, in the period since 1979 an unprecedented volume of local government legislation has been enacted. Of greater significance than the volume, however, has been the nature of this legislation. Basically the Government have been attempting to alter the nature of the framework by imposing specific duties on local authorities, curtailing administrative discretion by imposing detailed statutory procedures on local decision-making and by centralising discretionary decision-making by vesting broad powers of intervention in the Secretary of State. Elsewhere I have referred to this in terms of a shift in emphasis from a *functionalist* to a *normativist* style of law.[63]

[63] M. Loughlin, "Administrative Law, Local Government and the Courts" in M. Loughlin *et al.* (eds.), above, n. 7.

One longer-term impact of these changes may be to give the courts a more important role in supervising local authority decision-making. Indeed, since 1979, disputes have increasingly been fought out in the courts. However, so far these disputes have arisen mainly because of the discretionary powers vested in, and used by, the Secretary of State. Moreover, these legal disputes have largely arisen as part of a broader ideological conflict between urban authorities pursuing the policies of municipal socialism and those interests opposed to these strategies; ratepayers, Conservative controlled local authorities and the Government.

As a result, legal relations between central departments and local authorities are marked by antagonism, complexity and uncertainty. There are several reasons for this state of affairs. First, because the institutions involved are relatively powerful and therefore have a fair degree of manoeuvrability, they may try to use the courts in a tactical sense in pursuit of their goals. The likelihood of tactical use of the courts, and of law generally, is increased by the fact of expenditure restraint (which causes reflection on the legal limits of powers) and also because of changes in the style of local government law (which creates both constraints and uncertainties). Finally, while the style of local government law is changing from functionalism to normativism, there is evidence that a change in the opposite direction is emerging in the courts, where a functionalist style seems in fashion. Consequently, the overall picture defies simple explanation. However, some of these trends may be illustrated through examples.

First, there was the bombshell of *Bromley L.B.C.* v. *GLC.* [1983] 1 A.C. 768 in which the House of Lords quashed a supplementary precept issued by the GLC's new Labour administration to finance their policy of fares reductions on London's public transport system. The Lords quashed the precept on the grounds that the fares policy was beyond the statutory powers of the GLC and also, since the effect of the policy decision resulted in loss of rate support grant, was also in breach of the Council's fiduciary duty to their ratepayers. On both points the Lords displayed the utmost incompetence. In terms of statutory construction they construed a technical accounting provision, section 7(3) of the Transport (London) Act 1969, as incorporating a limitation on the power of the GLC to make revenue grants. In so doing they overturned more than a decade of conventional wisdom and practice in the area of public transport policy. On the fiduciary duty issue it is clear that Lord Diplock, the only judge to examine the issue seriously, did not understand the nature of the block grant system since the strict logic of his analysis seemed to lead to absurdity.[64]

[64] M. Loughlin, *Local Government, the Law and the Constitution* (Local Government Legal Society Trust, 1983), pp. 45–47.

Nevertheless both prongs of the judgment provided the Government with potentially powerful weapons in their crusade against municipal socialism. All the Metropolitan County Councils, for example, were Labour controlled, all were providing revenue subsidies to their public transport undertakings, and two authorities, recently been won by Labour, had issued supplementary precepts to finance fares reductions. In *R.* v. *Merseyside C.C., ex p. G.U.S. Ltd.* (1982) 80 L.G.R. 639, however, the statutory construction weapon proved unsuccessful. The Divisional Court held that the County Council's supplementary precept was not invalid because the Transport Act 1968, establishing the basic legal framework governing public transport in the metropolitan areas, although similar to the 1969 Act contained certain distinctions of emphasis. This judgment, therefore, protected the public transport revenue subsidy policies of the metropolitan counties. But the Government, exploiting the uncertainties created by the *Bromley* decision, immediately introduced a Bill designed ostensibly to establish a "clear and consistent legal framework" for subsidising public transport, which would provide the basis for "a reasonable, stable and lawful subsidy regime."[65] The Transport Act 1983, however, in reality seemed designed primarily to exploit legal uncertainties created by the use of the fiduciary concept by the Lords, rather than resolve the uncertainties in the statutory framework.[66] We must therefore consider this second potential weapon.

The fiduciary concept, in the context of the new grant penalty arrangements, seemed a very powerful legal doctrine which could possibly be used to convert government targets for local expenditure into expenditure ceilings. For this to occur, however, the courts would have to apply the fiduciary concept strictly. In fact the lower courts refused to do so. In *R.* v. *GLC, ex p. Royal Borough of Kensington and Chelsea, The Times,* April 7, 1982 for example, a case in which the Royal Borough sought to challenge the validity of the GLC's 1982/83 precept, McNeill J., in rejecting the Borough's arguments, expressed concern that "the power of judicial review is increasingly . . . sought to be used for political purposes superficially dressed up as points of law. The proper remedy in such matters is the ballot box and not the court." The basic reason for this attitude was the emerging functionalism in the courts,[67] which had led them to retreat from intervention in conten-

---

[65] Department of Transport, *Public transport subsidy in cities*, Cmnd. 8375 (1982), para. 5.

[66] M. Loughlin, "Public transport subsidy, local government and the courts" (1983) 133. New L.J. 283.

[67] C. Harlow, "Public" and "Private" Law: Definition without Distinction" (1980) 43 M.L.R. 241; G. Samuel "Public and Private Law: A Private Lawyer's Response" (1983) 46 M.L.R. 558; L. Blom-Cooper, "The New Face of Judicial Review: Administrative Changes in Order 53" (1982) *Public Law* 250.

tious areas of public policy. Incidentally, this trend has also rebounded on local authorities which have attempted to use the courts tactically; Hackney London Borough Council, for example, discovered this when attempting to challenge the validity of the Government's target for that Council on the ground that the target must incorporate some concept of attainability.[68]

From the Government's point of view therefore the Transport Act 1983 has been rather unsuccessful. First, because it soon became clear that the courts were not prepared to use the fiduciary concept to require local authorities to follow Government guidelines on appropriate levels of support. But it has also failed because the cost-benefit analysis mechanism, which was devised to render justiciable the levels of revenue support provided, has vindicated those levels of support provided by the metropolitan authorities. It is perhaps too cynical to suggest that it is because of these failures of the 1983 Act that it has been followed both by the London Regional Transport Act 1984, transferring control of London's public transport system from the GLC to the Secretary of State for Transport; and the current proposals for the abolition of the GLC and the metropolitan county councils. But what is clear is that the 1983 Act can in no way be said to have established a "stable . . . subsidy regime."[69]

The changing style of local government law has certainly been used as a method of constraining the collectivist policies of local authorities. A good example is provided by section 23 of the Housing Act 1980, which gives the Secretary of State powers to intervene to ensure that council tenants are able expeditiously to exercise the statutory right to buy their freeholds. The scope of the power is very broad indeed and the form in which it is drafted suggests that the objective was to minimise the possibility of judicial review. This crucial point has been underplayed by legal commentators who have tried to "invent" principles of administrative law in an attempt to limit that power[70] or have sought to explain the case of *Norwich C.C.* v. *Secretary of State for the Environment* [1982] 1 All E.R. 737 in terms of judicial bias without examining the nature of the statutory power.[71] Another example of this trend may be seen in the form of the Rates Act 1984. The power of the Secretary of State to require undertakings of local authorities applying for redetermination of their expenditure limit ensured that all local authorities designated for rate-capping in 1985/86 refused to apply. By

---

[68] *R.* v. *Secretary of State for the Environment, ex p. Hackney L.B.C.* (1984) 148 L.G. Rev. 691.
[69] Above, n. 65.
[70] A. Arden, *The Housing Act 1980* (Sweet & Maxwell, 1980) 51/23.
[71] P. McAuslan, "Administrative law, collective consumption and judicial policy" (1983) 46. M.L.R. 1, 13–14.

doing so, however, those authorities may have effectively abandoned the possibility of certain types of court challenge to the rate limit, since the courts are likely to hold that a statutory mechanism exists for dealing with grievances and the authorities should have utilised it.

Nevertheless, the heightened consciousness over the legal limits of local authority discretion has led many local authorities to exploit the autonomy given to them by the old-style functionalist legislation. The most notable example was the position of Liverpool City Council in relation to their 1984/85 budget. Most of the ruling Labour group were not prepared to fix a legal rate on the rate support grant terms set by the Government. They were able to exploit the fact that the General Rate Act 1967 does not require district councils to fix their rate by a particular date in order to carry a position of budgetary deadlock several months into the following financial year. During this period they negotiated with, and obtained a package of financial concessions from, the Government before they eventually fixed their rate in July 1984.

But this mixture between autonomy and constraint in local government law has also been utilised by the Government. The Conservative government has not, for example, taken direct control over housing rents as it did in the Housing Finance Act 1972. But the new housing subsidy system in Part VI of the Housing Act 1980 has been operated in such a way as to make it extremely difficult for a local authority not to comply with Government guidelines on rental levels even though formally the authority retains control over the setting of housing rents.

Generally speaking, however, despite the volume of litigation in this period of conflict and instability in legal relations between urban local authorities and central government the courts have been unprepared to act as the arbiters of appropriate conduct. In *R.* v. *Secretary of State for the Environment, ex p. Brent L.B.C.* [1982] Q.B. 593 and *R.* v. *Secretary of State for the Environment, ex p. Hackney L.B.C.* (1984) 148 L.G.Rev. 691 (D.C.),[72] for example, they have refused to accept the argument that the reference to principles in legislation meant not merely that the same standard must be applied to all local authorities in that class but also that that standard should be rationally related to the objectives of the Act. However, given the nature of the constitution it must be doubted whether the courts are capable of acting as arbiters of central-local relations. Given the Government's effective control of Parliament there is little to prevent the Government using to the full the legal power of the state. Indeed in its conduct with local government this is precisely what has happened. Consequently, although it may not be particularly meaningful to argue that the Government have

---

[72] See also the decision of the Court of Appeal: *The Times*, May 11, 1985.

been acting unconstitutionally (since at this level this is to engage in ideological discourse), the Government has certainly failed to abide by constitutionalist standards of behaviour.[73]

Conclusions

Central-local government conflicts are largely the product of the economic crisis and the nature of the Government's response to this crisis. But there are longer-term structural changes which must be taken into account in any attempt to understand the complexities of these conflicts. When these factors are examined it becomes clear that conflicts between the large urban local authorities and the Government raise special issues. There are economic, social, political and ideological dimensions to conflicts along this axis. First, the combination of economic and the process of deindustrialisation, of cyclical and structural decline, has had a devastating impact on the economies of the major cities. Secondly, since modern local government services are largely social welfare orientated it is hardly surprising, given the impact of economic change, that urban local authorities have sought to alleviate the consequences for city dwellers by attempting to protect service levels. Thirdly, since the major industrial cities are the heartlands of Labour support the large urban authorities are primarily Labour controlled. It was therefore almost inevitable that the question of spending need would become politicised. Finally, there has been a more deep-seated ideological conflict between urban authorities and central government along the lines of collectivism or individualism as organisational principles.

The intensity of the conflict is reflected in the volume and nature of local government legislation enacted since 1979 and the number and type of disputes affecting local government coming before the courts. More specifically, an insight into the nature of the conflict is provided by examining the extent to which urban local authorities figure in this flurry of legal activity. Of the 18 local authorities designated for 1985/86 under the Rates Act 1984, for example, 16 are Labour controlled and 14 are undoubtedly authorities based on the major industrial cities. Also, the current proposals to abolish the strategic authorities in London and the metropolitan areas must be viewed both as a centralising measure and as an attack on Labour controlled authorities which have sought to protect and promote collectivist policies. And the Labour controlled urban authorities have figured prominently in legal disputes in the courts in recent years.

---

[73] M. Loughlin, "The importance of constitutional argumentation and constitutionalist values in the debate over central-local government relations" in *New Research in Central-Local Relations* (M. Goldsmith ed., Gower, 1985).

Given the nature of the British Constitution, the courts cannot safeguard a sphere of local autonomy. Rather they have provided one forum within which these conflicts have been fought out. This is not to say that there are not important issues of constitutional principle involved in these matters. But merely that, given the structure of the British Constitution, there are few safeguards on a central government intent on imposing their contentious policies on other governmental institutions. What I am suggesting however is that if public lawyers are to seek to understand the nature and significance of these legal disputes and legal developments they must examine broader socio-economic issues. In this essay the issues of economic change, its social and spatial implications, and the nature of political and ideological responses provide the basic framework for understanding contemporary legal relations between central departments and local authorities.

Chapter 5

DE-LEGALISATION IN BRITAIN IN THE 1980s

NORMAN LEWIS

I have chosen to address the issue of "de-legalisation"[1] by breaking up some common understandings and by reconstituting the argument concerning more or less "law" as matters of constitutionality. I shall adopt the view that most debates about regulation, de-regulation, privatisation and the like are theoretically inadequate and that instead I should address and synthesise problems of legitimation, legal theory and systems building for the better conduct of rational discourse.

I have long taken the view that law is a series of socially necessary tasks to be performed in any given organisational framework.[2] Procedures for the resolution of grievances, for planning and monitoring, for describing the legitimate anatomy of groups (their constitutions) are necessary conditions of social intercourse. On that level then, to talk about "more or less" law is to contradict oneself and to engage in riddles. This is sometimes obscured by the practice of sanctifying one particular historical form of law, "the high bourgeois" or gesellschaft form, and relegating all others.

It is at this point that the question of legitimation arises. Which procedures for performing these necessary tasks are collectively acceptable and which not? This is the problem of constitutionality which is so characteristically ignored in Britain by lawyers and political scientists alike. Because Britain has no "foundation document," no "ark of the covenant" the tendency has grown up of identifying "the constitution" with a descriptive series of pragmatic working practices which habit of mind and tendency do the practitioners of this art no intellectual credit whatsoever. More recently some scholars have implicitly attacked this practice for its propensity to obscure the

---

[1] "De-legalisation" was the theme for a seminar series at the European University Institute where an earlier version of this paper was presented in March 1984. An expanded version is available under the same title as a EUI Working Paper, 1985.
[2] K. Llewellyn 1940. The Normative, the Legal and the Law Jobs. Yale L.J. 49, 1355 (1940); N. Lewis, "Towards a sociology of lawyering in public administration" (1981) *Northern Ireland Legal Quarterly* 32, 89.

realities of operational public power.[3] However, even the work of Daintith, much more perceptive than that of most British public lawyers, has so far failed to pursue its own internal theoretical logic. Thus, if it is both useful and *legitimate* to trace the intricate webs of government through "dominium" as he describes it (the power of the purse, the contracts, the concessions, the franchises, etc.) then we must be told why. It is the issue of legitimacy which lies at the heart of this problem for, like Daintith, I shall wish *accurately* to explain the workings of our constitution which cannot be a matter of subjective preference.[4] In doing so I shall ex-necessitate be describing *legitimate* public power (or identifying non-constitutional or illegitimate behaviour) and it is difficult to see how legitimate public power can be identified, defended or even constructed without public debate. Raw public power is of course a different matter but the very concept of legitimation imports a public discussion of parameters, even if the discussion marks off *some* behaviour as no-go areas. But it is the discussion which will justify the exceptions.

In a forthcoming book[5] I argue that to expose our constitution adequately we must turn our cultural claims (*e.g.* the rule of law) in on themselves and draw out their implications, thereby exposing imma-nent categories. This "immanent critique" I argue reveals a constitu-tion based on the twin premises of openness and accountability. Any other treatment which affects to describe the British Constitution is likely to be operating on an agenda of hidden values and will fail to carry either consensual or philosophical conviction.

The modern British State[6] is a typically complex modern welfare state where socio-economic processes are extraordinarily dense and where government is no longer simply concerned with facilitating the market and protecting property rights.

> "The economic activities of private entities are regulated to vary-ing degrees; the extent and visibility of the socialization of their formerly 'private' conduct depends upon the regulatory mecha-nism employed. Moreover the state has gone into the business of supplying primary goods and services (including protection against market risks) to its citizens. Given that the state has become in significant respects both the regulator and the competi-

[3] T. Daintith, "The Executive Power Today" in *The Changing Constitution* (J. Jowell ed., Oxford University Press, 1985); K. Middlemas, *Politics in Industrial Society* (1979).

[4] Sir W.I. Jennings, *The Law of the Constitution* (5th ed., London V.P., 1959), p. 37.

[5] N. Lewis and I.J. Harden, *The Rule of Law and the British Constitution* (Hutchin-son, 1986 (forthcoming)).

[6] B. Jessop, *The Capitalist State* (Martin Robertson, Oxford, 1982).

tor of private economic concerns, the interesting questions are who or what controls its expanded activities and by what power or authority does he do so."[7]

I have argued elsewhere[8] that in Britain the traditional parliamentary claims for overall legitimation fail to carry any real weight or conviction; that to borrow a phrase from an American source, the electorate "buys representation in bulk-form."[9] I have argued, in agreeing with a former Permanent Secretary to the Treasury, that traditional assumptions concerning Cabinet government are now no longer sustainable and that the major locus of public power in Britain is focussed around a federation of the great departments of state in conjunction with their client groups.[10] Given that Britain has no federal consititution nor developed principles of public law constituting a *rechsstaat*[11] we are desparately short on mechanisms which are directed to produce legitimate outcomes through rational political choice and discourse.

The Separation of Law and Politics

Part of the difficulty in encouraging constitutional lawyers in Britain to engage in institution-building through law in order to assist in delivering on constitutional claims and expectations is that the "rule of law" paradigm irrationally separates out law from politics. This "virtual obsession" was largely, though by no means exclusively, a product of nineteenth-century history.[12]

Given that the thrust of this chapter is towards arguing for a reasoned decision-making process through a revised concept of law, then the barriers which define the spheres of influence of law, administration and politics must be broken down lest we hinder the deployment of resources necessary for rational and efficient policy-making. I agree with K.C. Davis that "the danger of injustice lurks in unchecked power, not in blended power,"[13] though we must reiterate our commitment to the broader Llewellynesque, socially necessary

---

[7] R. Austin, "The Problem of Legitimacy in the Welfare State" (1982) *Pennsylvania Law Review* 130, 1510.

[8] N. Lewis and I.J. Harden, "Sir Douglas Wass and the Constitution: An End to the Orthodox Fairy Tales" (1984) 35 N.I.L.Q. 213–230.

[9] J. Choper, *Judicial Review and the National Political Process* (1980).

[10] D.E. Ashford, *Policy and Politics in Britain* (Blackwell, Oxford, 1981).

[11] K.H.F. Dyson, *The State Tradition in Western Europe* (Martin Robertson, Oxford, 1980).

[12] M.J. Horwitz, *The Transformation of American Law 1780–1860* (Harvard, 1977), p. 130. See M. Arthurs, *Without the law* (Toronto, 1985).

[13] K.C. Davis, *Administrative Law Text* (1958), p. 30.

concept of law. The following remarks seem to us to make the point well:

> "As a political actor [government] assumes responsibility for deciding what ends are to be pursued and what resources it is prepared to commit in dealing with problems such as pollution control or discrimination in employment. . . . But government must then proceed, as a *legal* actor, to establish the agencies and mechanisms by which public ends will be furthered. In principle, . . . these institutions [should be] designed to bring maximum objectivity to the elaboration of public policy. . . . "[14]

In other words we are not seeking to replace politics by law but to harness legal institutions to the exploration and facilitation of policy-making so that the optimum conditions for political choice are created.

Constitutionality: the Public/Private Divide

Constitutionality, the legitimate atmosphere for public action, naturally poses questions concerning the existence and/or desirability of marking out the boundaries between the public and private spheres. Whatever constitutes the public sphere, it is clear that action within it should accord with settled constitutional principles, specifically in relation to procedural matters. As to the substantive behaviour, that, unless one adopts some version of natural law thinking,[15] is very much a "local" or contingent issue. The public sphere's relation to private behaviour, varying over time and space, time and place, must, I would urge, be equally characterised by the same settled principles. Given that these, in Britain certainly and most compellingly in the United States, must be constituted by canons of openness and accountability we ought to be able to map out the relationships, the tensions between the boundary fences, and the degree of compenetration occuring between "state" and "society" at any given time.[16] This has never been systematically attempted by British constitutional lawyers so that much essentially public behaviour has gone unscrutinised, at least in an overt institutional sense.

In the classic liberal state the clear distinction between public and private was crucial to its legitimacy. The private sphere was supreme while the public was primarily charged with facilitating the activities of the private sphere.

---

[14] P. Nonet and P. Selznick, *Law and Society in Transition: Toward Responsive Law* (1978), p. 112.

[15] D. Beyleveld and R. Brownsword, "Law as a Moral Judgment vs. Law as the Rules of the Powerful" 23 *American Jo. of Jurisprudence* 79 (1983).

[16] G. Poggi, *The Development of the Modern State* (Hutchinson, London, 1978).

"The public sphere was ostensibly operated according to democratic principles; the hierarchy and dominations that characterized the private sphere were explained by the market."[17]

The corollary was that legal thought was concerned to create a clear separation between constitutional, criminal and regulatory law—public law—and the law of private transactions—torts, contracts, property and commercial law.[18] What is not always appreciated, however, is that this development was historically specific and by no means characterised English law over a long historical period.[19] However the "immutable laws of capital" seemed to make it necessary for regulation to be kept at a minimum,[20] even though when occasion demanded the public and private streams commingled as witness the injection of private capital into "public" utilities, with the state guaranteeing limited liability.[21] Indeed it now seems clear that private power began to become increasingly indistinguishable from public power precisely at the moment, late in the nineteenth century, when large-scale concentration became the norm. These very concentrations became to a large extent the cause of government intervention and a major impetus to the emergence of the Welfare State.

It has to be said that although in Britain institutional machinery for moderating competition between interests which seek to capture or privatise part of the state machinery is very underdeveloped, the phenomenon itself it not. The exploration of North Sea Oil is a case in point for it has been cogently argued that forces pushing for the co-option of offshore safety into the broader generic machinery of onshore safety administration found themselves in competition with the Department of Energy itself which was being pushed by national and international oil interests to give higher priority to the requirements of commercial production.[22]

The overall failure to examine the finer details of public/private intercourse is also in evidence in relation to the general debate on regulation. As I have argued elsewhere,[23] regulation can and does

---

[17] Austin 1982 at p. 1517, see n. 7, above; Habermas, 1979.
[18] Horwitz, 1982, see n. 12, above; P.S. Atiyah, *The Rise and Fall of Freedom of Contract* (Clarendon, Oxford, 1979).
[19] Sir William Holdsworth *A History of English Law* (Methuen, London, 1938), Vol. XI, p. 518.
[20] W. Carson, *The Other Price of Britain's Oil* (Martin Robertson, London, 1982), p. 302.
[21] K. Davies, *Local Government Law* (Butterworth, London, 1983), p. 33; Horwitz, 1977, pp. 110–114. See n. 12, above.
[22] Carson, n. 20, above at p. 297.
[23] N. Lewis and I.J. Harden, "Privatisation, De-regulation and Constitutionality: Some Anglo-American Comparisons" (1983) 34 N.I.L.Q. 297–229.

occur in the public sector as the private. While in both "domains" regulation, especially in Britain, can be formal or informal. The relationship of British Airways and the Civil Aviation Authority clearly makes this point while the other commercial nationalised industries have been subject both to the very occasional formal ministerial direction and to extreme pressure of the less formal variety. I argued at the time that ownership and regulation are conceptually distinct and that at least four combinations are possible; namely, private ownership with or without regulation and public ownership with or without regulation. When de-legalisation is discussed however, private ownership without regulation seems to be the model generally assumed. I take the view that this is of itself misleading for a number of reasons, just a few of which we shall outline shortly. Briefly, however, I would argue that various informal processes may link public and private decision-making even in the absence of formal regulatory mechanisms. Even so, given that the state sees its role in part as being to create conditions for markets to flourish, then it is thereby and immediately involved in private ordering, while we know for example that favourable conditions of a highly preferential kind are as capable of being offered by the public sector to the private as by the public sector to another part of the public sector. Recent concern over the links between British Oxygen, (BOC) a publicly quoted company, and the National Health Service (NHS), a formal part of British Central government, fired by a large growth in BOC's profits taken from health care makes the point neatly.[24] I shall develop this later. However there remains much to say in relation to the increasing compenetration of state and society.

Networks: the British Passion

A much discussed issue of network linkage in modern government in recent times has been the issue of corporatism, whereby government purposes are sought to be effected through representative groups who then, for the benefits which they can bargain with government, seek to deliver government policies through their constituencies. This is not the place to pursue well-worn arguments surrounding these developments save to say that corporatist tendencies not only create another dimension on the public/private plane but for the most part operate only subject to informal mechanisms which are not in any regular sense "accountable." They allow government to proceed "by other means" and as such are simply an example of performing law-jobs covertly without regard to the underlying principles of legitimation which we

[24] *The Guardian*, January 6, 1984.

insist inform the true British Constitution.[25] I have argued that the real importance of the debate surrounding various versions of corporatist thought lies in exposing another part of the working of the processes of British Government, of identifying private/public linkages and of highlighting problems of accountability and constitutionality. In this respect corporatist ebbs and flows are of a piece with the thrust of our general arguments concerning the need to legitimise the process of public action through our informing set of immanent expectations. That public institution-building is called for to take the informal legal and para-legal processes out of the shadows. This issue is evaded by speaking of such developments as "de-legalisation," the contraction of the state and the like.

In discussing the bewildering array of networks which conceal the nature of public/private relations we touched upon the British Oxygen affair. It is worth drawing this out a little though we would not wish to suggest that the problems surrounding the public interest in this matter are anything other than symptomatic of the difficulties in lending constitutional credibility to government/private sector commercial relationships. In early 1984, the House of Commons Public Accounts Committee decided to examine an exclusive contract which the Department of Health and Social Security has given to BOC and which would allow the Company to extend its monopoly in supplying medical gases and equipment to the National Health Service. A joint non-government investigation by *The Guardian* and the College of Health, a body set up in 1983 to protect health service consumers, was the occasion for the heightened public interest. The report draws attention to the confidential nature of price negotiations between the DHSS and BOC, to the existence of an exclusive contract for which other contractors were not allowed to bid and, *inter alia,* to the fact that some 30 per cent. of the group's £150 million operating profit in the preceding financial year came from its health care business. Less than 10 years ago it constituted less than 10 per cent. It is nearly 30 years since the monopolies and restrictive practices legislation was used to examine these matters and the undertakings which the Monopolies and Mergers Commission (MMC) extracted would now need to be considerably re-vamped if they were to be properly policed by the Office of Fair Trading (College of Health 1984).

Networks and Re-legalisation

I have referred constantly to the networks of power in Britain and I now need to say a little more on this level before I can bring the

---

[25] Lewis and Wiles, "The Post-Corporatist State?" (1984) 11 J. of Law and Society, 65–90.

preceding strands of my argument together. Reiterating that public power in Britain resides essentially in the great Departments of State together with their client groups, it needs to be heavily stressed that the institutional forms assumed for the exercise of public power are heterogeneous to say the least. In a range of areas, governmental power is mediated through formal quasi-government and quasi-non-government agencies.[26] However, it is safe to say that with the possible exception of the Civil Aviation Authority most of these bodies exercise power without any very stringent form of public law control; no rule-making procedures, grievance procedures, independent appeal mechanisms or the like. Although in many ways I would favour an expansion in number of such bodies, the way they currently operate in Britain tends to obfuscate decision-making to a considerable degree. The reason for this is that they often operate with a veneer of independence which disguises the strong pressure exerted by Whitehall for which it is prepared to accept little responsibility; indeed even the extent of that pressure is clouded beneath blankets of sophisticated and tutored forms of secrecy.[27]

Informally bargained outcomes, the decisions and non-decisions accommodated through networks of civility and conviviality represent very substantially the operation of the "law jobs" of planning and monitoring and resolving grievances (albeit ordinarily in an atmosphere of organised non-disclosure). Given what I have argued about the compenetration of the public and private spheres and given our concept of law it becomes then something of a nonsense to talk about de-legalisation in its ordinary meaning. If I argue that the immanent underlying principles informing British constitutional expectations are openness and some form of accountability then our task becomes that of re-legalisation through institution-building based on these legitimating principles.

I shall later turn to discrete areas of public administration to illustrate the foregoing but a few remarks might be in order at this juncture. Thus, it has been recently argued that "anti-trust" regulation both in Britain, the United States and the EEC is to a large extent regulation by bargaining.[28] Although the British Nationalised Industries are now subject to the jurisdiction of the MMC, these remarks were directed to the private sector. However, long before the Competition Act 1980, regulation through bargaining and informal processes characterised

---

[26] A. Barker, *Quangos in Britain* (Macmillan, Hong Kong, 1982); N. Lewis, "Who Controls Quangos and the Nationalised Industries?" *The Changing Constitution* (J. Jowell ed., O.U.P., 1985).

[27] Lewis and Harden (1983) *op. cit.*

[28] B. Boyer, *Fifty Years of Regulatory Reform in the United States*, Paper to Conference on Regulation in Britian (Oxford, 1983).

the way successive governments handled their dealings with those industries. Government intervention over pricing, borrowing, pay negotiations and investment in the interests, variously, of counter-inflation policy, industrial policy and macro economic policy had taken place through informal and unaccountable processes which by-passed the formal legal authority to give directions to those industries.[29] Some of the same problems emerge in relation to the operation of competition policy. Although the machinery adopted is much more formal and public than is the case across much of British Government, considerable leverage is still employed by the Secretary of State himself without engaging the machinery as such. I have no doubt that the rather complex institutional arrangements have the potential to deliver an open and public examination of these matters even if considerable improvement in this respect currently needs to be effected. Indeed a reformed set of procedures such as these could well have considerable analogical potential. Nonetheless the Secretary of State's role seems to me still to be insufficiently structured and institutionalised for me to be satisfied that a sufficient degree of openness is secured. Unsurprisingly perhaps, the British courts have also ensured that his discretion will rarely be supervised.[30] Even the official government position is that "decisions on merger references are taken on a case by case basis rather than by applying a rigid set of rules."[31]

Government Action, Inaction and Constitutionality

I argue elsewhere[32] that in Britain the underlying expectations of openness and accountability mean that the activities of all public actors and their agents are the proper subject of public scrutiny unless a strong case to the contrary can be made out, that case in its turn having to run the gauntlet of public and reasoned scrutiny. Given that I have made out a case, even in the course of this paper, that public actors have extensive links, formal and informal, with private ordering and given that it is in Britain a constitutional axiom that Parliament can exercise omnicompetent power within its subject territories then it follows that the relationship of public actors to private concentrations of power is a matter of constitutional vitality too. This in turn poses questions about the instrumentalities and institutions for illuminating this relationship, a matter to which we have already adverted. I shall

---

[29] Nedo Report on Nationalised Industries. For a discussion of this see Prosser below, pp. 174 *et seq.* (1976); J. Redwood and J. Hatch, *Controlling Public Industries* (Blackwell, 1982).

[30] *R. v. Secretary of State for Trade, ex p. Anderson Strathclyde* [1983] 2 All E.R. 233.

[31] HMSO 1978. *A Review of Monopolies and Mergers Policy*, Cmnd. 7198.

[32] Lewis and Harden (1986). See n. 5, above.

have more to say on this issue shortly. However, baldly stated, these propositions fail to identify an important element which I have only hinted at in my remarks concerning competition policy in particular and *ex parte* contracts more generally.

It ought to be commonplace that public actors these days operate as much through legally conferred discretionary powers as through legal duties. Indeed the literature on discretion is now too voluminous to need more than a passing nod. However, very little distinctly *constitutional* attention has been directed to this matter, at least in the United Kingdom. Interest in rule-making procedures, for example, has been substantially confined to circumstances where the executive either proposes to act or has already acted without a sufficient degree of openness to satisfy the critics. But as K.C. Davis pointed out some little time ago,[33] the non-exercise of power is really quite often as interesting as its formal exercise. Especially, I might add, where it is the result of network conviviality, bargained outcomes and the deliberations of the cosy embrace. In other words, not least in the practices of British Government. There are numerous ways in which procedures could be devised for exposing the thinking processes of Ministers when they decide not to refer a merger to the MMC or not to press ahead with a piece of legislation originally favoured, or indeed why it had rejected some policy options in favour of others. A growing literature surrounding the issue of inaction or non-decision-making is beginning to appear in the United States and has, I believe, considerable significance for Britain which is much more in need of institutionalising its constitutional practices. Let me speak briefly to some of the American literature:

> "Administrative inaction occurs at least as often as administrative action. Its effects can be just as influential. When the will of Congress is not properly implemented, people lose benefit of legislative action and faith in the ability of government to effectuate social change. Judicial review of agency non-implementation of a statute is both necessary and proper to give effect to the congressional intent and to assure the legitimacy of the administrative system."[34]

Some movement has occurred towards the development of a court-enforced duty for agencies to speak to the non-implementation of programmes[35] and thereby to fill an accountability gap by forcing

---

[33] K.C. Davis, *Discretionary Justice* (University of Illinois Press, Chicago, 1971).
[34] P.H.A. Lehner, "Judicial Review of Administrative Action" Columb. L.Rev. 83, 627–689 (1983).
[35] R. Steward and C.R. Sunstein, "Public Programs and Private Rights," Harvard L.Rev. 95, 1193 (1982).

agencies to listen to the claims of the electorate. All this has to be seen in the context of the Freedom of Information Act, the Government in the Sunshine Act and various executive orders which together demand that the agency accumulate a fairly complete record of subjects that have become the object of agency consideration. Combine this with the requirement to produce contemporaneous records sufficient to show the public and the court its data, methodology and reasoning and they are on notice to keep an up-to-date record of anything that may be of concern to the public.[36]

In concluding this section I would add one item. Though adopting the position that this level of institution-building is demanded at the normative consitutional level I would add the rider that the demands of "efficiency" point in the same direction. Though not wishing to engage a refined dialogue about the nature and forms of efficiency we would rest here on one contemporary-sounding argument; that of rationality crises in times of increased organizational complexity and the corresponding need to "ground" rationality in learning processes.

In general terms let it be said that modernity tends to be accompanied by economic crisis management, confusion in the face of complex socio-economic processes and cognitive limits of mechanisms of political-legal control.[37] This is one of the reasons why broad delegations of power have been acceptable for the American administrative agencies and why the development of cable in Britain ought, it is said, to be conducted through general as opposed to detailed regulation. The industry, it is urged, is likely to grow in ways which are currently impossible to forecast.[38] In the world of banking we have been told that an era of financial innovation and institutional change, though observable, is not easily susceptible to quantitative study.[39] More broadly we are constantly told that the system cannot keep its own promises whether in terms of social regulation, macro-economic policies or in relation to non-market interventions. This has been well documented in Britain though it has been seen to be a more broadly-based problem suffused with difficulties surrounding inadequate programme formulation, information or implementation capacities.[40]

A States-side Excursus

I believe that the history of regulation in the United States points up a

---

[36] Lehner (1983), at p. 635. See n. 34, above.

[37] G. Teubner, "Substantive and Reflexive Elements in Modern Law" Law and Soc. Rev. 17, 239–285 (1983), at p. 268.

[38] Sir Norman Hunt, *Report of the Inquiry into Cable Expansion and Broadcasting Policy*, Cmnd. 8672 (1962), at p. 13.

[39] J.S. Fforde, "Competition, Innovation and Regulation in British Banking" (September, 1983) *Bank of England Quarterly Bulletin* 363–376.

[40] Reich (1983), pp. 8, 35; Ashford (1981), see n. 10, above.

number of key issues that any re-examination of the relationship between the governors and the governed in Britain ought to take on board. First it is clear to us that in developing the "hard-look doctrine" the Federal Courts were right in insisting on a rejection of the crystal-ball approach to the resolution of tough questions.[41] On the other hand there has been a clear move away from the rigid constraints of formal rule-making on the record in recent years with both Congress and the Courts fighting shy of it. Rather there has been a move towards flexibility dependent however on producing a "substantial enquiry" and a "thorough, probing, in-depth review."[42] The search then has been to avoid formal adjudicative procedures, whilst going beyond the arbitrary and capricious test. The latter, known as "soft" judicial review, sometimes less charitably as the "lunacy" test has been strongly evident in Britain when judicial review has been available at all.[43] The "unsolved problem of regulatory reform is to perfect an interest-representation model which will import political checks into the administrative arena."[44]

The flexibility of "hard look" then has been generally welcomed in that participation can take the form of conferences, consultation with industry committees, mixes of written and oral comments all directed at avoiding the unsatisfactory nature of the trial-type process. What is vital is to provide "recorded agency reaction to crucial submissions" which is basic to effective judicial review.[45] This can be seen to demand different levels of detail in differing contexts and whereas environmental impact statements and regulatory impact analyses[46] might be thought necessary on some occasions, less rigorous methods of producing discourse will serve on others.

In the United States there now seems general accord that regulatory procedure requires a new flexibility which respects traditional concerns for accuracy, fairness and acceptability, but which meets the need for more efficient administration. The strength of informal hard-look rulemaking resides in its unique combination of flexibility, expedition and fairness. The ability to "go outside the record" makes it much like the political process itself.[47] Change is clearly in the air to ensure that flexible models are developed which provide comprehensive and

---

[41] *Natural Resources Defence Council* v. *Morton* 458F. 2d 827, 837 (D.C. Cir. 1972).
[42] *Citizens to Preserve Overton Park* v. *Volpe* 401 U.S. 402, 415 (1971).
[43] *Associated Picture Houses Ltd.* v. *Wednesbury Corporation* [1948] 1 K.B. 223.
[44] Boyer (1983). See n. 28, above.
[45] Verkuil, P.R., "Judicial Review of Informal Rulemaking" Virg.L.Rev. 60, 185 (1974).
[46] Lewis and Harden (1983), at p. 219. See n. 23, above.
[47] American Bar Association (ABA) *Federal regulation: roads to reform* (1979); Verkuil (1974). See n. 45, above.

rational standards. Underneath all these proposals lies a *cri de coeur* about democratic societies in general;

> "It is necessary for democratic institutions to adapt their workings so as to meet the necessities of modern governmental agendas. Should this fail to occur, democracies may fail to sustain acceptable standards of executive performance, or alternatively power will seep away to hidden bureaucracies, or to some type of 'business government,' leaving political institutions increasingly formalistic."[48]

In Britain, these concerns are especially pointed. For largely fortuitous reasons there is the occasional breakthrough whereby the zero-sum, "all-or-nothing" nature of judicial review of executive behaviour is dented. Thus, warts and all, the role afforded to the Social Security Advisory Committee under the Social Security Act 1980 to cause the Secretary of State to take a "hard look" at objections to proposed regulations relating to the supplementary benefit scheme is to be welcomed.[49] Elsewhere the Civil Aviation Authority has been praised for breaking the mould of administrative law in Britain. These, however, are isolated developments. In general, procedures for major policy initiatives in Britain are defective in terms of both democratic conventions and the efficient absorption of the contributions of broad-based "publics."

Developments in Britain in the 1980s

It should be clear from the foregoing that important questions of legitimation through law, of constitutionality, have been substantially suppressed for some little time past. The last two decades have, it is true, seen an upsurge of interest in administrative and public law controls which at the time of writing seems to have "peaked" in the shape of the recently established pressure group, the Freedom of Information Campaign. However, there can be little doubt that events since 1979 have quickened the pace of unaccountable government and consequently have quickened the pulses of some constitution-watchers.[50] Quite apart from significant changes in the machinery of government itself there has been a commitment to some measure of de-regulation and a large measure of privatisation. Absent the machinery for examining these developments which have lain at the

[48] P.E. Self, *Administrative Theory and Politics* (Allen and Unwin, London, 1972).
[49] Social Security Act 1980, s.10(4); HMSO 1982. *First Annual Report of the Social Security Advisory Committee per 1980–1*, App. 3; HMSO 1983c. *Second Annual Report of the Social Security Advisory Committee per 1982–3*, Chap. 3.
[50] Lewis and Wiles (1984); Lewis and Harden (1983). See n. 23, above.

heart of this paper, it has been easier to make a clean break in the public/private arenas than might have been the case elsewhere.

On all manner of issues it is clear that machinery to examine major public matters in settings which encourage cognitive development and the monitoring of approved programmes does not exist or is inadequate for the task. This is true not only on the level of innovation but on that of quality control. For instance, it took a string of scandals on the Lloyds insurance market to effect changes, not the least of which was the appointment of an outside chief executive with the specific job of cleaning the Augean stables. Elsewhere the balance to be struck between the detailed regulation of specific practices and the need for general and effective public oversight of self-regulation or self-governance will require constant adjustment. I have committed myself to the view that a mix of types of legal framework will be required for the optimum ordering of public affairs but in Britain at the moment I have no confidence that the means for securing that optimum ordering are available. Let me now turn to discrete areas to make out the case for a "hard look" at providing optimum procedural solutions for the resolution of current dilemmas.

Until the beginning of 1984, the sale of public assets undertaken since 1979 was reported to have provided large speculative gains for investors given that the selling price was in aggregate some £400 millions less than current share prices. Moreover this was achieved by selling assets off primarily to pension funds and thereby exchanging one unaccountable set of bureaucrats in the West End for another in the City of London.[51] Many of these decisions are being taken, it needs to be added, without any [public] discussion of what regulation, if any, will need to be emplaced specifically on account of the decisions to sell off being taken.

Examples are legion but let us look briefly at coach and rail competition in a deregulated market. The Transport Act 1980 removed, *inter alia*, licensing constraints on long-distance coach services. The change took place after 50 years of stability and was bound therefore to have aroused considerable interest. There have been some surprising consequences of this decision but we will restrict ourselves to one issue alone. The major growth for coach passenger travel has been on routes where British Rail already provide not only a high frequency of service, but in most cases their best services. British Rail estimate that the financial loss from coach competition was £12 million in 1981 and £15 million in 1982 which represents a loss to the taxpayer. This has clearly added impetus to BR's determination to amend its pricing structure in favour of "cheap deals," which a government-sponsored report has

---

[51] *The Guardian*, January 12, 1984.

doubted is in the long-term interests of the industry.[52] The hard-look at this issue is, more often than not, exhausted by debates in the House of Commons and in Committee, the standard British forum for the scrutiny of matters of major moment. A recent review by the CAA is a notable, if contentious, exception.[53]

All of this naturally locks into the general unaccountability of the Nationalised Industries. Institutions can be created to help overcome the impotence in not being able to set and monitor objectives through public law techiques as was shown by the admirable study of United Kingdom nationalised industries in 1976[54] but until now the political will has been manifestly missing.

Cable

The Hunt Report has been largely accepted uncritically by the Government[55] and so in describing the outline of the proposals I shall conflate the Report and the Government response. Basically the Government's strategy can be summarised as follows; cable investment should be privately financed and market led. Regulation should be as light as possible and the regulatory framework flexible so that it can adapt as technology constantly changes what is practicable and economic. A small number of key safeguards will be needed with a new cable authority having the central role of promoting and overseeing the development of cable systems. The process of franchising cable operators will stand at the heart of the Authority's activity and flowing from it will be the Authority's responsibility for monitoring the performance of cable operators.

It is too early to speculate on the likely performance of either the Cable Authority or the new cable industry at large but some warning bells need to be sounded. The White Paper says that most of the detailed procedures for the franchising exercise will be for the Authority to determine and it will decide to what extent it wishes applicants for franchises to enlarge on their proposals in public rather than in private. Given the somewhat unsatisfactory history of the Independent Broadcasting Authority[56] this is an un-promising beginning. I think that there is a great deal to be said for the government not insisting on detailed regulations for the new cable system if for no other

---

[52] HMSO 1983. *Railway Finances* (The Serpell Report).
[53] Civil Aviation Authority, 1984. *CAP 500 Airline Competition Policy*, CAA; *The Guardian*, September 10, 1984.
[54] National Economic Development Office (NEDO), 1976. A study of U.K. nationalised industries (HMSO); Lewis (1985). See n. 26, above.
[55] HMSO 1983.
[56] Lewis, "IBA Programme Contract Awards," [1975] *Public Law* 317–340.

reason than that flexibility is part of a necessary learning process. However, I should like to be satisfied that the new Authority would operate publicly and through published standards and policies and that both its own performance and that of the franchise-holders should be subjected to guarantees that periodic monitoring of performance took place through some version of the "hard-look" doctrine ultimately enforceable in the courts.

The Regulation of Banking

I could develop a number of the preceding themes and illustrate the haphazard and disorganised nature of control or regulation over the insurance industry or the building society movement. The exercise would be easy to construct but instead I shall say just a little about regulation and banking in the belief that these few remarks will subsume what could be said about some of the other financial services before we turn to the Gower Report.

In spite of the vicissitudes of informal governmental pressures there has, until recently, been little external regulation of the banking sector which has traditionally been dominated by a handful of major institutions. Self-regulation by the banks, supported by the customary authority of the Bank of England, was sufficient at least to maintain adequate standards of liquidity and to preserve the quality of banking business. Nevertheless, within the context of general autonomy there have been variations with the early 1970s as a period of very substantial freedom from interference.

However, during the 1970s prudential standards outside the primary banking sector were undermined by competitive pressures and by demands for credit from borrowers, particularly in the field of commercial property, who lacked ready access to finance from the established sources. New lending institutions grew up in the secondary sector and by 1974 a major crisis had ensued. Apart from the building societies there was no comprehensive legislation governing the activity of deposit-taking and no single supervisory authority. A number of *ad hoc* statutory provisions emerged but it became clear that a new and more comprehensive framework was needed while impetus for reform came from the EEC with the First Banking Directive in 1977 which required the establishment of formal arrangements for licensing deposit-takers. The result was the Banking Act 1979, the central provision of which is that of general prohibition of deposits without specific authorisation from the Bank of England. The Act contains broad criteria relating to the conduct of banking business but leaves a wide measure of discretion to the Bank of England. The criteria have been described as raising "complex questions involving subjective decisions."[57]

There is much talk these days of financial supermarkets growing or of para-banking activities which are difficult to predict with any precision given the current state of money markets and of technology.

> "Innovation of this kind underlines the need for a parallel response from the supervisor, keeping under review both the legislative basis for supervision and the appropriate form of supervision, to ensure that new techniques of banking are both properly conducted and supervised."[58]

These remarks seem to me to be eminently in keeping with the concerns which I have expressed throughout the paper but I am bound to say that there is nothing in the Banking Act itself which impels anyone to keep this counsel and certainly nothing of an institutional sort to facilitate the exercises envisaged. In the British setting, this is likely to mean that any reviews undertaken will be to a greater or lesser extent "private" affairs. At the time of writing considerable ferment is detectable while the shape and nature of supervisory patterns remains uncertain, though with a preference for a "pragmatic" approach strongly evident in relation to financial services generally.[59]

Investor Protection

Leaving the clearing banks to one side, the most interesting developments in terms of money markets in Britain in recent years have related to the matter of investor protection in general and the City of London in particular. Many of the issues which we have touched upon in this paper have been raised during the course of these developments and they have culminated, in our sense at least, in the Gower Report.

In 1981, the Secretary of Trade asked Professor Gower to examine the protection available to investors in securities and to recommend legislative reform in the light of his findings. Professor Gower's brief extended beyond examining the Stock Exchange, but not only did the latter figure prominently in his deliberations but a number of matters supervened before his Report could be written. The Exchange had, in the last few years, twice been forced to defend itself before the Monopolies Commission and was, during 1983, doing so before the Restrictive Practices Court where its rule-book was under attack from the Director General of Fair Trading. Just before Gower reported, the

---

[57] J. Cooper, *The Management and Regulation of Banks* (MacMillan, London, 1980), at p. 256.
[58] Fforde (1983), at p. 368. See n. 39, above.
[59] *Bank of England Quarterly Bulletin* 1984, Vol. 24, pp. 40–53.

issue was informally settled out of court on the basis of an understanding between the Council of the Exchange and the Department of Trade and industry.[60]

I shall not here detail the nature of the accords between the Council of the Stock Exchange and the DTI. Instead I only remark that the implementation of these measures is to be monitored by the DTI and the Bank of England to ensure the evolution and development of the Stock Exchange as an efficient, competitive and suitably regulated central market which affords proper protection to investors. Gower himself regards this as a considerable advance and one which "completes the conversion of the Stock Exchange from a private club to a recognised self-regulatory agency within a statutory framework of control."[61] I make no comment on this judgment and would merely say that whatever is happening in the Square Mile, it is not de-legalisation but re-legalisation, the legitimacy of which will be much debated in the months and years to come.

Gower pins his colours very clearly to the mast of self-regulation, subject, we hasten to add, to effective oversight backed by limited regulation. He clearly regards the financial markets as being over-regulated in some areas if by that I mean the regulation of fine detail. His position can be best summarised as being that the scandals which have so beset the City of London in recent times are less the result of self-regulation than of the fact that such self-policing has not always been subject to effective surveillance.[62] It is then by this standard that his recommendations have to be judged and I am bound to say at the outset that I am less than overwhelmed by the likelihood of this being achieved under his schema. However, in some respects this is a mere aside.

Gower is suggesting then that for a very important sector of British power and influence, self-regulation with effective oversight is the way forward, and that detailed regulation is not the most effective way of delivering on the public interest. What is crucial, and Gower himself accepts is crucial, is the effectiveness of the oversight. In this respect we believe that DTI oversight in the culture of British politics is likely to be less effective than a self-standing commission, provided always that its constitution was to be informed by principles of openness and accountability of a sort currently lacking for most quangos.[63] I shall return to this theme at the end of this chapter but I regard the kind of framework suggested by Gower as being one kind of means of

---

[60] Secretary of State, H.C. Deb., cols. 1194, 1195. July 29, 1983.
[61] Gower, L.C.B., *Review of Investor Protection, Report Part 1*: Cmnd. 9125 (1984), para. 5.06.
[62] *Ibid.* para. 1.10.
[63] Lewis (1985). See n. 26, above.

re-legalising an important area of public concern. Effective self-regulation, effective oversight, effective ombudsmen and grievance mechanisms (all of which find some support in Gower) seem more likely to produce rational discourse and an evolving learning process than does a strict regulatory regime whose inflexibility and fierceness can easily cause it to fall into relative desuetude.

Conclusions

I have argued that an analysis of Britain's working constitution is long overdue; that public power and its relationship with private configurations is inadequately charted in the constitutional literature and that this in substantial measure relates to a failure to examine the legitimation foundations of the British compact which to an important degree are expected to be characterised by notions of openness and accountability. Over many years, public power (in the widest sense) has been exercised in a largely covert manner through networks of conviviality which obscure the workings of the British state. Law-jobs, social processes, get done then only in small degree under the public gaze and if our constitutional expectations are to be enfranchised and encashed then legal processes need to be re-examined and relegitimated.

In this belief I hold no especial brief for traditional forms of law and, indeed, for the most part regard them as less relevant to the problems of the late twentieth century British state than a "revised model" of administrative or public law much more dependent upon procedural devices directed at producing "hard-look" and rational discourse. In contemporary Britain however, much remains to be done before pledges will be honoured.

I have objected to the unseemly haste of the Hunt Report but nevertheless am prepared to accept that general oversight as opposed to detailed regulation can provide the opportunity to respond flexibly as the industry develops in ways which are difficult to forecast at any given time. I am sympathetic to the idea of a light regulatory touch and the adoption of a reactive rather than a proactive style.[64] But my belief is based upon a conviction that such complexity requires a public learning process and not upon any ignorant version of marketism.

Thus with new learning situations especially, it is less than sensible to prescribe from the centre, a disease to which the British are particularly prone. But if I am serious about such claims then effective sources of knowledge must depend to a considerable degree on public participation of varying kinds simply to ensure the cognitive competence

---

[64] Hunt (1982), at p. 13. See n. 38, above; HMSO 1983, at p. 13.

of the organisation concerned, quite apart from any larger notions of consent. Freedom of Information, which I espouse vigorously[65] is probably a pre-requisite but it is only that, and considerable expertise in planning and evaluation through cost benefit and other techniques will need to come in train if justice is to be done to any effective decision-making process. This version of the legal process will need to sunder the connections with a number of Anglo-Saxon legal traditions, not least in the administrative law sphere.

Although exposing *ex parte* communications is notoriously difficult to guarantee through law, it seems to us vital to make the effort, most particularly in a system which is riddled with institutional veins of familiarity. It is worth reminding British lawyers that the American Administrative Procedure Act obliges members of agencies to place on the record written communications, memoranda of oral submissions and other responses oral and written received from one party to the proceedings only. Much administrative law reform since 1946 has represented an attempt to catch new variations of informal and improper pressures. It is surely time for British lawyers to address their minds to such matters within the heart of the governmental process.

Where then are we led? The central policy dilemmas confronting the British state need, in the light of expectations underlying our polity, to take place in an atmosphere characterised by the best information available from all interested parties. Our system does not currently encourage this.

We need to examine experiments in the field of "loose" and "soft" regulation and to monitor the effectiveness of oversight in the public interest. We need also to think about institutions which will be able to scrutinise the costs and benefits of alternative policies and programmes, not least to ask when self-regulatory techniques are worth pursuing and when not. All of this means institutionalising a "hard look" at tough choices. I am prepared to offer a variation of Sir Douglas Wass's standing Royal Commission as a beginning. A British Administrative Conference with teeth could start to chew on such a programme.[66]

Much of the literature concerning legitimation and rationality crises, of the need for grounded or bounded rationality and institutional learning processes finds us an eager public. However, its theoretical attractions apart, the particular problems of the British State[67] with its extraordinary concentrations of executive power, make it required and persistent reading. That it should focus on the empirical circumstances

[65] Lewis and Harden (1984). See n. 8, above.
[66] *Ibid.*
[67] Ashford (1981). See n. 10, above.

of current public dilemmas with a view to suggesting conceptual categories for legal institutions in the 1980s and beyond is my passionate belief.

References

College of Health, 1984. The nation's lifeline: An investigation into the relationship of the DHSS and BOC. (London College of Health).

Department of Trade, 1982. *The Nationalised Industries Consumer Councils, A Strategy for Reform.*

A. Gewirth, *Reason and Morality* (Chicago, 1978).

C. Harlow, *Commercial Interdependence; Public Corporations and Private Industry* (Institute of Policy Studies, London, 1984).

P. Harter, "Negotiating regulations—A cure for malaise" (1982) *Georgetown L.J.* 71, 1.

M.J. Horwitz, *The Transformation of American Law 1780–1860,* (Harvard, 1977).

Simar Lazarus, *The Genteel Populists* (Holt, Rhinehart and Winston, New York, 1974).

P.H.A. Lehner, "Judicial Review of Administrative Action" Columb. L.Rev. 83, 627–689.

R. Stewart, "The Reformation of American Administrative Law" Harvard L.Rev. 88, 1667–1813 (1975).

D.M. Trubek, "Complexity and Contradiction in the Legal Order: Balbus and the Challenge of Critical Social Thought about Law" Law and Soc. Rev. 11, 529–569 (1977).

R.M. Unger, "The Critical Legal Studies Movement" Harvard L.Rev. 96, 561–675 (1983).

Chapter 6

DEMOCRATIC CONSTITUTIONALISM AND POLICE GOVERNANCE

LAURENCE LUSTGARTEN

I

The title of this essay deliberately encapsulates one of the characteristic limitations of the debate over the role of the police in the British[1] constitution. The issues have been discussed in relation to political theory—conceptions of liberty, democracy, social order and the rule of law. Clearly these considerations, and their institutional corollaries, are vital, indeed fundamental. But to restrict the debate within their boundaries ensures that it will remain unsatisfactorily inward-looking, and lead us to treat matters that are historically contingent, even accidental, as though they were essential elements of a democratic polity. This produces a wholly unwarranted exaltation of the status quo.

A glance across the North Sea or the Channel makes one point very clear: there is no necessary connection between democracy and any particular mode of organisation and control of the police. Unless one is to assert that democracy speaks only the Queen's English, a view over the water produces the unsettling conclusion that England is very much in the minority among democratic nations in the extreme degree of self-governance it permits its police, and—a separate but connected point which increases the importance of the first—in the breadth of discretion they exercise within the structure of criminal justice. Some of the difference may be due to divergent concepts of democracy, or divergent histories of the growth of the state in England and on the Continent.[2] But a good deal of it must also be attributable to

---

[1] Apologies to those north of the Border: despite the use of word "British," although a few references are made to Scottish experience, no real attempt is made here to analyse Scottish legislation or case law.

[2] See especially K. Dyson, *The State Tradition in Western Europe* (Martin Robertson, Oxford, 1980), pp. 36–47, emphasising the uniqueness of Britain in this respect. An attempt to relate features of criminal process to political tradition and ideology, which draws a sharp distinction between Anglo-American and Continental traditions, is found in Damaska, "Structures of Authority and Comparative Criminal procedure" 84 Yale L.J. 480 (1975), hereafter cited as *Damaska*.

differences in the sphere of criminal justice, more particularly in structure and institutions. As this aspect has been ignored entirely in the debate over what has come to be called "police accountability,"[3] I want to begin this essay by examining its importance, perhaps even overstating it in order to shift the perspective from which the problem is normally viewed. The exaggeration stems in part from the fact that I am talking in terms of ideal types, not empirically precise descriptions. I then want to rejoin the mainstream and discuss the issues in more traditional constitutional terms.

II

The English police operate in the context of an adversarial, not inquisitorial, system. (The difference is neatly symbolised in the style of criminal prosecutions: Reg *versus* Smith becomes Az JS VII/103–85 or BGHSt 26, 263 in German.) In practical terms, this means a system in which the trial is of much greater importance. It is true that most accused persons plead guilty even when facing serious charges,[4] but the police must do their work in preparation for the possibility of a proceeding which Professor Damaska describes as a "party contest" rather than the Continental "official inquiry."[5] This trial is governed by rules erecting relatively high evidentiary barriers to conviction; in the adversary system "there is a greater divergence between what the police actually know and what can be introduced as evidence at trial."[6] Moreover, the verdict at that trial is reached by persons without legal training who, unlike mixed Continental tribunals, need not give reasons for their decision. Thus the English police take an avowedly partisan stance in a system in which partisan contest is supposed to produce truth. And the evidentiary barriers reinforce bureaucratic and resource imperatives of avoiding trials in the vast majority of cases by producing guilty pleas. This is impossible in Continental systems, where the accused is not permitted to plead guilty.[7] This gives the

---

[3] "Accountability" is often used as a weasel word. What is really at issue is the degree of control various political institutions are to have over the police. Accountability in the sense of after-the-fact explanation means acceptance of a limited degree of control, a point recognised by its more candid exponents. *Cf.* G. Marshall, *Constitutional Conventions* (Clarendon Press, Oxford, 1984).

[4] For statistics, see A. Bottoms and J. McClean, *Defendants in the Criminal Process* (Routledge and Kegan Paul, London, 1976), pp. 105–108.

[5] *Damaska*, p. 481, n. 1.

[6] *Ibid.* p. 523, n. 109. In this quotation and that in the previous footnote, Professor Damaska draws upon his earlier article, "Evidentiary Barriers to Conviction and two Models of Criminal Procedure" 121 U.Pa.L.Rev. 506 (1973).

[7] A.V. Sheehan, *Criminal Procedure in Scotland and France* (HMSO, Edinburgh, 1975), pp. 26–27. See J. Langbein, *Comparative Criminal Procedure: Germany* (St. Paul, Minn. West Pub. Co., 1977), pp. 96–97, for a description of the West German procedure (Strafbefehl) analogous to a guilty plea but which is only operative in relation to payment of "penance money for petty infractions."

English police substantially greater incentive to seek to obtain a confession from the suspect; more generally and ominously, it would seem to be a constant pressure leading them to overstep their powers against those they "know" are guilty.[8]

The role of the police in conducting investigations is also very different. "French police are expected to prepare an investigative record that is complete and formally correct, available to the defence as well as the prosecution and able to withstand a searching examination [by a judge at trial]."[9] The investigative police are called *police judiciaire,* and in this capacity are subject to the supervision and control of the *procureur,* a member of the magistracy who sees his role as that of a judicial officer; in some difficult cases they are directed by a judicial figure, the examining magistrate. Even though in the great majority of criminal incidents, which inevitably involve minor matters, the police will conduct their investigations entirely on their own,[10] this structure creates a radically different ethos among the police, and in practical terms—notably their career ladder and the supervision and investigation of their conduct by both judicial and non-police administrative superiors[11]—places them in a much more subordinate position to judicial and ministerial hierarchies. The activities of the German police, for example, are subject to review in the administrative law courts under the legal principle of "proportionality," which permits judges to determine whether they could have used methods less restrictive of personal liberty in pursuit of legitimate ends.

Further, there is nothing in England corresponding to the principle of compulsory prosecution. Although this is subject to countervailing principles and practices, it serves as the point of departure for the decisions to be made in individual cases. In particular, on the Continent the discretion not to prosecute is not exercised by the police, who are required to report all offences that have come to their notice to the public prosecutor.[12] It is the latter, a much more formidable figure than his quasi-counterpart in most English-speaking countries (a point taken up below), who exercises the discretion.

Finally, and here one begins to move away from consideration of

---

[8] McConville and Baldwin, "The Role of Interrogation in Crime, Discovery and Conviction" (1982) Brit. J. Crim. 165 emphasise the overwhelming importance of obtaining statements from a suspect, and the centrality of police interrogation, rather than the trial, in criminal justice.

[9] Langbein and Weinreb, "Continental Criminal Procedure: 'Myth' and Reality" 87 Yale L.J. 1549, 1554 (1978).

[10] Goldstein and Marcus, "The Myth of Judicial Supervision in the French System of Criminal Procedure," 87 Yale L.J. 240, 247–250 (1978).

[11] A point emphasised by Langbein and Weinreb, *op. cit.* in relation to both France and Germany: 87 Yale L.J. at 1555 and 1560 respectively.

[12] *Damaska*, pp. 502–503; A Sheehan, *op. cit.* p. 20.

criminal procedure strictly speaking to wider political institutions, Continental police are so much a part of a centralised, nationally uniform structure that, to quote a distinguished comparative lawyer, "It may be said with only a modicum of exaggeration that both in England and America a police system in a continental sense hardly exists."[13] Professor Damaska bases this rather startling conclusion on the absence of "the dominant structural principle of all continental systems," namely centralisation of police and prosecution corps, within which "central authorities issue binding general directives to local officials and can give specific instructions on the handling of a particular case."[14] This fundamental difference is doubtless in some ways connected to equally significant differences in political culture and institutions, which in turn may reflect a basic difference in political philosophy concerning the relationship between the individual and state authority.[15] What is of critical relevance, however, is that none of these features, so alien to the English experience, makes Continental countries any less democratic or libertarian, nor makes their police into greater instruments of political oppression.

Thus the police in England work in what, in comparative terms, is a very unusual context. Their task is to play an avowedly one-sided part in an adversary contest in which the accused may present a contrary version of the facts, and in which a verdict will be delivered by lay persons whose reasons remain inscrutable and from whose judgment of acquittal there is no appeal.[16] They are entirely independent of judicial supervision, and the notion of a judicial or even quasi-judicial role is no part of their occupational ethos. They are unrestricted by ministerial control in relation to particular cases and adoption of general practices. They cannot be required to act in particular ways in order to achieve uniformity in enforcement practices throughout the country. They alone decide whether to investigate, how to conduct the investigation and, save for minor exceptions where the Director of Public Prosecutions must be consulted, whether to charge a suspect and what charges to lay. Viewed from the east, the scope of their authority, and the lack of control over its exercise, is awesome.

---

[13] *Damaska*, p. 511.
[14] *Ibid.* pp. 487–88. A caveat should be entered here, however. Centralisation does not necessarily entail direct control; it can co-exist with constabulary independence, as in the case of the Royal Canadian Mounted Police.
[15] See *Damaska,* Pt. IV, for one attempt to relate these ideological influences to the structure of criminal justice in the Anglo-American and Continental traditions.
[16] In West Germany, both prosecution and defence enjoy liberal rights of appeal, which is one reason why, as also in France, the verdict must be fully reasoned. See J. Langbein, *op. cit.* pp. 63, 84–85.

III

The adversarial, as opposed to inquisitorial, nature of English criminal justice thus has profound implications for the constitutional position of the police. Yet even with the genus of adversarial systems, the *species Anglica* contains some virtually unique features, whose effect is to extend the range of unchecked police power still further.

Perhaps the most obvious is the absence of a separate institution responsible for prosecution of offenders. Put another way, the police in England and Wales combine the functions of investigation and prosecution, thus possessing a degree of control over the processing of suspected lawbreakers that has few equals even in adversarial systems. The police not only decide whether to arrest and charge a suspect; they also decide whether to proceed with prosecution and on the specific charge to be brought, which often determines which court will hear the case. In relation to minor offences, they may physically present the case to the bench. More important, in their use of solicitors, whether specifically engaged or employed by the local council, they retain the dominant role as client, a relationship noted and criticised by the Royal Commission on Criminal Procedure.[17] It is the police, rather than a lawyer, who retain control over the proceedings, and if they choose to drop the case, there is no equivalent of the French *action civile* which might enable the victim to force the authorities to undertake further investigations on proceedings.[18] By contrast the private prosecutor in England must assemble his own case, without the benefit of police powers of questioning and search for evidence, let alone the resources to conduct an investigation.

This combination of functions has a clear historical origin. In theory the police prosecute as private individuals who happen to have information about lawbreaking by the accused. This now patent fiction exists because only surprisingly recently have they come to stand in the shoes of victims of crime: not until around 1870 did they replace private associations as the most frequent initiators of criminal prosecutions.[19] It may be thought that the creation of an independent prosecution service, as promised in the White Paper of November 1983,[20] will radically limit their role. Evidence from other jurisdictions suggests that the real change may be less than one might expect. The Scottish

---

[17] Cmnd. 8092 (1981), para. 6.5.

[18] Sheehan, *op. cit.* pp. 20–22 explains the role of the *partie civile*.

[19] On these associations, see D. Phillips, *Crime and Authority in Victorian England* (Croom Helm, London, 1977), Chap. 4, and his subsequent paper, "Good Man to Associate and Bad Men to Conspire" in *Prosecution and the Police in Britain* (D. Hay & F. Snyder eds., forthcoming), Chap. 5. The date of 1870 is an approximation offered by Douglas Hay in conversation.

[20] *An Independent Prosecution Service for England and Wales,* Cmnd. 9074 (1983).

procurator fiscal occupies in strict law a supervisory position over the police; indeed under Scottish law a Chief Constable may be required to initiate a particular investigation at the direction of a Fiscal.[21] Recent research into the way fiscals in various offices actually conduct their work, however, suggests that they are largely dependent upon the police as "reporters" of crime. In only 6 per cent. of cases did the prosecutor request further information from the police; in all the rest he proceeded entirely upon the material in the file they had prepared. In only 8 per cent. of cases did the lawyer, purportedly an independent professional serving the public interest, drop the charges laid by the police.[22] Similarly, an earlier study of the Crown Attorney's office in Toronto concluded that "In effect great confidence is placed by the prosecuting authorities in the competency of the police officer on the beat, for his decision to arrest is adopted as their decision to prosecute."[23] The emotional sense of being "on the same side" and the personal relationships that grew up as individual prosecutors and police repeatedly worked and socialised together reinforced the tendency for the prosecutor to serve as a sort of police advocate, rather than an independent check. Only in the higher courts, where more experienced lawyers dealt with a small number of the most serious cases were "police pressures" effectively resisted.[24] As the White Paper envisages a system similar to that of Ontario, in which full-time lawyers primarily function as a courtroom processing and pleading service which only comes into operation after the police have laid the initial charge, it is unlikely that the effective police dominance of the prosecution process will be much diminished.

⁄ A very different type of prosecutor would be required to diminish the pre-eminence of the police in the prosecution process. The only example in countries with adversarial systems is the American District Attorney or his federal counterpart, the United States Attorney, whose office was significantly based on the French model, which commanded admiration during the early years of the new republic.[25] As well as handling cases brought to him by the police, the District Attorney can initiate his own investigations. Within his office under his command are a large number of investigators who enjoy law enforcement powers identical to the police; and there is a tendency in large urban areas for some of them to be deployed on difficult and complex

---

[21] Police (Scotland) Act 1967, s.17.
[22] S. Moody and J. Tombs, *Prosecution in the Public Interest* (Scottish Academic Press, Edinburgh, 1982). The figures quoted in the text are from pp. 47 and 57, respectively.
[23] B. Grosman, *The Prosecutor* (Univ. of Toronto Press, Toronto, 1969), p. 27.
[24] *Ibid.* pp. 44–50.
[25] Grosman provides a good brief description: *ibid.* pp. 13–14.

cases which the police are believed to be less capable of managing.[26]
The District Attorney thus generates an important part of his own
caseload, and may receive reports of crimes directly from the public. A
very important consequence of his investigatory capability is that the
District Attorney may pursue police corruption or other misconduct
with adequate legal powers to compel information employed by an
expert staff who are not fellow police officers. The obstruction that so
effectively made a fiasco of Operation Countryman[27] could have been
more readily overcome by a determined District Attorney. The proposals for independent investigation of complaints against the police in
England have always been bedevilled by the absence of any pre-
existing body of skilled and experienced investigators whose friend-
ships and careers lie outside the police organisation, a deficiency the
proposed prosecution service will do nothing to remedy.

IV

'Thus in the edifice of English criminal justice the police are the
keystone. Institutions with which elsewhere they would have to share
or to which they would have to subordinate their powers are either
non-existent or have left them undisturbed on their patch.' And comparative analysis at a quite different level further emphasises the
extraordinary freedom from restraint they enjoy. This is the level of
constitutional structure, and can be seen in sharpest relief by comparison with certain salient features of the American system.

The first point is that the absence of the American brand of federal-
ism, with parallel systems of criminal law, means that there can be no
equivalent of federal law enforcement officials who can prosecute
venal or brutal local police on charges of federal crime. This machinery
has sometimes been of value in instances of maltreatment of racial
minorities or widespread corruption. More important, the existence of
federal constitutional rights has given rise to what has been called a
"constitutional tort"— a civil action for damages in federal court for
denial of any of those numerous rights by public officials, including the
police. In England, victims of police misconduct can avail themselves
only of the protections afforded by the common law, which comprise a
much narrower range of rights and interests, embodied in actions for
false imprisonment, assault and trespass. Though the so-called "sec.
1983 action" is flawed in many respects, thousands of Americans

---

[26] The Royal Commission visited and described one such D.A.'s office in San Diego,
California: *op. cit.* para. 6.33.

[27] For a good description, see A. Doig, *Corruption and Misconduct in Contemporary
British Politics* (Penguin Books, Harmondsworth, 1984), pp. 245–252.

invoke its provisions annually.[28] It can provide a means of redress and, at least potentially, a deterrent to police misconduct, that has no parallel here.

Two further controls on the American police derive from constitutional provisions. The Fourth Amendment requires that arrests and searches be based upon "probable cause," a more stringent standard than the "reasonable suspicion" sufficient for the so-called "stop and frisk"—or on the street "pat down" for weapons justified by the potential danger to the officer.[29] It is the lower, more permissive standard of reasonable suspicion which governs major police power of arrest in England[30] and now, under the Police and Criminal Evidence Act 1984, a general power of search as well.[31] Thus the English constable may quite lawfully exert far greater control over the ordinary citizen, in the sense of arresting and searching him and his home in circumstances indicating a lesser degree of likelihood that he has committed a crime, than is available to the American policeman. Correspondingly, of course, the citizen cannot lawfully resist or seek redress for intrusions that satisfy this minimal criterion.

Moreover, the English courts have steadfastly refused to adopt the exclusionary rule in cases where the police have obtained evidence unlawfully. This rule, judicially derived from the Fourth Amendment though not found in its text, was from 1961 to 1984 interpreted to require that matters unlawfully obtained be automatically excluded as evidence in court.[32] The approach in England, as in all other common law jurisdictions, is to admit reliable evidence however obtained,[33]

---

[28] For two important criticisms, including extensive empirical evaluation, see Newman, "Suing the Lawbreakers" 87 Yale L.J. 447 (1978) and Project, "Suing the Police in Federal Court" 88 Yale L.J. 781 (1979). The latter study, p. 781, n. 31, reveals that the number of s.1983 actions against the police trebled to over 6,000 per annum between 1971 and 1977.

[29] *Terry* v. *Ohio*, 392 U.S. 1 (1968). There are, however, a number of exceptions, *i.e.* circumstances in which a search may constitutionally be conducted on the basis of less than probable cause.

[30] Criminal Law Act 1967, s.2 now replaced by s.24 of the Police and Criminal Evidence Act 1984.

[31] s.1. See also ss.18 and 19.

[32] *Mapp* v. *Ohio*, 367 U.S. 643 (1961) announced a general exlusionary rule applicable to state as well as federal prosecutions. However, in *U.S.* v. *Leon*, 104 S.Ct. 3405 (1984) the Court created a novel exception, denying the exclusion where the evidence is seized in the good faith execution of a warrant subsequently found invalid. Some fear that this ruling portends further relaxation of the rule.

[33] The leading case is *R.* v. *Sang* [1980] A.C. 402. There is now, under s.78 of the Police and Criminal Evidence Act 1984, a discretion to exclude evidence, the admission of which, in the light of the circumstances in which it was obtained, "would have such an adverse effect on the proceedings that the court ought not to admit it." The meaning of this section—quickly cobbled together by the Government after Lord Scarman had persuaded the House of Lords to accept presumptive exclusion of all unlawfully obtained evidence—is anyone's guess. Mine is that the discretion will seldom be exercised.

leaving the problem of punishing and preventing police illegality to civil actions for damages, criminal prosecutions, or internal disciplinary procedures. Since these machanisms seem to be remarkably ineffective in curbing police abuses, one might advocate adoption of the exclusionary rule if there seemed a credible case that it would have a serious deterrent effect on police misconduct. However, American studies do not support any such conclusion; the only defensible position on this empirical question is agnosticism.[34] These studies, however, by their nature cannot identify instances where the police officer was deterred from making an unlawful search[35] because he was concerned about possible suppression of evidence, or put another way, where he complied with legal standards in order to ensure that the evidence would be admissible. The exclusionary rule may thus exert some undetectable influence towards inhibiting unlawful practices by American police, which would have no counterpart in English law.

From comparative analysis there emerges a striking conclusion. Police in England work within a system whose ethos is that of partisanship and competitiveness, in which the surest way to "victory" is aborting formal combat—the trial—by obtaining the other side's "surrender"—a guilty plea or at least a confession. This system equips them with wide powers of compulsion and intrusion, along with the motivation (they would say the necesssity) to use them. They enjoy a unique dominance within the institutional structure of law enforcement. In a liberal society, this degree of coercive authority prima facie calls for vigilant external control. Yet the police in England are subject to fewer constitutional, legal and political restraints than in virtually any other Western democracy. This paradox is the signal feature of the problem of police governance.

V

Constitutional thinking about the police in Britain has been bedevilled by a particular conception of law, or more precisely, by the identification of policing with a highfalutin notion of The Law. In most people's minds, law is the apotheosis of fairness and justice; hence law enforcement is seen, not so much as requiring higher standards than other government services, but as not a service at all—as something higher

---

[34] See sources cited in Newman, *op. cit.* p. 448, n. 3. The Royal Commission considered only one or two of these articles, but reached the correct conclusion. See paras. 4.125–126.

[35] Most of the studies concerned illegality in searches, rather than arrests or obtaining confessions. Exclusionary rules apply to these situations as well. A few studies of the *Miranda* rule have been conducted: see Y. Kamisar *et al, Modern Criminal Procedure* (5th ed., St. Paul, Minn.: West Pub. Co., 1980), pp. 631–635.

than the merely "social" or "political." The equation of law with justice may be explicable historically, because until about a century ago criminal law was the main embodiment of the state, and maintenance of order (of a particular kind) and protection of person and property was its major service. The conception of justice implied was a very narrow one: wholly proceduralist, suited only to a market economy and excluding any elements of social justice or communal responsibility. In the present day, this equation is positively harmful, for it retards the desperately-needed development of a constitutional ethic for a welfare state. It is not a denial of the importance of personal security to insist that policing—of which law enforcement is only one component[36]—is but one of many governmental functions essential to a decent society, and that *all* public services should be required to meet the same rigorous standards of justice and be subject to the same powerful mechanisms of democratic control.

Policing, then, is a public service. Generally in a democratic polity it is expected that public services be responsive to the public. In Britain, several mechanisms have been created to achieve this. Most establish ways in which elected representatives can supervise the conduct and exercise of powers of state officials; in a few limited areas, the citizenry is enabled to participate, or at least be heard directly, in the making of particular kinds of decisions. Supervision and participation are the two principal modes of democratic control. Principal, but not twin: the predominance of the former reveals the limited character of the democracy Western states have managed to achieve. Supervisory powers generally entail establishing broad lines of policy for officials to follow; appointing, and in some instances discharging, senior administrators; questioning and making representations to officials on behalf of constituents aggrieved by the decisions or behaviour of their subordinates. Allied to these is the ability to command attention of the media to pursue grievances when the authorities prove unresponsive.

In relation to the Civil Service and local government, the supervisory mechanisms currently in operation are seriously defective: a matter largely of design failure but also of inadequate maintenance. Nonetheless the rudiments are there, and the principle that supervision is an essential element in the working of democracy is unquestioned. Yet in relation to policing, the mechanisms are all but non-existent, and even the principle remains bitterly controversial.

Despite pronounced trends over the past two decades towards centralisation, and co-ordination of training and activities undertaken

---

[36] The vast bulk of police activity is actually taken up by order maintenance, traffic control and above all, a whole congeries of social service tasks. See, *e.g.* Punch, "The Secret Social Service," in *The British Police* (S. Holdaway ed., E. Arnold, London, 1979), Chap. 7.

by forces of vastly increased size, policing remains a function of local government. Outside the Metropolitan Police District, the representative democratic body is the police authority. This may be the police committee of a local authority or, where the force serves more than one authority, a specially created committee containing nominees from each constituent part. However, unlike all other local authority bodies, statute requires that one third of the membership of this committee consist of magistrates,[37] who are selected by their colleagues and are never at any time subject to the discipline of election. The police authority can only appoint the chief constable, his deputy, and assistant chief constables with the approval of the Home Secretary[38]; it requires similar approval for their dismissal, which can only be "in the interests of efficiency."[39] (The greater autonomy from central control in the selection of education officers and social services directors accorded local authorities in recent years[40] has emphatically not extended to the police.) Appointments and promotions to ranks below these levels are now wholly the responsibility of their chief constable, subject to central government regulations; the same is true of discipline within the force. Chief constables are not required to discuss policy or operational decisions with the police authorities, though in practice many will defend their actions after the fact; they need only submit a very general annual report.[41] The police authority may call upon the chief constable to provide a written report on a specified matter; if, however, he believes such a report would contain information which "in the public interest ought not to be disclosed, or is not needed for the discharge of the functions of the police authority," he may appeal to the Home Secretary who is thus the ultimate arbiter of whether the information must be provided.[42] Police authorities are, despite a few well-publicised exceptions, pliant bodies whose members view themselves as a sort of cheerleader corps for their force. In the one authority that received extensive study, the members were disproportionately elderly and viewed their work as entirely non-partisan and apolitical.[43] This last point is a matter of attitudes and behaviour rather than of legal

---

[37] Police Act 1964, s.2 as amended.
[38] *Ibid.* ss.5 and 6.
[39] *Ibid.* s.5(4), and note also s.29.
[40] *e.g.* the repeal of the requirement that local authorities require approval by the Secretary of State before appointing a Director of Social Services (Local Authority Social Services Act 1970, s.6(4)) by the Local Government, Planning and Land Act 1980, s.183(3).
[41] Police Act 1964, s.12(1).
[42] *Ibid.* s.12(3).
[43] Brogden, "A Police Authority—The Denial of Conflict" (1977) 25 Soc.Rev. 325. See also Dean, "The Finger on the Policeman's Collar" (1982) 53 Pol.Q. 153 for a journalist's useful anecdotal account.

structure, but the two must surely interact; if a committee has no real power, councillors concerned to represent their constituents effectively and make their mark politically will choose to concentrate their energies elsewhere. Above all, no contemporary police authority has ever tried to lay down policy guidelines for the police force for which it is purportedly responsible. It would be quite bereft of the legal power to do so.

The position in London is simpler, if no more satisfactory. The police authority is the Home Secretary. He is in theory accountable to Parliament, and indeed London M.P.'s can table Parliamentary Questions about police activities within his jurisdiction, and receive somewhat more detailed responses than would be available to representatives of all other constituencies for which a local police authority is the legally responsible body. Nonetheless it is idle to pretend that the political head of a Department in which policing shares attention with, amongst many other things, immigration, nationality, race relations and the prison system, can exercise more than the most perfunctory superintendence of a force of 27,000, even with the support of a specialist Division of civil servants. There is continual liaison between the Home Secretary, his civil servants and senior Metropolitan Police officials, but even formulation of policies with major political implications is in the end left in the hands of the Commissioner; *a fortiori* the control of the conduct of constables on the street. Indeed in an organisation suffering severely from elephantiasis, practical responsibility for officers' behaviour, and indeed for critical operational decisions, rests several levels down the command structure. To Londoners seeking to exert direct influence over those who serve them, the Metropolitan Police are literally out of control.

In the relationship between the chief administrative authority and elected representatives, policing is unique among local government functions. Indeed, foreign policy and military matters apart, no other area of government activity claims this degree of immunity from democratic control. This extraordinary situation can be explained historically. That is, an interpretation based upon verifiable fact may explain what balance of material and ideological influences have produced this strange result. Explanations will vary with period of time considered—for the constitutional position of the police has altered radically in the past century and a half—and the relative emphasis and priority the particular interpreter chooses to give to economic, institutional, ideological and legal factors. It is an interesting and important level of analysis, which very few writers have had the interest and imagination to attempt.[44] But whatever the historical determinants, the

---

[44] The most ambitious attempt is by a sociologist: M. Brogden, *The Police: Autonomy and Consent* (Academic Press, London, 1982). Though open to criticism on a number of counts, it is essential reading.

ultimate question is whether the present position should be maintained. That depends on whether it is acceptable as a matter of policy; and on an issue that goes to the core of the relationship between state and society, "policy" must be rooted in fundamental constitutional values.

In contemporary Britain, this means taking seriously the implications, some less immediately obvious than others, of liberalism and democracy.[45] At a minimum, liberalism in this context entails a paramount concern for the protection of human rights—such as those which the British government has pledged in several international agreements to respect—buttressed by effective controls against exercise of excessive and arbitrary power by state officials and satisfactory remedies where abuses occur. Historically, the liberal state has tended to emphasise judicial controls and remedies, a reflection of the fact that liberalism long preceded democracy, and that liberty of the subject was thought adequately protected by a profoundly elitist institution functioning in an avowedly undemocratic manner.[46] Tensions between liberalism and democracy exist at many levels, none more severe than that concerning the role of the judiciary in matters of public law. In the present context, the tension has two main sources. The first is that liberal institutions block the creation of democratic mechanisms of control, with liberal ideology serving to discredit (as "political") attempts to enlarge the sphere in which democracy functions. Secondly, the legal methods by which the police might be controlled under general principles of administrative law are either non-existent or debilitated by judicial refusal to become involved, in sharp contrast to the prevailing attitude in other areas of administrative action. Liberalism has abdicated in practice, clinging on only in its tenacious efforts to prevent democracy stepping into the breach.[47]

---

[45] It could also mean talking about what an avowedly socialist philosophy would yield. For one attempt to do so, see T. Jefferson and R. Grimshaw, *Controlling The Constable* (Frederick Muller, London, 1984), Chap. 5. A great more needs to be done. I have chosen to restrict myself to discussing liberalism, if only because the socialist future seems increasingly to be receding, if not vanishing down a black hole.

[46] I pass over the important question whether the vast bulk of the population was ever able to use legal institutions effectively to protect their rights, as well as the even more important issue of the relative worth of the substantive rights to different social classes.

[47] Despite bold statements made in the first *Blackburn* case, *R.* v. *Commissioner of Police for the Metropolis, ex p. Blackburn* [1968] 2 Q.B. 118, about the responsibility of the police to the law, the courts have never reviewed a decision to prosecute or not to prosecute in particular cases, nor have they ever ordered a chief officer to alter his policies towards particular types of cases. See, *e.g. R.* v. *Commissioner of Police for the Metropolis, ex p. Blackburn (No. 3.)* [1973] 1 Q.B. 214 and *R.* v. *CEGB, ex p. Chief Constable of Devon and Cornwall* [1981] 3 W.L.R. 967.

Precisely because the present essay is concerned primarily with the democratic element in the constitutional value structure, it must reject the conventional separation of substance and structure. The proposition advanced is that the substantive criminal laws which the police enforce, and the powers of arrest, search, surveillance, data collection and ancillary matters they are granted by law, predispose if not require them to behave in a manner hostile to the values of liberalism and democracy. A corollary is that there exists an unbreakable link between what the police do on a daily basis and the way they may be expected to respond to attempts to ensure that they are subject to democratic control. The relationship between substantive criminal law, the law of criminal procedure, and the problems of police governance have barely been explored, indeed only recently perceived. The conjunction is pithily expressed in the title of the Police and Criminal Evidence Act 1984, the first time matters of police governance and police powers have appeared within the covers of the same statute.

It is sufficient for the present to support the proposition with a few examples. When the legislature creates crimes of almost infinite vagueness, in which the gravamen of the offence is the policeman's perception of the suspect's likely future behaviour—as with the now-repealed "sus" law and analogous legislation in local acts which remain in force—or when it confers powers of search on the expansive grounds of "reasonable suspicion" backed by the ability to arrest on charges of obstruction those who resist peacefully, however innocent of the suspected crime,[48] it implicitly instructs the police to place a low value on the liberty of the subject. Ditto when the courts support police decisions to break up public meetings and now apparently, to seal off whole counties from intending pickets, when they claim to be preventing a breach of the peace.[48a] When common law and statute give the police power to detain people without charge and deny them access to solicitors or even the opportunity to inform their family of their whereabouts for lengthy periods, it is not surprising that they are unreceptive to claims that they routinely violate human rights. Their near-total power over suspects and persons in custody stems less from

---

[48] It is no defence to a charge of obstruction of a constable in the course of his duty (Police Act 1964, s.51(3)) that the victim of the search was innocent of wrongdoing. So long as the search was based on "reasonable suspicion" the victim is bound to comply. The PSI study (below, n. 55) found that of 1.5 million stops made annually by the Metropolitan Police, less than one in twelve yields an arrest. "Reasonableness" is clearly a flaccid standard.

[48a] *Moss* v. *McLachlan*, *The Times*, November 29, 1984. For commentary, see East and Thomas, "Freedom of Movement: *Moss* v. *McLachlan*" (1985) 12 J.L. & Soc. 77.

unlawful behaviour and abuse of power than from the authoritarian substance of the law itself.[49]

However, the police are no longer merely the passive receptacle of the lawmakers' illiberalism. In the past decade or so, beginning with the tenure of Sir Robert Mark as Commissioner of the Metropolitan Police, police representative organisations and individual chief constables have overtly entered the political arena and attempted to influence legislation and public policy. These efforts have ranged from disquisitions on the state of the nation's moral health to active lobbying of the Royal Commission on Criminal Procedure to adopt particular proposals for the extension of police powers. The latter endeavour by Mark's successor Sir David McNee and the Association of Chief Police Officers (ACPO) achieved striking, though not total, success. This politicisation of the police, which extends equally to representatives of the lower ranks, has been documented beyond doubt.[50] It means that they can no longer be seen as merely servants of the legislature but rather as an institution carrying a significant responsibility for the content of substantive and procedural criminal law. This change in their role is of constitutional magnitude. It undermines one of the central pillars of the doctrine that the police are, and should be, wholly independent of normal democratic control. Their attempt to influence the outcome of the political process implicitly recognises that their work is fundamentally political, in the broad sense of matters which entail judgments about moral values, favour certain interests over others and require weighing competing claims for scarce resources. It follows, unless one accepts the startling proposition that state officials are the ultimate source of democratic political authority, that those engaged in carrying out political decisions must ultimately be subordinate to elected representatives. Since the Police Federation and ACPO now seek to influence public opinion in like manner as, say, the National Union of Teachers, they should expect that policing policy, like education policy, will ultimately be determined by the political authorities. Of course not all police work is political in the broad sense, still less in the partisan sense, any more than is the daily work of teachers in the classroom. Yet that notwithstanding, no-one doubts the primacy of the local authority education committee and the DES as policy-making bodies. Nor do they challenge the legitimacy of selec-

---

[49] This is to state more broadly a point made very persuasively about the law of criminal procedure by Doreen McBarnet in a series of articles and her book *Conviction* (Macmillan Press, London, 1981).

[50] Kettle, "The Policing of Politics and the Politics of Policing" in *Policing the Police* (P. Hain ed., John Calder, London, 1980), vol. 2; Reiner, "The Politicisation of the Police in Britain" in *Control in the Police Organization* (M. Punch ed., Mass, M.I.T. Press, Cambridge, 1983), pp. 126–148.

tion of heads by school governors, who are soon to consist of a majority of parents, the nearest approximation to users of the service identifiable in this context.[51] Unless there is something radically different about police work from any other function of government, the same principles must apply. And even if some such difference does exist, or exists in relation to a specific aspect of policing, the police entry into the political arena has made it that much harder to respect. Yet realistically it seems no more likely that they will withdraw from the arena, reverting to their traditional stance—still largely maintained in Scotland[52]—than that the NUT will remain silent on education issues or the British Medical Association will cease to attempt to influence health policy and spending in the NHS.

Indeed, these analogies point to yet another critical similarity between the problems of police governance and those of government generally. The police increasingly see themselves as a professionalised body of experts whose claim to freedom from "interference" rests as much on superior knowledge and skill at their craft as on the abstractions of constitutional theory.[53] They claim the same status and restriction from lay control that is asserted in the name of professionalism by teachers, doctors, planners and lawyers. One response might be to deny that professionalism is an appropriate label for police work. This, however, is to assume that there is something called professionalism which is objectively identifiable and that the only problem is whether policing satisfies its criteria. A more fruitful approach is to question the validity of the label itself. The point is most succinctly made in Bernard Shaw's comment, "all professions are conspiracies against the laity." The claim of professionalism is often a means by which an occupational group asserts powers in the sense of autonomy from public or governmental scrutiny.[54] These claims to self-regulation now receive increasing skepticism from a public which has seen or had to live with the planning disasters, cases of wrongful confinement to mental institutions, maltreated children and inflated fees that have followed from treating decisions requiring human empathy or political choice as matters of technical expertise beyond the abilities of the uninitiated. In this respect the police leadership is trying to cloak itself in a mantle that is coming apart at the seams.

---

[51] White Paper, *Parental Influence at School,* Cmnd. 9242 (1984).
[52] P. Gordon, *Policing Scotland* (SCCL, Glasgow, 1980), Chap. 8, emphasises this characteristic of the Scottish police hierarchy.
[53] Holdaway, "Changes in Urban Policing" (1977) 28 Brit.J.Soc. 119.
[54] See further, T. Johnson, *Professions and Power* Macmillan, London, 1972), and M.M. Larson, *The Rise of Professionalism* (U.Cal. Press, Berkeley, 1977).

VI

Public debate about police governance and police powers has polarised around two opposed images. The first, historically dominant and still held by most middle and "respectable" working class people and virtually all the elderly, is that of the police as guardians—the preservers of safety and order. The second view, unfortunately increasingly shared, particularly amongst the young, ethnic minorities, politicial activists broadly on the Left, and civil libertarians, is that of the police as danger—overbearing, authoritarian, destructive of personal liberty.[55] The truth is that they are simultaneously both, but for different categories of people. The experience of the police of the *Daily Telegraph* reader in Barnet is light years away from that of an unemployed teenager in Newcastle, let alone his black equivalent in Lambeth. The middle aged property owner who decries "political interference" with the police and demands that they be "left to get on with the job" may simply be unaware, or refuse to believe, that the police frequently behave in an oppressive and discriminatory way. But whatever his knowledge, he certainly does not expect that the police will behave that way towards him. Those who advocate the widest latitude for the police are the least likely to experience its effects. Conversely, those who are at the sharp, or perhaps blunt, end of police power—not the genuinely guilty, though they too are entitled to reasonable treatment, but those innocent of crime who are repeatedly stopped and searched, insulted, bullied, or denied their legal rights—give inadequate recognition to the need to support the police in legitimate measures to control crime. (A reader of literature produced by various community monitoring groups and like-minded commentators would conclude that the police singlemindedly devote their time to harassment and intimidation and that the incidence and fear of crime is largely an invention of the right-wing press.) The result is that the discussion has resembled two people talking, if not shouting, past each other.

The most fruitful approach to the problems of policing in a liberal democracy is to start with first principles. Lord Scarman, in his Report on the Brixton Disorders, spoke of "two well-known principles of policing a free society," which he identified as "consent and balance" and "independence and accountability."[56] The first refers to the

---

[55] The PSI survey of Londoners, D. Smith, *Police and People in London* (Policy Studies Institute, London, 1983), vol. 1, revealed a massive degree of distrust and suspicion of the police among Afro-Caribbeans of all ages, and a surprisingly high proportion of whites under 24 who believe the police "often" use excessive force in arrests or violence at police stations, or employ threats or unreasonable pressure when questioning people. See especially the Tables on pp. 252 and 255.

[56] *Report of an Inquiry into the Brixton Disorders*, Cmnd. 8427 (1981), para. 4.55.

divergent functions of policing, the second to the question of governance under consideration here. Independence and accountability, however, are not first principles. They derive from a conception of social order and must, like any alternative, be justified in light of such a conception.

I would suggest that a conception appropriate to democratic constitutionalism may be derived from the work of the philosopher John Rawls.[57] Although entitled *A Theory of Justice* it is not devoted to specifying substantive outcomes. Rather it is concerned with underlying principles, and above all with the method by which those principles would be agreed. Rawls is fundamentally concerned to abolish interest, particularly self-interest, in that process of agreement. He therefore concludes that rational people would agree to those principles of justice which they would accept in total ignorance of whether they would be favoured or disfavoured when the principles came to be applied to them. They are the principles that would be chosen in "reflective equilibrium," not those designed to produce the greatest possible gratifications of an individual's desires.

Most of the discussion of Rawls's principles seems to have been in connection with economic or material inequalities. Yet they are of abundantly fruitful potential in relation to issues of power and political order. Rawls himself thinks they would produce agreement on "constitutional liberty"[58] but he restricts his discussion of such matters to a very abstract level. In an attempt to bring Rawlsian theory somewhat closer to the street, I would suggest that no structure of power be regarded as just unless rational persons would agree that, within its contours, they would willingly be subject to those whose material interests were radically different from their own. Hence no relationship of power would be justified unless the person in the superior position would agree to exchanging roles with those occupying the subordinate position.

This is emphatically not a prescription for anarchy or "license": it is a fundament of constitutionalism. A rational person will consent to such an allocation of power provided it is subject to limits and controls restricting its use solely to the purpose for which it was granted. He will do so for all the reasons that mutual dependence and division of labour are essential features of modern society. In so far as the exercise of their specialist functions requires the police to be granted power over others, he will correspondingly insist that it be exercised subject to effective control. More concretely, this requires that the police—who

---

[57] J. Rawls, *A Theory of Justice* (Harvard U.P., Cambridge, Mass, 1971).
[58] He says this most explicitly in an essay, "Constitutional Liberty and the Concept of Justice" in *NOMOS VI* Justice (C. Friedrich and J. Chapman eds., Atherton Press, New York, 1963), pp. 98–125.

possess a virtual monopoly of legitimate violence in the name of the political order—be subject to a regime of control which ensures that everyone, regardless of social or economic conditions, is subject to identical standards of treatment. Thus the favoured suburbanite, acknowledging the claims of justice, should support the regime of police governance most likely to ensure that the Byker or Brixton teenager is treated with the same respect as himself, and that the safety, property and security of a Bengali family in Spitalfields are maintained at the same level as his own. The disadvantaged youths must correspondingly acknowledge their responsibility to support and co-operate with the legitimate activities of the police.

The critical practical question is what such a regime would look like. The most severe restriction affecting a local structure is that it must take the substantive laws as given, however much majority sentiment may disagree with them. The notion of parliamentary sovereignty requires no less, and is a permanent constraint on the degree to which community feeling can direct law enforcement. However—a point that needs much more discussion than it can receive here—law enforcement is only one function of the police; the maintenance of order, or at any rate of public decorum, and provision of all sorts of social services actually occupy the great predominance of the ordinary constable's time.[59] On these matters, Parliament is largely silent.

Discussion here must be limited to sparse statements of principle. The first is that priorities of policing—which offences are of gravest concern to people and should receive particular attention and resources—should be decided by democratically chosen representatives, not the police themselves. Such choices are necessitated by the inevitability of scarce resources; and they are pre-eminent examples of value choices, which administrative officials have no particular competence to make. The formulation of priorities, however, cannot encompass decisions to treat non-criminal activities as criminal or conversely to refuse to enforce a particular law. This is yet another implication of parliamentary sovereignty.

"Priorities" may of course be short-term and shifting according to altered circumstances—a blitz on drunk driving at Christmas, or increased patrols in a particular area in response to a spate of burglaries. Reaction to public feeling or growing awareness among police leadership of particular inadequacies, *e.g.* in the response to victims of racist attacks or rape, may lead to additional or reorientated training in handling these cases. Such decisions, however, lie towards the opposite end of a continuum from decisions about purchase of certain types of equipment, or particular uses of such equipment, or

[59] See source cited in n. 36 above.

matters of organisational capability like the establishment of specialist squads. The second point is that whilst these may seem merely technical, they in fact raise controversial financial or value questions, and must be decided by elected representatives. Whether to establish a drug or obscene publications squad, rather than one devoted to commercial fraud or investigation and prevention of racist attacks, is a political choice in the sense in which that word is used in this essay. So is the acquisition of plastic bullets and CS gas, because possession of such weaponry must inevitably shape police response to street disturbances in a way that will have serious long-term consequences for their relations with the public. And whilst those managing the police organisation are best situated to decide whether computers will help them carry out their work, matters such as the nature of the material stored and the ability of those about whom data are collected to ensure the accuracy of the information, are political questions because their resolution requires deciding how to accommodate the conflict between freedom and privacy and the need for intelligence to assist in detection of crime.

Thirdly, the police should be treated no differently from any other public body in the standards of managerial efficiency and value for money required. This would seem crashingly obvious, particularly in times of Rayner scrutinies and rate-capping, except that they are presently subject to less financial control than any other institution. Thus budgetary decisions of combined police authorities—those, like Avon and Somerset, serving more than one county—are not subject to review by their constituent councils. In London the picture is even starker: after the Home Offices has approved their global expenditure figure, the police themselves simply announce their own precept and levy it on the boroughs directly. It is inconceivable that any other service would receive such complaisant treatment.

Fourthly, whilst investigation or surveillance of specific persons or specific crimes should remain entirely under the direction of the police, generalised activities like patrolling or search operations in particular areas, roadblocks and the like—which inevitably result in large numbers of innocent persons being subjected to stops, searches and questioning—should be subject to disapproval by elected representatives of those areas. Having been informed why the police regard the particular measures as necessary, they are the appropriate persons to decide whether the gain is worth the intrusions and conflict that may result. Conversely, it is equally legitimate for elected representatives to insist upon particularly rigorous action, for example against unlawful conduct by pickets. If they were to decide to deploy a massive number of police on extended picket duty, their constituents would have to live with the consequences—long-term absence of local police, less effective detection of crime, higher expenditure due to overtime. It is perfectly legitimate for politicians to decide that these are acceptable costs; and it is up to those they represent to disagree and press for a reordering of priorities. The essential point is that, precisely because of these multiple consequences, these are political decisions, and should be clearly presented as such, not disguised as technical or "operational" ones. The role of elected representatives here is part of what should be a fundamental aim of the practice of policing: to contribute to popular participation in law enforcement and to create a climate in which the police are seen as a service, not a force. This may be optimistic in a society as stratified as Britain today, but it is not Utopian.

Fifthly, where the police themselves have adopted generalised policies to deal with particular classes of offender or offence—*e.g.* to caution juveniles or first offenders, or not to prosecute teenagers engaging in sex below the age of consent if consent in fact existed—these should be put to elected representatives for approval. Usually such decisions are not controversial (although one could think of others that would be, *e.g.* non-prosecution of those possessing small quantities of cannabis) but it is the constitutional principle, not the substantive policy, that is of greatest importance. Such decisions are presumably based upon judgments about public feeling or the dangers of excessively rigid law enforcement, yet they involve deviations from the strict duty of equal and evenhanded enforcement. It is only democracy, not administration, that can supply the legitimacy for deviation from that duty.

Sixthly, all managerial and technical decisions not coming under the foregoing heads should be left to police management, which would periodically inform its political superiors of its work. This is simply good administrative practice; as has been said in an analogous context, it is unnecessary and unwise to bark alongside one's own dog.[60] The vast bulk of day-to-day management and administrative decisions fall into this category, and it is to be expected that those who specialise in these matters will make better decisions than part-time politicians who are outside the organisation. This conclusion applies uniformly to all government services; heads and teachers are best left to decide the organisation of the timetable and techniques of instruction, as is the engineering department to assess the condition of streets and sewers.

Finally, the decision to investigate, arrest and charge in a particular case must remain wholly a matter for the independent judgment of the officer in charge of the case. It is important to identify the precise justifications of this principle, for they are quite distinct from the

[60] A. Barker *Quangos in Britain* (Macmillan, London, 1982), p. 18.

extravagant claims that are routinely made about the constitutional status of the police. The requirement of independence in this sphere has little to do with the nature of law or criminal process, and everything to do with the nature of the decision to be taken. Positively, the decision requires objective and honest application of a rule or standard of conduct; negatively, improper considerations such as favouritism, racial or political bias and the like must be rigorously excluded. This is no less true of teacher's grading of an examination. Unduly favourable marking of the script of an influential business-man's child, or conscious or unconscious devaluation of the work of black pupils, is as objectionable as police favouritism or racism—for precisely the same reasons. It is the betrayal of the impartiality required of the person in whom a public trust has been placed. Fairness, moral scrupulousness and professionalism rightly understood—as standards of work and ethics—are expected of all services, most of which, like education or social work, are under political control. Independence of decision is one means by which they are achieved. Presumably as a society we place greater trust in the independent specialist than in his political masters because the latter are supposed to bargain, compromise and deal as part of their craft, though these too are subject to moral and legal limits. Impartiality and like treatment of like cases are demanded of the policeman, not because he is the servant of the Monarchy, the Law or some other abstraction, but because they are the imperatives of a liberal democracy. And the policeman is entitled to demand that other public officials be subject to the same rigorous controls and mechanisms of redress as himself.

When a democratic polity grants such independence to its servants, it is entitled to insist that the resulting power is properly exercised. This requires a dual system of control. The first element is internal. It consists primarily of training, discipline and reward for good perform-ance within the service, and is the responsibility of senior management. On a day-to-day basis, they will have the field largely to themselves, and must therefore respond seriously to criticism from the public of their subordinates' performance, and be able to demonstrate the effectiveness of their methods of supervision.

The second element is external, the role of elected representatives. They may act as a conduit for particular complaints, but their primary responsibility is to ensure that an effective internal control system is in operation. Once satisfied of this, they can concentrate their attention on the matters of political and policy choice which the division of labour of representative democracy allots to them.

VII

It is obvious that the regime sketched here would greatly enlarge the degree of democratic participation in governance of the police.[61] It would also—a point deserving more attention than space permits—represent a major reassertion of local, as opposed to national, influence. I have argued that the constitutional principles of liberal democracy require no less. There is also a practical argument: that the alternative—a continuation of the present situation of creeping national control and the literally irresponsible authority of the chief constable at local level—is a blueprint for an increasingly alienated and militarised police force. Constitutional principles are intimately connected to the quality of policing and thereby to the quality of democratic life.

---

[61] Even more so if coupled with a more influential role in policy-setting for local consultative bodies than is now required by s.106 of the Police and Criminal Evidence Act 1984.

Chapter 7

DECISION-MAKING AND ITS CONTROL IN THE
ADMINISTRATIVE PROCESS—AN OVERVIEW

Patrick Birkinshaw

Introduction

By way of introduction a few points need to be made about the title to
this essay. First of all, although the title refers to "decision-making,"
we should not be blind to the existence of "non-decision making," by
public agents. This might occur where a power to initiate or embark
upon a programme, course of action or whatever is not exercised. It
can involve those occasions when decisions are taken which exclude
certain interests or items from the political agenda. A substantial body
of work has been directed towards this phenomenon in the United
States and subtle forms of relief have been geared towards combating
unauthorised non decision-making.[1]

Secondly, the term "Administrative Process" is a convenient though
rather vacuous phrase covering a multiplicity of functions, *fora* and
activities. This study is not confined to challenge by individuals upon
routine decisions made under statutory authority. It affords a broad
interpretation to "administrative" to include Governmental and
legislative activities. House of Commons Select Committees for
instance are departmentally related and are concerned with the policy
of departments and their performance and expenditure—"to find out
what the Executive is doing and to hold it publicly accountable"
although not all are convinced of the Select Committees' efficiency.[2]
Standing Committees, and Parliament as a whole play an important
role in supervising legislation, both primary and delegated. Clearly the
activities of Parliament are crucial in our study. What of decisions

---

[1] And which extend far beyond the scope of Order 53 relief, or *Anns* v. *Merton
L.B.C.* [1978] A.C. 728; see P.H.A. Lekner, "Judicial Review of administrative
inaction" 83 Colum. L. Rev. 627 (1983); R. Stewart, and C.R. Sunstein, "Public
programs and private rights" 95 Harvard L. Rev. 1193 (1982); Chayes, "Public
Law Litigation and the Burger Court" 96 Harvard L. Rev. 4 (1982). N. Lewis,
Chap. 5.

[2] D. Wass, *Government and the Governed* (1984), Lecture 4. A. Davies, *Reformed
Select Committees: The First Year* (1980).

151

made under prerogative as opposed to statutory authority? The use of prerogative power in administration is more common than generally imagined so it too must be embraced by this essay, though it is ironic to realise that the exercise of some of the most important prerogatives are devoid of any control save political rebellion or insurrection—declaration of war for instance or the appointment of a Prime Minister. This overview of decision-making in the administrative process will include those decisions which possess a very high policy content—there is no equation of administrative with the routine or uncontroversial. Which "administrative power" is the subject of examination? Is concern focused upon the public sphere or the private sphere? Large scale industry can face and cause administrative and bureaucratic problems not dissimilar in scope or complexity to those of government bodies. My concern is with decision-making within the public sphere—in those institutions which constitute the "loci of official power." This may sound simple enough to the unwary but the latter phrase contains acute problems of definition and delineation in marking out the extent of official power; in determining, in other words, the boundaries of the "State."

Thirdly, what is meant by control? Do we mean determining what a body can decide or making it accountable for what it has decided? Control can be good if it reduces irresponsibility, corruption or inefficiency. It can be deleterious if it is inimical of responsibility, impartiality or initiative. Control is a stronger term than accountability, but this essay is concerned with both concepts. Control is usually exercised *ex ante,* before a decision is made or made effective. The degree of control can be loose and flexible by, for instance, setting a body of standards, principles or broadly drafted rules to act as guidelines in decision-making. Alternatively control can be total where, for example, a commission is given broad powers to investigate and recommend to a minister a certain course of action, which the minister can reject out of hand if it conflicts with governmental policy. Control is achieved in the latter case ultimately by denuding the commission of executive power.

It is more usual to talk of accountability as an *ex post facto* feature after a decision is taken. It could take the form of accounting to an elected or appointed assembly; of providing grievance procedures, tribunals or courts in which a decision will have to be justified; that it is in accordance with accepted criteria of good administration, within the rules, within the law, or within tolerable leeways of fairness. Control and accountability can take place over a period of time where a programme is monitored and constantly assessed; or control can be achieved by time itself where a body is given a definite life-span to achieve a given task. There can be fiscal control and accountability where public money is concerned.[2a] Control and accountability may be achieved vertically,[3] to bodies or groups or individuals who stand above a decision-maker in an hierarchical allocation of power. They can be achieved horizontally to peer groups or downwards by inviting participation or comments from members of society at large, by engaging in consultation or public inquiry exercises. Control and accountability can be achieved by free elections at periodic intervals. In our constitution, we place pre-eminent importance upon this method. M.P.s are recalled to their constituencies to face their electorate, whom if re-elected they represent. Assembled in Parliament there are no controls which may be exercised upon what they do collectively or what—short of a defaulting monarch—they may enact.[4] This, European Law notwithstanding, is the ultimate "Truth" of the constitution and its utility for a powerful executive exercising control over a united majority party is ultimately what the Rule of Law means in the British state.

Control in the British Model of Representative Democracy

The model of representative democracy as it developed within a British context made claims to two fundamental and distinct forms of control and accountability which disciplined the exercise of public power. The most important was political control. Traditional wisdom perceives M.P.s elected upon and responsible for a mandate. Ministers are responsible for their exercise of power and departmental administration to M.P.s in Parliament. Legal control, however, was maintained by an impartial judiciary upholding the Rule of Law and insisting that the exercise of power by the Executive and its officials must be justified by reference to a legal or traditional authority. Legal authority was located in statute, statutory instrument or common law, the latter of which presumes that individuals, including officials, can do whatever is not prohibited or unlawful. Traditional authority was located in prerogative and common law.

By the nineteenth century the model incorporated various claims which purported to legitimate the exercise of public power. In the first place, politics and law were to be separate and distinct realms. Secondly the common law was to cede pride of place to politics as expressed through legislation. Judges had the power of interpretation,

---

[2a] See E.L. Normanton in Smith and Hague, n. 3.

[3] See A. Barker, in *Quangos in Britain*, A. Barker ed. (1982). And see Smith in B.L.R. Smith and D.C. Hague (eds.) *The Dilemma of Accountability in Modern Government* (1971).

[4] Though Marshall places emphasis upon the power of constitutional conventions to control Parliamentary "excesses," *Constitutional Conventions* (1984).

but judges' law was inferior to politicians' law. What made the "tyranny of the majority" acceptable was the assumption that the Executive would not intrude unnecessarily into the private realm and that legislation would not abuse the pattern of rights and privileges which the common law had moulded for "Free-born Englishmen." Common law alone, and not any separate and specific body of public or administrative law, would define individual entitlement and right in the absence of specific legislative provision. The third feature of the classical model was that although the law as applied by the judges was to be common law, common to the public and private realms, the distinction between public and private realms—or the State and Civil Society— was to be maintained at all costs. The State would provide "essentials" such as a system of law and justice, an army and navy, police forces, prisons. The creation of the wealth of the nation would be the preserve of individuals operating through the market place in the private realm. Inescapable "natural laws" of supply and demand would determine the appropriate level of the price of exchanges; equivalents would be determined by the market, and bargaining to an agreement would cement the exchange. The fittest survived, the weak had only themselves to blame. The rhetoric insisted that any State laws which sought to regulate the market or shape positively the future of individual lives, in other than very limited spheres, were wide of the mark. In reality, the common law and statute had a profound impact in shaping individual preferences and dictating the nature of development of the private realm, both here and in the United States[5] and even in the eighteenth century the legislature had been employed to alter irremediably the basis of property relationships and social organisation.[6]

The above is well documented; so too is the gradual compenetration throughout the nineteenth and twentieth centuries of State and Civil Society as the State assumed increasing regulatory powers to redress the excesses and imbalances caused by market forces and the State's own "neutrality" in the governance of human affairs.[7] Increasing regulation of the erstwhile private economy; introduction of institutional machinery to help assuage the ruptures caused by conflict between the forces of capital and labour[8]; the impact of "war efforts" upon the State's assumption of greater responsibility for control of essential industries as well as its increasing responsibility for organising

---

[5] P.S. Atiyah, *The Rise and Fall of Freedom of Contract* (1979); M. Horwitz, *The Transformation of American Law* (1977).

[6] E.P. Thompson, *Whigs and Hunters* (1977); D. Hay in *Albion's Fatal Tree* (1977).

[7] G. Poggi, *The Development of the Modern State* (1978).

[8] K. Middlemas, *The Politics of Industrial Society* (1979). O. Kahn-Freund, *Labour and the Law*, P. Davies and M. Freedland eds. (3rd ed., 1983).

public health and welfare, education and regulation of the environment are all well catalogued. These interventionist and centralising
tendencies transformed the classical model of a balanced representative democracy beyond recognition. Not only did the official organs of
authority—the departments of state, local authorities, public boards
and corporations—grow enormously in terms of manpower, expenditure and powers but there emerged a bewildering arabesque of non
departmental bodies, governmental agencies, tribunals, intermediary
organisations representing the interests of particular groups or clien-
teles to the governors as well as a host of private organisations which
were allowed to regulate their domestic affairs and members in return
for basic compliance with the governmental will. By the middle of the
twentieth century, the degree of compenetration and interdependence
defied complete attempts to distinguish the private and public realms
successfully.

The "Problem" and the Antidote

All of this increased enormously the power of Government, or more
specifically the ministers. The shell of power was in parliamentary
legislation, its substance was in statutory instruments, departmental
rules, codes of practice, ministerial circulars and letters, White Papers,
statements of intent, government contracts and in the informal deals
struck between mighty departments and their client groups. All the
features, in other words, of government by *dominium* through the
power of the public purse,[9] government by enormous delegation to
official, quasi official and "private" self-regulating bodies. Government, in other words, by processes over which Parliament had little
real effective control and which courts were ill-equipped to understand
or tackle. Governments have not, however, always had their own way,
and at various times Parliament has made efforts to redress centripetal
tendencies. But Parliament has invariably lacked the tenacity, inclination or knowledge to grapple with executive power in its myriad forms.

In 1932, the Committee on Ministers Powers (the Donoughmore
Committee) reported on "the powers exercised by or under the direction of (or by persons or bodies appointed specially by) Ministers of the
Crown by way of (a) delegated legislation and (b) judicial or quasi-
judicial decisions, and to report what safeguards are desirable or
necessary to secure the constitutional principles of the sovereignty of
Parliament and the supremacy of the law."[10] A problem had been
perceived, but the antidote was a realisation of ideals forged in the past
to restore the *status quo ante*. The Statutory Instruments Act 1946

[9] T. Daintith, in *The Changing Constitution* (J. Jowell and D. Oliver eds., 1985).
[10] Cmd. 4060 (1932).

reaffirmed to some extent the importance of Parliamentary scrutiny of delegated legislation, ultimately by special Joint and Standing Committees and laying procedures. There is an obligation to publish the draft regulations and consultation is widespread, but it is the case, strange to say, that from the perspective of publicity, safeguards for affected interests were reduced by the 1946 Act in comparison with those contained in the Rules Publication Act of 1893. Many authorities insist that Parliamentary control is far from real.[11] The procedural safeguards are certainly exiguous in relation to affected interests when set beside those applicable under the Administrative Procedure Act 1946 of the United States as developed by federal judges. On the judicial and quasi-judicial powers, the report displayed some confused thinking and set faith in increased controls from our "high courts of law."

It was the Franks Committee which in its report on *Administrative Tribunals and Enquiries*[12] displayed a far more incisive awareness of the two legal realms: the legal proper which was the appropriate area for legal concern, precise procedure, rigorous standards, reasons for decisions, open decision-making, in short the courts; and the administrative realm where procedural and substantive safeguards in the exercise of administrative power were paltry if not non-existent. In the latter domain, there was little structural constraint to encourage what the Committee termed the basic desiderata of "openness, fairness and impartiality" in administrative decision-making. Its recommendations and the Tribunals and Inquiries Act (consolidated in 1971) are landmarks in accountable and responsible decision-making. The legislation, described by Lord Denning as a "new chapter in a Bill of Rights" provided for independent membership for many tribunals; that reasons for decisions generally be given after tribunal and inquiry hearings; open hearings; publication of procedural rules made by delegated legislation; rights of appeal or challenge to courts of law on points of law; and limited the opportunity to exclude judicial review of decisions of tribunals established prior to 1958. It brought, in short, more exacting procedural standards to certain areas of administrative activity. This was the strong point of Franks.

The constructive suggestion of Franks that a body should have oversight over tribunals and inquiries and should act as an independent superviser, critic, expert and Government advisor with the necessary powers to deliver the goods was only partially met by the

---

[11] See H.L. 51, H.C. 169 (1977/8), paras. 9–12, cited in C. Harlow and R. Rawlings *Law and Administration* (1984). See incidentally *R. v. H.M. Treasury ex p. Smedley* [1985] 1 All E.R. 589.

[12] Cmnd. 218 (1957).

creation in 1958 of the Council on Tribunals. It was denied the powers and resources to fulfil the role which Franks envisaged for it, its most important suggestions are often ignored by Government and it lacks the ability or opportunity to take an overall grasp and assessment of the tribunal structure as a whole. This is meant as no disrespect to the membership of the Council and its quality, rather as a criticism of successive Governments which failed to provide the resources to allow the Council to make a significant impact.

The Committee's weaknesses, as well as its omissions, have become more obvious subsequently and indeed Franks was aware of many, if not all, of them. He remarked with some irony that ad hoc non statutory inquiries, such as the one into Crichel Down, were outside his frame of reference in spite of the wide belief that it was the inquiry into that fiasco which led to Franks's own investigation. The more covert, more informal and non-statutory responses to complaints or crises escaped scrutiny.

A fundamental limitation inhered in the philosophy of the report itself. The Committee did not investigate the "policy" which established either a tribunal or "hearing" in the first place. It took for granted that its own investigation was caused by disputes between "the individual and authority" and it saw as its main interest the investigation of the conduct of tribunals—a function of adjudication it maintained, not administration. The second limb of its terms of reference—basically public inquiries or hearings following which recommendations are made to a minister—contained, it believed, a large policy element in the Minister's decision which it was inappropriate to control by an adjudicatory framework. In advocating "openness, fairness and impartiality" to be the controlling features in decision-making with which it was concerned, the Franks Committee saw these *desiderata,* especially impartiality, being trimmed where there was a policy factor which had to weigh in the Minister's decision. There is a tendency to see "Policy" as if it is something which is clearly separable from implementation of decision-making or its effects. Policy, however, suffuses the whole of the administrative process—who makes decisions, where, how, through what procedures and according to what constraints? Policy is subliminal and cultural—all of which Franks thought beyond examination. And the policy element is very often the very element in a decision which, as Franks realised, individuals wish to attack. To say that this is not proper because the appropriate forum for challenge is Parliament contains a presumption that that institution is properly informed about a project and has appropriate time to debate or investigate fully the essential features. However, bodies as diverse as the Outer Circle Policy Unit, the Royal Town Planning Institute, the Council on Tribunals and in a different manner Sir Douglas Wass have all perceived this not to be so.[13] The confusion displayed by Franks on policy was recently echoed by the House of Lords in *Bushell* v. *Secretary of State*[14] where Viscount Dilhorne giving a judgment with the majority and Lord Edmund Davies dissenting, both relied upon Franks to justify their respective decisions that the factual basis supporting a policy was, or was not, part of the policy itself. If it were, as the majority held it was, then no cross examination could take place upon it.

More specifically, the thrust of Franks was individualistic. That is not necessarily bad. Far from it. Franks helped to achieve essential safeguards for the individual *vis á vis* statutory tribunals and inquiries. But many of the underlying problems caused by such bodies were brought about by policies of increasing collectivisation and centralisation of resource allocation and distribution which Franks would not, indeed could not address. Looking at tribunals themselves, many have argued that resort to them by departments helped to hide behind a facade of impartiality highly contentious political choices concerned with: public relief of poverty; State subsidy for the infirm, the sick, the unemployed; movement of finance capital; the extent of profiteering in the provision of essential facilities such as rented accommodation. Adoption of modified legal/adversarial standards in a more informal context has helped the administration sell contentious programmes as a matter of rule-juggling over individual entitlement and has deflected, many believe, attention away from the appropriate level of State distribution to groups and classes.

The term "tribunal" also covers varying institutions which Franks did not distinguish adequately. A basic distinction has been made between "court substitute" tribunals such as the type referred to in the preceeding paragraph which adjudicate in individual disputes between a department and an individual, and "policy-making" tribunals. The latter bodies invariably make decisions or recommendations which carry great significance for the wider public interest in areas of monopolies and mergers, aviation and transport policies, economic and industrial regulation or industrial relations to name a few. Government could never accept a decision of such tribunals as binding upon it after a process of adjudication displaying "openness, fairness and impartiality." Governments invariably reserve the right to appoint the members and to hear appeals from the decisions of such bodies; or their reports are only recommendatory as *R.* v. *Secretary of State for*

---

[13] *The Big Public Inquiry* O.C.P.U. (1979); *The Public and Planning: Means to Better Participation etc.* Royal Town Planning Institute (1982); *A Fairer and Faster Route to Major Road Construction*, N.E.D.O. (1984); Wass n. 2 above; the Council on Tribunals is drawing up a code of practice for "Big Inquiries."

[14] [1981] A.C. 75.

Trade, ex p. Anderson Strathclyde recently reminded us when the Secretary of State rejected a majority report of the Monopolies and Mergers Commission.[15] Such bodies are not afforded the benefit of independence and impartiality as Government is not prepared to allow ultimate control of such bodies to slip out of its hands. Yet there are policy-making tribunals which are under the supervision of the Council on Tribunals and presumably are expected to operate according to Franks's criteria and in a judicial manner. This poses two major problems.

First of all, they are not judicial bodies in any traditional sense but wider-ranging regulatory or recommendatory agencies which *may* exercise certain judicial functions. But such a body operates within a policy framework set by the Government. The importance of the activity such a body is regulating necessitates that the appropriate level of regulation is governmental—but government has not the time, expertise or inclination to regulate the activity itself. It appoints a body to regulate for government but within parameters set by the sponsoring department which can issue guidelines, directives or hear appeals. The problem then becomes how can such institutions operate and be controlled in a manner which is fair, open and accountable. In this respect the record of many such agencies or bodies is mixed, with better practices frequently stifled by Government entering into informal and off the record deals effectively undermining the efforts of its agencies. Conversely, there is always the risk, from Government's point of view, that the relationship between a department and its agency will be misunderstood, and that the judges will see the agency as a truly independent judicial body which should not be subject to improper interference from the department—the saga of the *Laker Airways*[16] litigation is a fine illustration of such a judicial approach when the Court of Appeal interpreted very narrowly the scope of the Guidance which the Department of Trade could give to the Civil Aviation Authority.

Franks works best, then, when his standards are applied to tribunals which adjudicate on individual issues. Even in this class of tribunal, the Government has increasingly sought to circumvent the "impartiality" of certain tribunals. In social security, for instance, while we have witnessed legislative movement towards a more rational, presidential system of tribunals, the combined social

---

[15] [1983] 2 All E.R. 233.
[16] *Laker Airways* v. *Department of Trade* [1977] Q.B. 643. The Court of Appeal ruled that the Department was attempting to issue Directives under its powers to issue Guidance and was also undermining the statutory duties of the C.A.A. See Baldwin (1978) *Public Law* 57 for an interesting critique of the decision and more generally *Regulating the Airlines* (Oxford, 1983).

security tribunals, it has been noticeable that the Department of Health and Social Security has increasingly reversed the effects of decisions by statutory instrument. The Chief Adjudication Officer and Chief Supplementary Benefit Officer have prevented publication of a Social Security Commissioner's decision so that prospective applicants could not use it as a helpful precedent.[17] The cost of social security is seen as a constant scourge to a Government which has placed its faith in economic regeneration via drastic reductions of public expenditure and a minimum role for the State. If independent judgment cuts across political ideology, independent judgment will have to suffer. The Social Security Advisory Committee, for instance, is an advisory body appointed by the Secretary of State which he is under a duty to consult in respect of regulations made under relevant enactments. A copy of the Commission's report must be laid with the draft regulations and the Secretary of State must express to what extent he has followed the report or his reasons for not doing so. There is an escape route in cases of emergency.[18] The Secretary of State, motivated by a desire to reverse the effects of a Commissioner's decision, has laid regulations before full consultation had been achieved and against the advice of the Committee,[19] as well as resorting to the emergency provision rather enthusiastically.

Franks was concerned with open decision-making in statutory tribunals or "opportunities to be heard" under statute. He was not concerned with those processes which do not pursue statutory procedures, but utilise instead non-statutory ones whether of a formal or informal nature, whether adjudicatory or otherwise. Further, bodies which would seem to fall within the first of Franks's terms of reference have escaped his recommended safeguards, *e.g.* in immigration, adjudication officers, including the Chief Adjudication Officer, are appointed by the Minister and not the Lord Chancellor—whatever safeguard that is! There is no right of appeal to a court of law from Immigration Appeal Tribunal decisions. The Parole Board,[20] until recently the Foreign Compensation Commission,[21] Gaming

17 The Child Poverty Action Group has made complaint to the Lord Chancellor about this matter.

18 Social Security Act 1980, s.11.

19 *The Guardian*, March 29, 1984. See the Prime Minister's statement: H.C. Deb., Vol. 65, col. 654 (October 25, 1984).

20 *R.* v. *Secretary of State for the Home Department, ex p. Findlay and Others* [1984] 3 All E.R. 801, H.L., where the Parole Board was not consulted by the Home Secretary before the imposition of a minimum 20 year sentence for certain categories of murderers, and for their acceptance see *The Times*, July 9, 1985.

21 *Anisminic* v. *F.C.C.* [1969] 2 A.C. 147 where the House of Lords took the opportunity to extend their power of review of tribunals' decisions; see Tribunals and Inquiries (F.C.C.) Order, S.I. 1984 No. 1247.

Board[22] and Legal Aid Committees as well as Boards of Visitors[23] exercising judicial disciplinary functions in our prisons are not under the supervision of the Council on Tribunals although all are statutory bodies. We should not be blind to the fact that developments subsequent to Franks have sought to render accountable some of the more "ephemeral" of administrative decisions, made after less formal procedures than tribunals or inquiries.

Ombudsmen and Ombudsmania

The office of the Parliamentary Commissioner for Administration followed the recommendations of the 1961 Whyatt Report in 1967.[24] The Report had an important impact in shaping the eventual nature of the PCA which took the form not of an independent agency to act as an Ombudsman proper, but rather of an adjunct to Parliament to investigate complaints against scheduled departments and agencies. The PCA can only be contacted by complainants via M.P.s.[25] and he is expressly prevented from tackling the merits or the policy content of an administrative decision. He can impugn maladministration in the making of a policy decision, but not the policy itself. Now, there is policy and policy, a point noted by several official reports.[26] If we concentrate on routine departmental policy, as opposed to policy of a high political significance which is *terra prohibita* in its entirety, it can be seen that the PCA has come close to the merits of decision-making when pursuing maladministration—"bias, arbitrariness, neglect, incompetence, delay, turpitude, etc." But it has not been an open attack. The PCA is concerned with procedure not substance. The legislative process is outside his jurisdiction, though after prompting from the Select Committee he will ask for reviews of statutory instruments, statutory regulations which are not statutory instruments and departmental rules which are alleged to be causing individual hardship.[27]

All of the above should begin to impress us with the success which claims about the undermining of ministerial responsibility and reduc-

---

[22] *R. v. Gaming Board for Great Britain, ex p. Benaim and Khaida* [1970] 2 Q.B. 207.
[23] *R. v. Board of Visitors of Hull Prison, ex p. St. Germain* [1979] Q.B. 425. Cp. *Ex p. Tarrant and Another* [1984] 1 All E.R. 799 and *Ex p. Anderson* [1984] 1 All E.R. 920.
[24] Parliamentary Commissioner Act 1967.
[25] Known as the "Filter arrangement." Sir Cecil Clothier has disapproved of the system, and for his suggested reforms, see H.C. 322, para. 7 (1983–1984). For proposals to extend the jurisdiction of the PCA over various non-departmental bodies, see H.C. 619 (1983–84).
[26] H.C. 303 (1964–1965). The distinction between "routine" and "significant" policy can often be impossible to discern.
[27] For regulations which are not statutory instruments, he may well have wider powers to question maladministration in the process leading to their final draft.

ing the role of an M.P. as the citizen's champion, etc., had on limiting the scope and extent of PCA investigations and reports. His powers were closely hedged in, a feature which is obvious when we look at the areas which he is not allowed to investigate. Two of the most controversial have been personnel matters relating to the civil service and armed services, so that the G.C.H.Q. fracas[28] was not amenable to his investigation, and Government commercial and contractual transactions.[29] Government invariably argues that its commercial and contractual affairs are not suitable for investigation as they are not "governmental" in the sense of being within the preserve of Government alone! Governments in the past have pursued the realisation of their policies by their contractual powers and it is a major omission that the PCA is unable to investigate complaints into the somewhat limited field of maladministration in such relationships. The Comptroller and Auditor-General, revamped under the National Audit Act 1983, can investigate value for money in Government contracting in relation to departmental expenditure, but he is not allowed to question the fairness or placement of contracts or removal of tenderers from approved lists. Nor can He question any matter which impinges on governmental policy in relation to contracting, although the Public Accounts Committee has recently made critical comments about the methods adopted by the Government to sell off public corporations into private hands and to place public subsidies or unconscionable profits into the pockets of private contractors or manufacturers.

The reports of the PCA have no binding force; a department "negotiates" around a recommendation of an *ex gratia* payment and the constraining hand of Treasury influence will operate behind the scenes where it is expected that acceptance of a recommendation will lead to significant expenditure.[30] In 1983, 715 complaints were received by the office; 809 were disposed of in the year and 605 of those were rejected. Of 198 full investigations, 42 per cent. were found to be wholly justified. Out of a population of over 55 million, these are very low figures. One should not deny the ripple effect that an investigation and finding of maladministration will hopefully have on improving administration. But the PCA *was* created essentially as an aid to the aggrieved individual; only secondarily was he concerned with supervising or improving departmental administration. This latter task has

---

[28] *Council of Civil Service Unions* v. *Minister for the Civil Service* [1984] 3 All E.R. 935 (H.L.).

[29] Though those transactions involving compulsory acquisition of land are within his competence. See Sched. 3 of the Parliamentary Commissioner Act 1967 for excluded subjects and S.I. 1983 No. 1707.

[30] Which may require statutory authorisation.

fallen to the Select Committee on the PCA pressing home points made by the PCA in his reports.[31]

The Ombudsman theme blossomed in the late 1960s and 1970s and still thrives. The National Health Service, Northern Ireland, Local Government in England, Scotland and Wales, all have ombudsmen and he has appeared in the private sector in the insurance and banking worlds. Creation of an Ombudsman has been urged for prisoners' complaints, police complaints, nationalised industry complaints and data protection—the Home Office in fact refers to the Data Protection Registrar performing "Ombudsman duties." From the governors' point of view, the "safeness" of the PCA system can be gauged by the fact that the Commission for Local Administration in England and Wales was modelled on the PCA—quite remarkable given the cultural and traditional differences in the practice of central and local government. The position of the CLA is more invidious inasmuch as the equivalent to the Select Committee is the Representative Body and it is comprised of the very interests which the CLA investigates: members of the local authority representative bodies, the GLC and the National Water Council.[32] The water industry is the only public utility or nationalised industry which has an Ombudsman.

Where Government opts not for an Ombudsman but a special agency to deal with complaints or problems arising from, *e.g.* racial discrimination, equal opportunities or policing, the scope of the agency's jurisdiction is not confined by allowing it to investigate only some equivalent of maladministration, but by other devices. The Commission for Racial Equality has been, as many suggest, deprived of appropriate funds and assistance by central, local and quasi government; it has been presented with aims which are vague and confused, and with an investigatory procedure which is so prolix that it has become the happy hunting ground of judges chastising technical slips with gay abandon while finding it difficult to suppress sentiments inimical of the Commission and what it seeks to achieve.[33]

---

31 Two of the *causes célèbres* of the PCA: Sachsenhausen and the collapse of the Vehicle and General Insurance Co., where reversals of ministerial decisions were achieved, followed inept ministerial statements to Parliament, not a Select Committee report.

32 Although the dead-hand of the Representative Body is obvious from a reading of CLA annual reports, the CLA is often more vigorous in its investigations and condemnation of authorities than is the PCA. The CLA certainly appears to be countenancing the possibility of legal action to enforce decisions against recalcitrant authorities.

33 *C.R.E.* v. *Amari Plastics* [1982] Q.B. 1194; *C.R.E.* v. *Hillingdon L.B.C.* [1982] A.C. 779; *R.* v. *C.R.E. ex p. Prestige Group plc* [1984] 1 W.L.R. 335; *Mandla* v. *Lee (Dowell)* [1983] 2 A.C. 548 and *Science Research Council* v. *Nassè* [1980] A.C. 1028.

With the Police Complaints Board, the changes introduced by the Police and Criminal Evidence Act 1984, which *inter alia* replaces the Board with the Police Complaints Authority, will do little other than allow the police themselves to investigate the vast majority of complaints against officers and ensure that in spite of a duty upon chief officers and police authorities to consult with local communities there will be no hard opportunity to discuss policies behind policing. The Act will do little to ensure, within a democratic framework, the accountability of the police. Nor does the Act grapple with changing patterns of national and local administration and the impact of these changes upon police policy-making. The police, it could be argued, are a special case as there is no-one to call to account within a political arena for decisions on operational policy; police are not required to be answerable in a political sense, it is argued, as that would in some measure destroy their political neutrality.[34]

What the episode illustrates more specifically is the all-prevailing protection of policy at every level in our public administration. The changing nature of the British State resulted in a vast accumulation of power in Government and its departments and accessories. The ordinary political and legal processes had lost their ability effectively to control or legitimate the changing role of Government, hence the proliferation of the official reports, statutory changes and innovations which we have witnessed. But all the devices encountered so far are premised on the belief that they can only interfere in a *very limited* sense with the administrative process. At the upper reaches of that process, in the policy field, the executive is as jealous as ever of its powers and prerogatives. But, it will be argued, it is accountable to M.P.s for the exercise of such power. That merely invokes the traditional "safeguard" of representative democracy, the limitations of which led to the proliferation of administrative "quality control" devices, none of which offered the opportunities for interested parties to engage in structured debate about the content of policy, or the creation of rules expressing policy, which can take place in agency rule-making in the United States. It is time to attempt an assessment of the nature of powers and decision-making which have eluded virtually any effective forms of control.

What Escaped the Diagnosis

It is surprising how much time Government departments spend pro-

---

[34] The Act has removed "double jeopardy" as an automatic defence, *i.e.* if the same facts constituted a criminal offence as well as a disciplinary charge, but the D.P.P. had refused to prosecute, then the former Police Complaints Board refused to press for a disciplinary charge; *see ex p. Madden* [1983] 2 All E.R. 253. See Lustgarten Chap. 6, for a discussion on police accountability.

cessing complaints themselves in an informal, or formal but unpublished manner or as a supplement to more formal statutory appeal or complaints' mechanisms. The department either does not hand the matter over to a tribunal or statutory hearing, or it exercises discretion to override a decision reached in accordance with a statutory appellate procedure such as immigration. I have written on this subject elsewhere and the practice really is pervasive.[35] The closer a matter or complaint touches upon important aspects of policy, the more enthusiastically a department keeps the matter within its own overall grasp: be the field education; grants to industry for regional and selective assistance; export credit guarantees; regulation of the investor and securities markets; immigration and deportation decisions; informal procedures in social security and welfare; or complaints by petition from prisoners to the Home Secretary. The details and variety in practice are rich and varied. And there is little to believe other than that the standard of decision is high. But virtually all the formal extra-statutory processes are not publicised; details are rarely provided on how they operate; they are invariably employed as an aid to discretion or to avoid a more rigorous and formal statutory process of hearing grievances or complaints. About these procedures we know relatively little. Powerful institutions can use the informality of relationship, especially if it is a continuing one with a department, to negotiate a favourable position against other competitors or interests. Because the relationship is screened by confidentiality, we have little or no assurance that all the issues are canvassed, all the alternatives considered, or all the policy options delved into. The scenario can be illustrated by decisions in 1983 and 1984 involving the Stock Exchange and self-regulation; monopoly investigations; health and safety regulation in the North Sea Oil Fields; British Oxygen's exclusive contract with the DHSS to supply gas for the NHS and the overpricing of armaments and drugs contracts to the advantage of private manufacturers and the disadvantage of British tax-payers. There is a close connection between informally resolved grievances and informally planned or bargained outcomes when the client groups of departments are powerful and influential. This phenomena is not peculiar to central government and its agencies and its development is well documented in relation to local authorities where informal resolution of complaints has been studied.[36] It is interesting too to observe in local government

---

[35] "Departments of State, Citizens and the Internal Resolution of Grievances" (1985) *Civil Justice Quarterly* 15, and *Grievances, Remedies and the State* (1985), Chap. 2.

[36] N. Lewis and P. Birkinshaw, "Taking complaints seriously" in *Welfare Law and Policy*, M. Partington, and J. Jowell, eds. (1979); "Local Authorities and the Resolution of Grievances: Some Second Thoughts" (1979) *Local Government Studies* 7.

the re-emergence of industrial "planning agreements" whereby industry trades its expertise, knowledge or autonomy in return for government concessions or opportunities to exploit resources or markets.

We have spoken of informal relationships. In central government there will doubtless be personal involvement by Ministers and senior civil servants in such relationships. For the more routine point of contact, the recent Personnel Management Review for the civil service stated that "much more responsibility should be delegated to civil servants, especially line managers operating away from Whitehall . . . civil servants should be encouraged to show their personal commitment to the priorities of their political masters rather than to Parliament or the needs of the public."[37]

If the general theme of our discussion is control and accountability in the public realm, then what are we to make of the informal networks through which the Government delegates effective executive powers while exercising wide-ranging patronage through powers of appointment? Here we encounter the field of non-departmental government, quasi-government or quangos and quangos to employ much overused acronyms[38] and which describe institutions from public corporations, such as those which manage nationalised industries to bodies which have no legal or formal constitutional status, and yet which stand in a significant relationship to Government. Some of these latter bodies are purely advisory; others are given permission to regulate their own affairs and their own members, either under a broad statutory umbrella or, in the absence of legislation, in return for promises that certain standards, or perhaps Governmental wishes, will be maintained. Such features figure largely in accounts of corporatism. At present, Trade Unions have, to a great extent, been expelled from the charmed circle of those incorporated, but in a British context commentators have noted how newer interests have moved into the lacuna caused by the absence of the TUC amongst others.[39] Likewise, commentators are describing the development of "welfare corporatism" whereby special access to governmental influence is extended to house builders; building societies and insurance companies, financial institutions or groups providing private medical facilities. A recent example was the committee of inquiry into retirement pensions, earnings

---

[37] *The Guardian*, May 24, 1983.
[38] Quasi autonomous non-governmental, and governmental, organisations. See A. Barker, *op. cit.* See Pliatzky, Cmnd. 7797; Civil Service Department *Non-Departmental Public Bodies* (1981); H.C. Deb., Vol. 68, cols. 57–58 (November 19, 1984).
[39] N. Lewis and P. Wiles "The Post-Corporatist State?" (1984) *J.L.S.* 65; K. Middlemas "The Supremacy of Party" (1983) *New Statesman* June 10 and 17; N. L. Harrison *Corporatism and the Welfare State* (1984).

related state pensions, company pensions and a "new portable pension scheme." It is no exaggeration to say that the inquiry was concerned with billions of pounds. It was chaired by a Secretary of State (only once before has a minister chaired such an inquiry) had four other ministers as members, as well as members and advisers closely connected with private insurance and investment companies. Only one member was described as "independent" and significant spheres of interest were excluded from membership. The Government will argue that all this is to do with "private welfare" which is not provided by the State but which results from negotiation between the State and private bodies and is therefore apolitical. Supported by professional, managerial and skilled classes, the effect of such concessions and fiscal advantages is often to dissipate support for direct state provided welfare hitting in particular the poor and debilitated.

Informality then, is the problem to which we must give pressing thought.[40] Franks's criteria are valuable ones, but we need to make a reassessment of the machinery and relationships and procedures which constitute the working of the British State. Ensuing years will produce historians who will tell us whether the transitions which have been at the centre of political rhetoric in the past few years have been merely transitory or have wrought fundamental change. I refer to the widespread practice of privatisation of public assets; the contracting out to private companies for labour supply to public bodies, and deregulation of public control; the transfer to non-elected bodies of numerous functions of local government and the increasing central control over local government finance including unforeseen curbs on capital expenditure in local government by the Department of Environment. Indeed the increasing resort to financial controls on expenditure such as cash limits, financial targets, and external financing limits on nationalised industries, makes it very difficult to do any other than live a hand to mouth existence in the provision of services and disrupts long-term planning programmes. These are all administrative decisions, yet we lack effective procedures and mechanisms through which to assess and discuss major shifts in social, industrial, economic and environmental changes; in other words to evaluate "policy" and its impact upon society.

In response to this criticism, it can be argued that we have Parliament and that if Parliament were made too effective Government could not govern, or at least the Prime Minister, the Chancellor of the Exchequer, senior Treasury officials and the Bank of England could

---

[40] One point amongst many made by Patrick McAuslan in "Administrative Law, Collective Consumption and Judicial Policy" (1983) 46 Mod. L.R. 1. And see p. 7.

not govern. It is not denied that Parliament can, on rare occasions, act as a powerful corrective to Government excesses. But the nature and usefulness of the debate depends upon M.P.s. being fully informed on all relevant issues and upon Government revealing whenever possible the totality of its plans to M.P.s. No Government appears prepared to do that, any more than it would do away with the Official Secrets Acts. Even Select Committees do not have power as of right to demand the presentation of information, or the presence of officials for examination.

If lawyers place at the centre of their universe the realisation of ideals of control and accountability through procedural forms, I would add greater participation from the public in major decision-making to the *desiderata* of openness, fairness and impartiality. Through what procedures would the ideals be pursued? What follows is premised upon the necessity of seeing Parliament taking a more effective and combative role in examining governmental policy.

The Outer Circle Policy Unit several years ago suggested a Project Inquiry to inquire into major projects before a Standing or Select Committee of Parliament scrutinised general policy and before more traditional local inquiries discussed site-specific proposals.[41] The Project Inquiry would be expert, fully informed, would question the merits and would take place before there was a final commitment to a project. Costs out of public funding would also be allowed for participants.

For changes of constitutional significance, a permanent royal commission after the model proposed by Sir Douglas Wass could be an effective overseer of major constitutional, social and industrial change. He saw it possessing a "limitless remit." Its members, appointed by the Crown on the advice of the Prime Minister, would have power to draw up their own programmes of investigation and co-opt specialists as required.[42]

At a more mundane level, three suggestions may be made; first the time has surely come when the ombudsmen should be able to impugn the merits of bad decision-making and when their conclusions should be enforceable against bureaucracy. Secondly, there is the need for the creation of effective grievance procedures against nationalised industries. Existing mechanisms are woefully inadequate.[43] Thirdly, a statutory code of Good Administration for Government departments

---

[41] See the O.C.P.U. report and the R.T.P.I. report at note 13 above. Not all were pleased with the proposals to separate the policy investigation from the site specific investigation, *e.g.* the Council for the Protection of Rural England.

[42] Wass, *op. cit.* Lecture 6. And see too the proposals by Partington, Chap. 9.

[43] See Birkinshaw, *Grievances Remedies and the State*, Chap. 4.

insisting upon openness and publication of internal processes which affect the public or individuals should be introduced.[44]

It is unlikely that the changes advocated here will be accepted by Governments in the immediate future, any more than it is likely that legislative reform will be enacted to make central government less secretive. Even if introduced, it would be idle to expect change or improvement in the results of control and accountability over-night. The changes are means to a better end which places emphasis upon openness and accountability.[45]

One subject has not been covered in any detail in this essay, and that concerns the role of the courts in controlling administrative decision-making. Courts are important as control mechanisms, even though ultimate decisions are not their responsibility but Parliament's or the Government's. Courts can issue severe reprimands for haughty and unlawful government, but their impact is, as Professor de Smith said "sporadic and peripheral." Further, there is a widespread feeling that judicial intervention in administration is selective for reasons which themselves border on the political. Many of the recent cases in public law delve into highly sensitive and controversial subjects and while a political predilection may colour the outcome in some judicial decisions, it could well be that a lack of acquaintance and familiarity with public administration and a judicial armoury which is rather undeveloped and unsophisticated may also have contributed to confused or contentious stances. For the future, I believe the most interesting judicial development will be the blending together of constitutional, civil liberties and administrative law as the connection between these areas is more fully perceived, especially as a result of decisions of the European Commission and Court of Human Rights. More than anything else, these have forced us to have regard to the comparative poverty of legality in our "administrative process."[46]

---

[44] This was urged almost 15 years ago by Justice, *Administration Under Law* (1971).

[45] For local government and the Access to Information Bill, see my *Open Government, Freedom of Information and Local Government* (1985).

[46] *Malone against the United Kingdom* (1983) 5 E.H.R.R. 385; *Silver against the United Kingdom*, Judgment March 25, 1983; *Case of Campbell and Fell,* Judgment June 28, 1984. For the judgment of *Malone* in the European Court of Human Rights, see Judgment 4/1983/60/94 August 2, 1984. Note also the European Court of Human Rights decision in the case of *Abdulaziz, Cabales and Balkandali,* Judgment May 28, 1985.

Chapter 8

DEMOCRATISATION, ACCOUNTABILITY AND
INSTITUTIONAL DESIGN: REFLECTIONS ON PUBLIC
LAW

TONY PROSSER

The occasion of the one hundredth anniversary of the publication of
Dicey's "*Law of the Constitution*" is a fitting time for a re-evaluation of
the role and nature of public law in Britain. I have argued elsewhere
that to develop any intellectual coherence in approaching public law in
modern society this should take the form of fundamental re-assess-
ment of the theoretical basis for its study.[1] In this brief contribution I
will develop further the ideas stated there, although of necessity they
will remain highly schematic. I will pay particular attention to the
potential of differing theoretical forms for public law and to British
forms for the legitimation of state action through Parliament.

Conceptualising Public Law

It is all too easy (particularly in a fundamentally empiricist political
culture such as that of Britain) to treat a concept such as law as self-
evidently embodied in existing legal forms and institutions. The
problem with this approach, however, is that it prevents any theoretical reassessment such as I advocate, and can all too easily lead to legal
thought lagging far behind actual social development and the changes
induced by this in law. What comes within the sphere of the legal is an
essentially conceptual rather than empirical question, and one to be
established at the level of theory rather than of appearance. It is here
that any necessary real definitions of the legal enterprise can be
constructed.[2] More importantly, the forms in which the legal domain is
embodied are highly historically specific and, in a society of rapid

---

[1] Tony Prosser, "Towards a Critical Public Law" (1982) 9 *J. of Law and Society*
1–19.
[2] For an argument for such a real definition see Deryck Beyleveld and Roger
Brownsword, "Law as a Moral Judgement vs. Law as the Rules of the Powerful"
(1983) 28 Am.J. of Juris. 79. Needless to say, there is not the space for me to
attempt a similar project here.

170

change, the form of law may itself rapidly change and be transcended.[3] In stressing this I have something in common with recent writers who take an evolutionary approach to the development of law.[4] I do not here wish to justify evolutionary theory, but to stress the essential underlying point that though the concept of law may be absolute, the forms in which it is embodied vary and develop with social change as well as with changes in law itself. A related point is that the separation of law and politics characteristic of most conventional approaches to public law is also a highly historically specific view.[5] Indeed, many of the current problems in conceptualising public law can be seen as stemming from a crisis of formal rationality in law through which the autonomy of legal thought is no longer tenable even at the level of appearances.[6]

An important distinction which can illuminate these points is that made by Habermas between law as "medium" and law as "institution."[7] Law as medium is law as a means of actively intervening in social life for particular ends; it is "an independent socio-technological decisional process" and is a means of shaping the allocation of goods. Law as "institution" on the other hand, does not actively shape the outcomes of social processes but rather provides an "external constitution" in which they can take place. It is thus essentially procedural and is concerned to facilitate processes of social development. Teubner, one of the evaluating theorists referred to earlier, draws on the German theorist Luhmann to suggest that complex, differentiated modern societies are particularly well suited to the development of "reflexive" legal rationality in which law approximates to its latter role; it is a

---

[3] For an interesting account of debates within nineteenth-century legal education which were really about competing conceptualisations of law see Raymond Cocks, *Foundations of the Modern Bar* (Sweet & Maxwell, London, 1983), pp. 34–54, 93–102, 104–118, 178, 189–194, 199–209, 231–233. A classic account of this process of course is Morton J. Horwitz, "The Transformation of American Law" (Harvard U.P., Cambridge, 1977).

[4] Phillippe Nonet and Philip Selznick, *Law and Society in Transition: Towards Responsive Law* (Harper Torchbooks, New York, 1978) and Gunther Teubner, "Substantive and Reflexive Elements in Modern Law" (1983) 17 Law and Society Rev. 239–285 .

[5] See *ibid.* Discussion of this subject is inevitably undertaken in the influence of Max Weber's work; see Max Weber, *Economy and Society* (University of California Press, Berkeley, 1978), pp. 641–900.

[6] See Teubner, *op. cit.* pp. 239–246; *cf.* David Nelken, "Is there a crisis in Law and Legal Ideology?" (1982) 9 J. of Law and Society 177–189.

[7] Jurgen Habermas, *Theorie des Kommunikativen Handelns* (Frankfurt, Suhrkamp, 1981) and see Teubner, *op. cit.* pp. 270 and 275. The relevant section of Habermas' work is not yet available in English, though the earlier part of it is published as *Reason and the Rationalisation of Society* (Heinemann, London, 1984).

means of designing and constructing institutions within which processes of social development can take place. There is, incidentally, a similarity between this and the "interest representation" model associated with the work of Richard Stewart in relation to administrative law in the United States in which the legal function is seen as that of providing an alternative to the political process for the assertion of group interests.[8] I have also suggested elsewhere that, in Britain, welfare rights groups have benefited from the use of law not in terms of substantive results but in terms of the development of skills and opportunities for the use of a range of forums apart from the courts.[9]

Nevertheless, in Britain the role of public law as providing a means for the construction of institutions for the working out of developmental social processes has been largely overlooked. Yet it is possible to reconstruct public law as an expression of this. The resulting project has two aspects. The first is that of public law as a means of "mapping out the state"; of establishing public institutions and setting out their bounds and relations with each other and with private interests. This is the central role of constitutions, formal and informal; as Norman Lewis suggests in his contribution, because of the hidden nature of the constitution in Britain, this set of arrangements has to be discovered amongst a complex pattern of informal relations. At one level this aspect is essentially descriptive; however, it also has a strong normative element and much of civil liberties law falls here; as well as being concerned with the expression of rights, this area of law is concerned with the capacity for the mutual limitation of powers by different institutions.[10] Part of the normative concern will be for efficiency, with establishing a set of institutions which will work towards given goals at the lowest possible cost; however it will also strive for legitimacy, as I will discuss below.

The second role of public law is that of institutional design. Again, this is central in the writings of the evolutionary theorists referred to earlier. Thus in describing their concept of "responsive law" Nonet and Selznick state; "Legal energies should be devoted to diagnosing institutional problems and redesigning instutional arrangements" and stress the need for "New modes of supervision, new ways of increasing the visibility of decisions, new organizational units, new structures of authority, new incentives. . . ."[11] Teubner, in developing from this the

---

[8] R. Stewart, "The Reformation of American Administrative Law" (1974–75) 88 Harvard L. Rev., 1667–1813.

[9] Tony Prosser, *Test Cases for the Poor* (Child Poverty Action Group, London, 1983) esp. Chaps. 5 and 6.

[10] See Paul Hirst, "Law, Socialism and Rights," in *Radical Issues in Criminology* (P. Carlen and M. Collison eds., Martin Robertson, Oxford, 1980) pp. 79, 80, 96. I do not, however, share the general rejection of the concept of rights of this article.

[11] *Op. cit.* pp. 106–107; see also at p. 112.

concept of "reflexive law" also stresses the necessity of institutional design; "legal attention focuses on creating, shaping, correcting and redesigning social institutions that function as self-regulating systems."[12]

Thus institutional design is essentially procedural and aims at enablement and facilitation (which, incidentally, is not to say that legitimate institutional arrangements are compatible with an infinite range of substantive outcomes[13]). To what purposes should institutions developed in this way be committed, apart from simple facilitation, from simply getting basic jobs done? At first sight the evolutionary theorists referred to above might be seen as recommending the development of areas in which the market place is left free to determine solutions within a framework set out through law. This would be a misreading and in earlier work I have argued that the concepts central to public law, beyond mere facilitation, were to be participation and accountability.[14] I suggested that a transcendental[15] basis for this could be established in the work of Jurgen Habermas. I still hold by this earlier work, but I would here like to put the same argument in rather different words. I will again be drawing on Habermas' work to consider the creation and development of social learning processes.

The concept of a learning process originates within Habermas' somewhat complex neo-evolutionary theory; I will not attempt here to describe in full or justify this theoretical approach.[16] In brief, one will be familiar with Marxism with the approach to the development of the productive forces within a society as a process involving directionality, a process involving a set of stages each building on the previous one. According to Habermas, a similar process can be perceived in the realm of social interaction and consciousness.[17] The essence of this is the development of an increased capacity for problem-solving, for coping with the complexities of social development. This is composed both of conceptual capacities and of institutional arrangements. The conceptual element has been summarised by Luhmann in his theme that the character of modern positive law hinders the emergence of a socially adequate "learning law"; what is missing is a "conceptual system oriented towards social policy which would permit one to

[12] *Op. cit.* p. 251; see also p. 254.
[13] See Prosser, *op. cit.* n. 1, at p. 11, and Beyleveld and Brownsword, *op. cit.*
[14] Prosser, *op. cit.* n. 1.
[15] Habermas denies that his method is transcendental in the accepted sense; see, *e.g. Communication and the Evolution of Society* (Heinemann, London, 1979) pp. 199–205.
[16] For a recent exposition see "Toward a Reconstruction of Historical Materialism" in *Communication and the Evolution of Society, ibid.*
[17] See *Communication and the Evolution of Society, op. cit.* pp. 97–98.

compare the consequences of different solutions to problems, to accumulate critical experience, to compare experiences from different fields, in short: to learn."[18] The institutional embodiment of learning processes is seen by Habermas as the way in which democratisation of society can take place:

> "I can imagine the attempt to arrange a society democratically only as a self-controlled learning process. It is a question of finding arrangements which can ground the presumption that the basic institutions of the society and the basic political decisions would meet with the unforced agreement of all those involved, if they could participate, as free and equal, in discursive will-formation. Democratization cannot mean an *a priori* preference for a specific type of organization . . . ."[19]

Cultural capabilities in the form of learning processes may be embodied in specific institutions, including the legal system.[20]

The argument now suggests, then, that there is a close link between public law and processes of democratisation. This applies not to substantive legal provisions but to law as the means of design for institutions within which social learning processes may take place. These then serve to resolve problems of legitimation. My discussion so far has been at a high level of abstraction; I will spend the rest of this contribution discussing the extent to which there has been success in this enterprise in Britain, and in particular to examine the role of parliamentary legitimation within it.

Institutional Design and Public Ownership

Recent writers have stressed the striking lack of any coherent structure to institutional arrangements within the public law sphere in Britain.[21] Patrick Birkinshaw in another contribution to this volume points to the limited and inconsistent arrangements for overseeing administrative decision-making. To pick another example, the same has been true in the lack of sophistication in the design of institutions for state involvement in, and ownership of, industry.[22] Thus the major examples of

[18] Luhmann, "Evolution des Rechts" [1970] 3 Rechtstheorie 1. quoted in Teubner, *op. cit.* p. 264.
[19] *Communication and the Evolution of Society, op. cit.* p. 186.
[20] *Reason and the Rationalisation of Society, op. cit.* p. XI, and see Nonet and Selznick, *op. cit.* pp. 18–27.
[21] Familiar accounts are G. Ganz, "Allocation of Decision-Making Functions" (1972) *Public Law*, 215–231; 299–308, and S.A. de Smith, *Judicial Review of Administrative Action* (4th ed., Stevens, London, 1980), Chap. 1.
[22] For a fuller account see Tony Prosser, *Nationalised Industries and Public Control* (forthcoming) (Blackwell, Oxford, 1986).

nationalisation by the post-war Labour Government utilised the form of the public corporation, allegedly insulated in much of its action from political control. This was done with only limited understanding of the implications of using this model; previous examples, such as the London Passenger Transport Board, had been on a much smaller scale and were unlikely to become important in governmental economic management. In much of the planning for public ownership, there was the naive belief that a change in ownership, and the ending of the profit motive which was assumed to accompany this, would in itself result in the industries pursuing an unproblematic "public interest." The result was unconcern with the crucial questions of institutional design. Moreover, proposals for scrutiny through "measurement and publicity" contained in early proposals for public ownership were not implemented in practice.[23] Unsurprisingly, serious problems of the constitutional relations of the industries to government, of their role in general economic management, of participation of interests and of accountability have plagued the industries ever since. The major proposal for a fundamental reassessment of this, based around the design of participative institutional arrangements, was rejected by the Government in a White Paper of notable superficiality.[24] Lip service was paid in the White Paper to the role of corporate planning as a participative process involving the industries, government and outside interests. However, the opportunities for developing such a process through sophisticated corporate planning techniques (sometimes explicitly based around the concept of planning as a learning process) were not taken up, and corporate planning in many of the industries remains in a state of severe disarray.[25] Nor were attempts by the Labour Government of the mid-nineteen-seventies to use the National Enterprise Board as a new form of public ownership likely to resolve these problems. Whilst some attempt was made to provide a more rational structure through the publication of formal guidelines issued by the Secretary of State, major problems of accountability remained. In any event, even under the Labour Government the Board was never given the opportunity to assume the role of a major new instru-

---

[23] The phrase is from Sidney and Beatrice Webb, *A Constitution for the Socialist Commonwealth of Great Britain* (Longmans, London, 1920), pp. 186–202, 328–330, see also Herbert Morrison, *Socialisation and Transport* (Constable, London, 1933), pp. 169–171, 174–176, 227–229 and 288–297.

[24] The proposal was the National Economic Development Office, "A Study of UK Naionalised Industries: Their Role in the Economy and Control in the Future" (HMSO, 1976); The White Paper, Cmnd. 7131 (1978).

[25] For a description of the possibilities of corporate planning see Bernard Taylor, "New Dimensions in Corporate Planning" (1976) 9(6) *Long Range Planning* 80–105. For its failure in practice in relation to the industries see Committee of Public Accounts, H.C. 139 of 1983–84, paras. 9–12, 28.

ment of public ownership rather than simply supporting "lame ducks" and filling limited gaps in the private provision of investment finance. Had it been given the larger role, the problems of accountability would have been much more severe.[26] To bring my concerns more up-to-date, current plans for the privatisation and de-regulation of state-owned industry have displayed a striking lack of either coherent constitutional principle or of any sophistication in institutional design, as Norman Lewis demonstrates in Chapter 5. I will return later to a particular aspect of the accountability of state-owned industry; that of efficiency audit.

Democracy and Parliamentary Representation

Why has there been this poverty of constitutional and institutional thought in Britain? Much of the answer must lie in the extreme centrality accorded to Parliament as the location for representation and accountability under British constitutional arrangements. This militates against the development of other institutional forms for legitimation.[27] It is allied to a system of government which permits an exceptionally heavy concentration of power in a small group of ministers and senior civil servants. Douglas Ashford, in a recent work, has documented how this concentration results in a greater degree of insulation of policy-making from social pressures than is the case in other democracies.[28] Thus the outcome is closed policy-making centred around an extremely strong "elite consensus" with little opportunity for outside input or for self-correction:

"There is no official voice outside Parliament that provides a continuing critique of how well government is working. The French Cour des Comptes or the Conseil d'Etat, for example, are not only constitutional guardians, but critics of ministerial decisions, administrative orders, and even individual treatment by government . . . (In Britain) perhaps the greatest loss is that learning from past errors and experience depends on a remarkably small number of persons who in fact have very little time, and very little incentive, to make the critiques and evaluations of

[26] See Wyn Grant, *The Political Economy of Industrial Policy* (Butterworths, London, 1982), Chap. 5, especially pp. 116–119, and Douglas Mitchell "Intervention, Control and Accountability: The National Enterprise Board" (1982) 38 Public Administration Bulletin 40–65.

[27] For fuller discussion of this see N. Lewis and I. Harden, *The Rule of Law and the British Constitution* (forthcoming, 1986).

[28] Douglas Ashford *Policy and Politics in Britain: the Limits of Consensus* (Blackwell, Oxford, 1981).

policy effectiveness that are most pronounced in other democratic political systems."[29]

Thus, quite apart from any argument of principle in favour of more open government, the British constitutional system is such as to limit the development of knowledge through processes of argumentation, through in other words a learning process. Ashford also points to the fact that, despite a highly adversarial style of politics within Parliament, the Opposition has a minimal practical role in influencing government; indeed the position of Parliament as a whole has been summed up nicely in discussion of the management of public expenditure; "Parliament is the permanent and proper stranger whose very presence indirectly helps nurture the sense of community within the Executive."[30] The result of all this is something of a paradox; despite apparent argument and dispute over policy-making within the adversary system of British politics, the "elite consensus" remains immune to effective criticism. To explain this involves further examination of two related themes, one relating to changes in the function of Parliament, and one relating to changes in concepts of democracy.

Parliament and the Public Sphere

My argument now will be that the forms of parliamentary democracy in Britain reflect a particular historical set of circumstances which no longer correspond to the realities of social structure; in other words that there is a gap between social processes and legitimating structures. This form of argument is by no means new; a classic example is Bagehot's *The English Constitution* with its theme of the distinction between the dignified and efficient elements of the constitution.[31] Once more, the work of Habermas provides a fertile source of ideas. One of the central themes in his work has been the development and decline of the "public sphere" based on open discussion of political life. It acted as the means of mediating between the state and society and as an agency of public supervision of the state. The basis for its operation was the justification of opinions through "the procedures and presuppositions of free argument."[32] Through this supervision it performed the function of making transparent official action and decisions. It had a legitimating function but also went some way towards achieving

---

[29] *Ibid.* p. 16.
[30] Hugh Heclo and Aaron Wildavsky, *The Private Government of Public Money* (2nd ed., Macmillan, London, 1981), p. 245.
[31] William Bagehot, *The English Constitution* (Fontana, 1963), esp. pp. 61–62.
[32] See David Held, *Introduction to Critical Theory* (Hutchinson, London, 1980), pp. 260–267, and Ray Kemp and Phillip Cooke, "Repoliticising the Public Sphere" (1981) *Social Praxis*.

legitimacy; "the principle of supervision is thus a means of transforming the nature of power, not merely one basis of legitimation exchanged for another."[33] According to Habermas this sphere arose in the eighteenth century in Continental Europe and earlier in England; Parliament and parliamentary debate was one form in which the public sphere was made manifest. However, he argues that since that period, the decline in the separation of state and society and allied rationalisation processes have led to the transformation of politics away from providing such an opportunity for rational discourse.

Further elucidation of this theme can be found in the work (heavily influenced by Habermas) of Poggi.[34] He has described the "compenetration" of state and civil society which has resulted from a variety of causes which include the extension of the franchise, the growth of oligopoly and the development of trade unions and employers' organisations. This undermined competition and replaced it with more directly political bargaining processes.[35] Together with the growth of demands from other interest groups that the state take action on their behalf this led to increased state intervention and increased involvement of non-state bodies in representation and administration. This change in institutional responsibilities is not, however, reflected in formal political arrangements; "the state still functions in our time within and through *forms* derived from the liberal-democratic nineteeth-century constitution; it does so to an extent sufficient partly to disguise and partly to limit the changes in the *substance* of the political process, but at the same time it modifies and distorts the forms themselves."[36] Together these tendencies undermined the key role of Parliament in overseeing the state. In particular the role of Members of Parliament to act independently through debate (in so far as it ever existed) rather than as representatives of interests and of party programmes, was largely lost.

> "The open-endedness and creativity of the parliamentary process is thus diminished. Increasingly, parliament is reduced to a highly visible stage on which are enacted vocal, ritualised confrontations between preformed, hierarchically controlled, ideologically characterized alignments. . . . Under such conditions, parliament

---

[33] Jurgen Habermas, "The Public Sphere—An Encyclopedia Article" (1974) 1 *New German Critique* 49–55.

[34] G. Poggi, *The Development of the Modern State: A Sociological Introduction* (Hutchinson, London, 1978) Chap. VI.

[35] It would of course be quite wrong to believe that there had *ever* been a clear divide between state and society; see, *e.g.* Horwitz, *op. cit.* pp. xiv–xv and Chap. 14, but as Poggi makes clear the essential change is one of degree and of perception and separation.

[36] Poggi, *op. cit.* p. 121 (emphasis in original: note omitted).

no longer performs a critical, autonomous role as a mediator between societal interests; instead, its composition and operations simply register the distribution of preferences within the electorate and determine in turn which party will lead the executive."[37]

Similar themes can be seen in Beer's account of changing patterns of political representation in Britain.[38] His description of the "Old Whig" politics of the eighteenth century stresses the Burkean view of the M.P. as the independent "man of wisdom and ability," and the later form of "liberal democracy" incorporates a strong hostility to party discipline. This is contrasted fundamentally with the major role of party as determinant of parliamentary behaviour which accompanied what Beer terms the "collectivist" politics of the twentieth century. He sees this as characteristic of both Tory and Socialist democracy (to use his terms) and closely associated with government attempts to engage in economic management.[39] An accompanying theme in the studies by Ashford and by Beer is that, though the nature of political representation has changed dramatically, the forms through which representation took place did not change, nor was the apparatus of government restructured in any fundamental way. Thus after referring to exercises in building new constitutions in other countries, Ashford comments that "British leaders tended to look upon most of these nation-building exercises with scepticism, and even suspicion. In nineteenth-century Britain the requirements of modern democracy were simply superimposed on an existing governmental structure."[40]

At this point I should sound a note of caution. I do not wish to suggest that there was a lost age of rational parliamentary debate, destroyed by the strengthening of party discipline. The limited nature of the interests able to participate in any parliamentary approximation of the public sphere is obvious and is clear in all the studies referred to above.[41] Nor do I wish to suggest that the party system has somehow, through the reinforcement of adversary politics, detracted from rational debate which would otherwise have occurred. In a strongly class-divided society such as Britain any democratic politics is likely to take an adversary form; the alternative is the effective disenfranchisement of disadvantaged groups.[42] Rather, the point that I am making

---

[37] *Ibid.* p. 141.
[38] Samuel Beer, *Modern British Politics* (Faber, London, 2nd ed., 1982).
[39] *Ibid.* Chap. 3.
[40] Ashford, *op cit.* p. 14.
[41] Habermas, *The Public Sphere, op. cit.* pp. 54–55; Kemp, *op. cit.*; Beer, *op. cit.*, pp. 22–32.
[42] *Cf.* C.B. Macpherson *The Life and Times of Liberal Democracy* (Oxford U.P., London, 1977), pp. 64–69.

relates more directly to the lack of institutional development which has accompanied the fundamental shifts in patterns of political representation. It is now impossible to claim that Parliament provides a forum for rational debate which provides legitimacy for the political process as a whole. As the quotation from Habermas above suggested, democratisation of a society is not a process to be accomplished through a form of organisation preferred *a priori*; rather it involves the institutionalisation of social learning processes.[43] In current Britain, Parliament can no longer offer the sole location for such a process; thus we come once again to the need for institutional design through public law.

The Decline of Democratic Ideals

A further theme is relevant in developing this argument. This concerns the impoverishment of the concept of democracy which has occurred in the present century. The argument is one which has cropped up in a variety of writers, from Habermas to Sir Douglas Wass.[44] It is a major theme in the work of C.B. Macpherson and has been most lucidly stated by Carole Pateman.[45] The argument is that the concept of democracy as a learning process has been comprehensively devalued in political thought. Recent concepts of democracy have, Pateman claims, minimised the role of the participating citizen. She terms such concepts the "contemporary model" of democracy; the earliest major expression of this model was in the work of Schumpeter.[46] The model takes its departure from the critique of a "classical model" of democracy with a central participatory role for citizens. It is alleged that such a participatory role is empirically unrealistic in modern conditions and instead Schumpeter gives a modern definition of the democratic method as "That institutional arrangement for arriving at political decisions in which individuals acquire the power to decide by means of a competitive struggle for the people's vote."[47] Several elements of this definition are worthy of note. First, political competition for votes is the central element of this concept of democracy (it is indeed explicitly made comparable to competition in economic markets) and it is bereft of any role for the participating citizen apart

[43] Habermas, *Communication and the Evolution of Society*, *op. cit.* pp. 186–187.
[44] Douglas Wass, *Government and the Governed* (Routledge & Kegan Paul, London 1984), pp. 104 et seq.
[45] Macpherson, *op. cit.* Chap. IV. Carole Pateman, *Participation and Democratic Theory* (Cambridge U.P., 1970).
[46] Joseph A. Schumpeter, *Capitalism, Socialism and Democracy* (9th Impression, Allen and Unwin, London, 1961) Chaps. XXI–XXIII.
[47] *Ibid.* p. 269.

from periodically deciding between leaders.[48] Secondly, it purports to remove any moral connotations from the concept of democracy; rather than enabling social and individual self-development it provides merely for selecting leaders and does not have implicit in it any particular ends; rather it is a means for the achievement of other independent ideals.[49] In Habermas' terms it is thus a means towards instrumental rationality rather than communicative competence. Nevertheless, as Pateman shows, the theories she describes do have normative implications and these tend to suggest that the current Anglo-American democratic systems are near the ideal of the feasible democratic political system.[50] Indeed the competition for votes at election time with little other provision for citizen participation seems close to the way in which parliamentary democracy in Britain currently works.

Pateman responds to this by seeking to establish the "classical model" of participative democracy as a myth; she shows that the different writers who claimed to subscribe to such a view in fact had widely differing views as to the role of participation in democratic theory and practice. Nevertheless, she maintains that certain theorists can indeed be seen as proponents of participatory theories of democracy; in particular Rousseau, John Stuart Mill and G.D.H. Cole. In summarising their views, Pateman shows convincingly that the central element in their thought is democracy as a learning process, both individual and social. Thus, "it is the psychological impact of social and political institutions that is Rousseau's main concern; which aspect of men's characters do particular institutions develop? The crucial variable here is whether or not the institution is a participatory one and the central function of participation in Rousseau's theory is an educative one, using the term 'education' in the widest sense."[51] Pateman demonstrates that similar themes appear in the work of J.S. Mill and of Cole. Thus in Mill, despite the disappointing substantive proposals for implementing what appeared to him as democracy,[52] there was a major recognition of the relationship between individual and social development and the institutions within which this could take place. Moreover, this was not confined to the institutions of central government; "a democratic constitution not supported by democratic institutions in detail, but confined to the central govern-

---

[48] For the links between this theory and economic competition see *ibid*. p. 271, Macpherson, *op. cit.* pp. 79–80, and also his *Democratic Theory: Essays in Retrieval* (Clarendon, Oxford, 1973), Chap. X.

[49] Pateman, *op. cit.* p. 3, and Schumpeter, *op. cit.* p. 242.

[50] Patemen, *ibid*. pp. 15–16.

[51] *Ibid*. p. 24.

[52] Macpherson, *The Life and Times of Liberal Democracy*, *op. cit.* pp. 56–60.

ment, not only is not political free but often creates a spirit precisely the reverse."[53] This leads to a conception of society as composed of various political systems, each of which is potentially open to democratisation. As I have mentioned, Mill was not able to incorporate these theoretical principles into his actual proposals, but this was done more convincingly by Cole in his scheme for representation through associations on a functional basis.

Thus the central element in this work is the concern with democracy as educative, as the basis for a social and individual learning process, and the extension of democratisation to spheres other than the conventionally political. Both of these elements can be sharply distinguished from the concept of democracy put forward by Schumpeter and other "contemporary" theorists. It can be seen clearly that there is a close relationship to my earlier claims as to the role of public law; that of designing a variety of institutions within which a learning process could take place. Once more the link between public law and democratisation becomes obvious so long as one does not see Parliament as the sole institution for constitutional legitimacy.

Parliament and "Measurement and Publicity"

So far I have been discussing Parliament as an institution within which representation of interests takes place and in which deliberation on policy decisions is expected. I now will discuss a different element in Parliament's functions; that of a means of accountability. Accountability must mean the development and institutionalisation of the means for obtaining and publicly testing information forming reasons for decisions. It can thus also be seen as part of a learning process; to quote a recent writer on accountability of nationalised industries, it should be regarded as "a co-operative and improving process, whereby, in the course of explaining their policies, practices, and performances to a basically friendly but impartial, expert critic, managements perceive more clearly their strengths and weaknesses and the hazards and opportunities of their situation."[54] I will deal briefly here with one aspect of this; the role of Parliament in assessing the efficiency of nationalised industries. This is an example of what the Webbs termed "measurement and publicity," and which they saw as essential in the establishment of democratically controlled institutions.[55]

---

[53] John Stuart Mill, *Collected Works* (J.M. Robson ed., University of Toronto Press, 1965), p. 944, quoted in Patemen, *op. cit.* p. 30.
[54] Maurice Garner, "Auditing the Efficiency of Nationalised Industries: Enter the Monopolies and Mergers Commission" (1982) 60 *Public Administration* 409–428.
[55] *Op. cit.* pp. 186–202, 328–330.

My concern with efficiency audit of nationalised industries is one which concerns the ability of Parliament to scrutinise the use of public money. The general powers of Parliament to control and scrutinise expenditure are notoriously weak; this appears not only from the classic account of the management of public expenditure in Britain[56] but also in recent reports from Parliamentary committees, and is enhanced by the growing stress placed on government borrowing in the management of the economy.[57] As we have seen, the form of public ownership adopted after the second world war was based on the Morrisonian model of an "arm's length" separation from direct political control. In practice this did not prove politically feasible; even if it had proved feasible, what was neglected was that Morrison's model had incorporated as an essential element quite sophisticated machinery for "measurement and publicity"[58]; Apart from these proposals, effective scrutiny by Parliament would have had to involve access to the books of the industries by the Comptroller and Auditor-General, in order to be able to engage in detailed study and to provide expert assistance to the Public Accounts Committee. Such access was not provided, despite the fact that it had existed in relation to, for example, the pre-nationalisation Coal Commission. Instead, the accounts of the industries were to be audited in the normal way by commercial auditors; as the leading authority on public audit has described, such formal financial and regularity audit does not give any useful information as to efficiency.[59]

In the areas in which the Auditor-General had audit powers or access, his concerns have developed beyond financial and regularity audit to examination of economy and efficiency, and also the assessment of whether policies undertaken to meet established goals had effectively met them.[60] Moreover his examinations increasingly have become systems-based examining the adequacy of management information systems, control systems, etc., rather than criticising individual decisions.[61] In relation to the nationalised industries, concern for the extension of the Auditor-General access declined with the establishment of the Select Committee on Nationalised Industries from the mid-nineteen-fifties. This, however, was unable to undertake continuing efficiency studies of the industries and did not have the assistance of

---

[56] Heclo and Wildavsky, *op. cit.* esp. pp. 242–263 and lii–liii.
[57] See Select Committee on Procedure (Supply), H.C. 18, 1980–1, and Select Committee on Procedure (Finance), H.C. 24, 1982–3.
[58] Morrison, *op. cit.* esp. pp. 289–293.
[59] Select Committee on Procedure, 1977–78, H.C. 588, App. 43, by Dr. E. Leslie Normanton. See also Cmnd. 7845, para. 10.
[60] Cmnd. 7845, para. 10.
[61] *Ibid.* para. 14.

a specialised scrutineer like the Auditor-General. With the setting up of the new Departmental structure of committees in 1979, the Committee on Nationalised Industries no longer exists.

The last few years have seen an increased concern to extend the powers of the Comptroller to give him access to the books of the industries. In the late nineteen-seventies both the House of Commons Expenditure Committee and the Procedure Committee made recommendations which would have had the effect of extending the remit of the Auditor-General to cover the industries.[62] The proposals by the Committees were that, in principle, the Auditor-General should be able to follow public funds, or more specifically, monies voted by Parliament, wherever they went. The Green Paper in response,[63] however, argued that the scope of his examination should reflect only the extent òf Ministerial responsibility to Parliament; otherwise, it suggested, there would be no sanction to back up his proposals.[64] It resurrected the myth that day-to-day running of the industries was for management, not government and contended that the extension of the role of the Auditor-General to cover the industries would be seen by them as a serious threat to their commercial freedom of action and would probably necessitate greater government intervention in their day-to-day affairs.[65] After referring to the powers of the Monopolies and Mergers Commission to investigate industries (this will be discussed below) the proposals were rejected in the Green Paper.

The Public Accounts Committee then produced a report highly critical of the Government's attitude.[66] It stressed that the Paper had not tackled the fundamental question about the need for satisfactory accountability to Parliament for public expenditure; scrutiny arrangements had failed to keep up with the growth in public expenditure of this century.[67] The Auditor-General himself had recommended that he be given access to the books of the nationalised industries and other public corporations, including the National Enterprise Board. The Nationalised Industries' Chairmen's Group had however strongly opposed an extension of access in their evidence; the main arguments they used were that they were accountable to Parliament already through the sponsoring minister, that access would not contribute to their efficiency and might hinder their ability to operate commercially, and that there was already a proliferation of bodies investigating the

---

[62] Expenditure Committee, H.C. 535, 1976–77, Procedure Committee H.C. 588, 1977–78.
[63] Cmnd. 7845.
[64] *Ibid*. para. 26.
[65] *Ibid*. paras. 46, 49.
[66] Committee of Public Accounts, H.C. 115, 1980–81.
[67] *Ibid*. paras. 1.3 and 1.6.

affairs of the industries, in particular the Monopolies and Mergers Commission.[68] The Committee did not accept the argument that Parliamentary scrutiny should be limited by the extent of ministerial responsibility; as Parliament currently had to rely on information provided by ministers, it had no means of satisfying itself that ministerial intervention was itself soundly based. It also noted that the Auditor-General would not "second-guess" commercial decisions, as the industry chairmen had suggested, but had described to them that his concern would be "systems of control and of assessment by the industries . . . and also their relations with Government."[69] After considering a variety of arguments on principle and matters of practice, the Committee recommended that the books of the nationalised industries and all other public corporations including the National Enterprises Board, should be subject to the scrutiny of the Auditor-General; and access for him should be a condition of all grants or loans from Government departments to other bodies, whether operating commercially or not.[70]

The Report contained a number of other important recommendations concerning the Auditor-General; the Government replied in a very brief White Paper which was later described by M.P.s of all parties in highly derogatory terms; "an appalling and shameful response from the Treasury," "a timid, trivial and disappointing document . . . offensive to Parliament," "the most perfect example of 'Yes Minister' ever produced outside the BBC."[71] The White Paper resurrected the primacy of Ministerial responsibility; "This constitutional convention does not fit all cases neatly but remains the only effective means by which Parliament can hold to account those to whom money is voted."[72] It was considered that the extent of Ministerial responsibility should be taken account of in determining the range of the Auditor-General's audit and this, together with the existence of the Monopolies and Mergers Commission were used as arguments for not extending his powers to the nationalised industries or other bodies including the National Enterprise Board.[73]

It is worth saying a little more about two of the arguments used against the extension of access for the Auditor-General. The first is

---

[68] *Ibid.* para. 4.10, and evidence, questions 1006–1081 and App. XXV.
[69] *Ibid.* paras. 4.11, 4.15. For the Comptroller's views as to his role, see App. XLII.
[70] *Ibid.* para. 4.21.
[71] See the adjournment debate after over 300 M.P.s from all parties had signed an Early Day Motion calling for legislation based on the Report; 14 H.C. Deb., cols. 39–112, November 30, 1981. The quotations are from Joel Barnett at cols. 39–40, Edward du Cann at col. 60, and Sir Albert Costain at col. 83.
[72] Cmnd. 8323, para. 3.
[73] *Ibid.* paras. 10–12.

that the industries were already accountable through the Minister to Parliament. Apart from any general weaknesses in Ministerial responsibility to Parliament, recent studies have made it clear that Departmental arrangements for monitoring the industries are quite inadequate. Thus the major report by the National Economic Development Office in 1976 found that "boards are not effectively required to account for their performance in a systematic or objective manner—whether it be to Parliament, to Ministers, or other legitimate interest groups or to the wider public."[74] Despite attempts to improve relations in the 1978 White Paper, a report by the Public Accounts Committee on the Monitoring and Control Activities of the Sponsoring Department of three nationalised industries found major problems still existed; thus the corporate planning procedures claimed to be central to relations between industries and government had broken down in the case of two of the industries covered in the examination, and there were other failures to supply information by the industries and inadequacies of monitoring; for example, the Department of Industry had failed to recognise a breach by one industry of a condition attached to its external financing limit that certain funds should only be used on capital expenditure.[75] The Committee concluded that "sponsor department and Treasury control is insufficient to ensure that the industries keep to the planned use of public funds."[76] This problem is not one which affected only the traditional nationalised industries; a series of reports by the Public Accounts Committee was also critical of the arrangements for monitoring Rolls Royce (1971) and BL, both when they were under the auspices of the National Enterprise Board and later when they reported directly to the Department.[77] It should also be remembered that, even if ministerial monitoring was excellent, this would not necessarily result in more information being available to Parliament in view of the limited range of matters relating to the industries for which ministers have been prepared to answer.[78] Nor would it enable proper examination of ministerial interventions in the industries.

A variant on the argument that the Auditor-General's powers should not extend beyond the range of direct ministerial responsibility is that without direct ministerial powers no sanction is available to enforce the Auditor-General's recommendations.[79] The question of

[74] National Economic Development Office, *op. cit.* pp. 38–39.
[75] H.C. 139, 1983–84, paras. 14, 28 and 29.
[76] *Ibid.* para. 41.
[77] See 1976–77, H.C. 531; 1977–78, H.C. 621; 1979–80, H.C. 446; 1979–80, H.C. 779; 1981–82, H.C. 407; and 1983–84, H.C. 103.
[78] See 1976–77, H.C. 521, para. 47.
[79] See Cmnd. 7855, para. 26, Cmnd. 8323, para. 3 and 14 H.C. Deb., col. 111 (The Financial Secretary to the Treasury), November 30, 1981.

what sanction is available where there is no such direct responsibility has been neatly answered by Garner in an account of the Monopolies and Mergers Commission; "It is difficult to believe that the answer to that question was unknown to a government which was even then planning to dump the Chairman of the CEGB and which regards external financing limits as an essential instrument 'for exerting a sustained discipline to contain costs and raise productivity. . . .' "[80] The fundamental irony must be that the doctrine of ministerial responsibility, whilst appearing to be a means of ensuring accountability, has here been used as a means for preventing accountability which does not fit within neat nineteenth-century constitutional categories.

A second important argument used against extending the Auditor-General's powers is that it is unnecessary because of the powers of the Monopolies and Mergers Commission under section 11 of the Competition Act 1980. This empowers the Secretary of State to refer to the Commission any question relating to the efficiency and costs of, the service provided by, or possible abuse of a monopoly situation, by a nationalised industry covered by the Act. The central point which distinguishes this from the potential role of the Auditor-General is that it is a matter for ministerial discretion; it is the Secretary of State who decides which industries to refer, who decides the terms of the reference and takes follow-up action. As a concession after criticism of the Treasury White Paper, it was announced that a more regular system of references would be adopted in which each major nationalised industry would have at least one major reference every four years, and more effective follow-up procedures would be adopted.[81] This does not however change the essential role of these references which is of a means of Ministerial control rather than Parliamentary accountability; it is possible for government to confine the examinations to areas and times convenient to itself but not necessarily those of public concern. As Garner has put it, "Effectively, therefore, efficiency auditing has been introduced in a manner that considerably strengthens ministerial control whilst making only incidental and indirect contributions to accountability to Parliament."[82]

The later history of this tangled area can be dealt with briefly. After the White Paper, Norman St. John Stevas introduced as a private member's measure the Parliamentary Control of Expenditure (Reform) Bill which in its original form would have extended the

---

[80] Garner, *op. cit.* p. 426, quoting the Treasury and Civil Service Select Committee, 1980–81, H.C. 348, Vol. II, p. 45.

[81] See 14 H.C. Deb, cols. 48–9 (The Financial Secretary to the Treasury), November 30, 1981.

[82] Garner, *op. cit.* p. 425.

access of the Auditor-General to the books of nationalised industries (repealing the provisions of the Competition Act), other publicly owned corporations and any company of which more than 50 per cent. of the voting shares were publicly owned, and would have empowered him to undertake audits of the economy, efficiency and effectiveness of those concerns. In second reading of the Bill this was largely welcomed by M.P.s of all parties and the Bill was sent to Committee unopposed. The Treasury spokesman, had, however, expressed concern at the effect of the nationalised industry provisions and reference was made to a campaign by chairmen of the industries against it; at least one of them had threatened to resign if the Bill became law in its original form.[83] In committee much of the Bill was replaced by Government drafted amendments and the Government proposed that the clause in question be replaced by a somewhat unsatisfactory compromise, imposing a duty on private auditors to undertake annual economy, efficiency and effectiveness audits of the industries. After some fears by members of the Committee that the whole Bill might be jeopardised by the inclusion of this compromise it was rejected and the original provision covering the nationalised industries was taken out of the Bill.[84] Indeed, Stevas himself voted against it, presumably to prevent government opposition to it leading to the loss of the whole Bill. As enacted as the National Audit Act 1983 the legislation makes important reforms to the office of the Auditor-General and his staff and provides statutory authority for his established practice of undertaking economy, efficiency and effectiveness audits of government departments and extends this to certain other bodies mainly supported by government funds.[85] However the nationalised industries are specifically excluded from these provisions and the terms of the Act are not such as to cover publicly-owned companies such as Rolls-Royce and B.L. It might be added that the position of the successor to the National Enterprise Board, the relatively small scale British Technology Group is highly anomalous. It was formed in September 1981 by merger of the Board with the National Research Development Corporation but statutory effect has not yet been given to this. The accounts of the latter organisation had been audited by the Auditor-General and continue to be so audited, whilst those of the Board still do not fall within his powers. The Public Accounts Committee has recommended that he be given access to all the accounts of the Group, to which weight was added by the Committee's failure to find an adequate explanation of a major loss incurred by one of the Group's

---

[83] 35 H.C. Deb., cols. 1149–1214, January 28, 1983.
[84] See Standing Committee C, cols. 148–246, March 30 and April 13 and 30, 1983.
[85] ss.6–7.

wholly-owned subsidiaries.[86] Problems of lack of access also hindered the Committee in its investigation of serious allegations of impropriety in relation to the disposal of the Bathgate tractor assembly line by a susbsidiary of BL. Although the Committee did not find evidence to support the allegations, it stressed how the refusal of BL to allow access to its books had limited its ability to engage in investigations. Once more the Committee recommended the extension of the powers of access of the Auditor-General to cover such bodies.[87]

In this section I have provided an example, which could be usefully supplemented if space were available, of the limited extent of accountability through Parliament for workings of public institutions in the modern economy. It also illustrates the ease with which government is able to prevent any more effective assertion of Parliamentary accountability which might lead to criticism of government. It is now time for me to summarise the themes from this contribution as a whole.

Conclusion

My argument has thus been that public law's central concerns should be first the mapping out of the interrelationship of public institutions with each other and their relations with the private sphere. Secondly, the concern should be the design of institutions within which a learning process could take place through the institutionalisation of procedures for participation and accountability. I have suggested that the centrality of Parliament as a legitimating forum in the British political culture had resulted in a lack of concern with such institutional design in Britain, despite the ineffectiveness of Parliament as a forum for rational discourse and as a means of accountability.[88] It is time for us to think of the building of a variety of democratic institutions rather than concentrating on Parliament as *the* institutional form.

What are the current prospects for the development of new forms of democratic institution in Britain? Some of the evolutionary writers referred to earlier see the development of reflexive law as socially necessary in a functionally differentiated society.[89] Nevertheless, the current prospects for its development in Britain appear grim. Corporatist means of legitimation have been progressively dismantled under the present Government without new legal forms of legitimation having been created to replace them.[90] Yet the types of ideology

---

[86] 1983–84, H.C. 144, paras. 30–31.
[87] 1981–82 H.C. 407, paras. 2, 32–4.
[88] See Lewis and Harden, *op. cit.*
[89] Teubner, *op. cit.* esp. pp. 262–264, and Luhmann, *op. cit.*
[90] Norman Lewis and Paul Wiles, "The Post-Corporatist State?" (1984) 11 J. of Law and Society 65–90.

associated with Thatcherism, a somewhat unstable coalition of claims to economic liberalism and a "strong state," nevertheless seem to have had a remarkable force as legitimation.[91] As regards legal forms, the current constitutional developments, far from the "autonomous law" associated with neo-liberal writers such as Hayek,[92] are characterised by the unregulated discretionary powers and ad hoc intervention most notably illustrated by central government policies towards local government. Indeed, they seem closest to the least developed type of law referred to by the evolutionary theorists discussed earlier; that of "repressive law" with its cardinal features of the subordination of legal institutions to governing elites and rampant official discretion.[93]

Thus, from the viewpoint set out in this contribution prospects for public law development in Britain appear depressing. Nevertheless, the importance of generating the conditions for the subjection of public life to rational debate remains as important as ever. Most important of all, perhaps, is to engage in theoretical and empirical mapping of the British state and its relations to other institutions as a means of developing beyond the outdated orthodoxies which currently dominate constitutional thought. As the leading account of the management of public expenditure has put it:

> "At the hands of its interpreters, the British constitution is an oracle which can only tell you why any and every particular change contemplated will not work. . . . Its principles are ethereal bodies unable to offer any positive guidance but always ready to descend on any change as a violation of their spirit. To summon these Harpies, you need only suggest something different."[94]

If this contribution has had any value it will have been to suggest that it is timely and indeed possible to move beyond reliance on oracles.

---

[91] Andrew Gamble, "The Free Economy and the Strong State" in *The Socialist Register* (Ralph Miliband and John saville eds., Merlin Press, London, 1979).
[92] See F.A. Hayek, *The Road to Serfdom* (Routledge & Kegan Paul, London, 1944). *The Constitution of Liberty* (Routledge & Kegan Paul, London, 1960), and *Law, Legislation and Liberty* (Routlege & Kegan Paul, London), 3 vols. 1973, 1976 and 1979.
[93] Nonet and Selznick, *op. cit.* p. 51.
[94] Heclo and Wildavsky, *op. cit.* pp. 340–341.

Chapter 9

THE REFORM OF PUBLIC LAW IN BRITAIN: THEORETICAL PROBLEMS AND PRACTICAL CONSIDERATIONS[1]

MARTIN PARTINGTON

Introduction

Most writers on public law in Britain have called for reforms in that law. But most such calls have tended to be specific in character, focussing on suggestions for, *e.g.* new courts, or new procedures or new remedies, or on particular issues, such as controls over the administrative discretion, or the need for greater freedom of official information. It is certainly the case that if one looks at the reforms in public law that have actually occurred in recent years, they have developed in a completely piece-meal, fragmented fashion, with no sense of structure or coherence.[2] Some may argue that, in pragmatic Britain, this is the only way of doing things; that tinkering is better than no tinkering; and that, in any event, grand schemes would never be implemented. But fragmentation may also disguise laziness, a failure of effort to think more broadly about the kind of public law that our contemporary society needs.[3]

In a collection of essays published to celebrate the 100th anniversary

---

[1] This paper has developed out of and is a substantially revised version of a lecture delivered in the University of Newcastle-upon-Tyne and Newcastle Polytechnic in March 1984. I am grateful to those who commented on the lecture at the time; also to Professor D.G.T. Williams, Professor P. McAuslan, Dr. C. Harlow and, my colleagues, Dr. R. Baldwin and Dr. R. Dhavan for many additional suggestions. They bear no responsibility for what follows.

[2] Consider the following developments over the last 30 years or so: The Franks Report on Tribunals and Inquiries, 1957; The Tribunals and Inquiries Acts 1958, 1971; the Creation of the Council on Tribunals; the passing of the Parliamentary Commissioner for Administration Act 1967; the creation of local government commissioners and health service commissioners; the making of Order 53 Rules of the Supreme Court (Supreme Court Act 1981, s.31). These developments, though important, do not smack of a "grand strategy."

[3] There are notable exceptions to this generalisation: see in particular, Prosser, "Towards a Critical Public Law" (1982) 9 J. of Law and Soc. 1–19, and the works discussed therein; and, from an earlier generation, Robson, *Justice and Administrative Law* (3rd ed., Stevens, 1951).

191

of Dicey's work, it may be useful to ask the question of whether it is possible to devise, on the basis both of theoretical and practical considerations, a strategy for the reform of public law. This paper does not purport to set down a blue-print for such a strategic development. Apart from any other consideration, any given strategy will depend, as I hope to demonstrate, on the views one takes of the nature and purpose of public law. But it is hoped that the paper may nonetheless make a contribution to an important debate about an essential aspect of the ways in which we organise our society and run our affairs, by attempting to identify the main issues that need to be considered in the creation of such a strategy.

This paper is divided into four main sections. In the first, basic issues of principle will be discussed; in the second, the question will be posed as to whether current legal provisions relating to the accountability of government in Britain are adequate; in the third, there will be a consideration of developments in public law in Australia, where there has been an important attempt to devise a coherent legislative strategy for the development of public law; and in the final section, some broad conclusions will be drawn.

I. *Some Basic Issues*

(a) *Theories of public law*

All writing on public law is underpinned by some theoretical perspective, however dimly perceived or narrowly conceived. Furthermore, the theoretical perspective adopted in relation to public law also assumes (either explicitly or implicitly) a theory of the role of the State, and the nature and extent of the power which it is appropriate for the State to exercise in that society.[4]

At one end of the scale, some public lawyers and other political theorists (from Dicey onwards) have clearly been worried about the expanding scope of public power. They appear to wish that state power should be restricted to a limited range of fundamental issues such as the maintenance of law and order and the defence of the realm. Other assertions of the state's power they would claim are improper and should be left to other mechanisms, in particular market mechanisms. In discussing public law, therefore, they suggest that the primary purpose of public law should be to create techniques by which controls, in particular legal controls, should be placed on the exercise of public

---

[4] For an introduction to the theoretical positions outlined in the next three paragraphs see the excellent discussion in C. Harlow and R. Rawlings, *Law and Administration* (Weidenfeld & Nicolson, 1984), esp. Chaps. 1 & 2: "Red Light Theories" and "Green Light Theories."

power. Such writers have recently been described as "red-light" theorists, advocating a *control* model for public law.

By contrast, other public lawyers take a different view of the role of the state, arguing that the exercise of power by the state over a wide range of social and economic policies is the quite proper, indeed inevitable, response to the inadequacies or failures of alternative mechanisms, especially the market. This view of the existence and exercise of public/state power is thus more benign than that of the "red-light" theorists. Indeed, they would argue that since the purpose of the exercise of public power is to achieve broadly accepted political, social and economic objectives, the primary responsibility for ensuring that such objectives are met should be through the *political* system, not the legal system, and that public law, as such, should play a relatively unimportant part in controlling the exercise of power by the state.[5] Those who offer this kind of analysis have been described as "green-light theorists," who prefer to see accountability of government achieved primarily through the *political* process, rather than through the law.

Yet others, adopting what might be described as a middle position (the "amber theorists"), would concede the desirability and need for the exercise of public power and thus reject the view that public law should be seen exclusively in terms of the *control* of such power, but would argue that reliance on traditional political techniques for promoting accountability and control, such as parliamentary questions, political debates, ministerial responsibility, select committees, and the like, is, as a matter of practical reality, inadequate, and that forms of political control need to be buttressed by forms of legal control. More recently it has been argued that, in addition to measures of control, or accountability, another objective of public law should be to encourage the *participation* of citizens in the decision-taking processes of government.[6]

The three theoretical positions outlined above are only crude models; an infinite range of alternative possibilities exists within these broad parameters. But they do serve to highlight the bases on which any strategy for reform of public law must be founded. If one is not explicit about one's theoretical starting point, it is unlikely that any coherent view will emerge.

[5] This is not to assert that the actual interventions by the State have always achieved their objectives; for an analysis of this issue, with a conclusion that intervention has tended to be more beneficial than non-intervention, see V. George & P. Wilding, *The Impact of Social Policy* (Routledge & Kegan Paul, London, 1984).

[6] This point is made, particularly, by Prosser, above, note 3. See also J. Ely, *Democracy and Distrust: A Theory of Judicial Review* (Harvard U.P., Cambridge, Mass., 1980).

Underlying this paper, therefore, is the proposition that the so-called "amber" theory of public law is the most useful basis for considering questions of the reform of public law in Britain in the late twentieth century. This assumes that it is appropriate for the state to exercise a wide range of public powers; the primary means of setting limits to the scope of that power must be by way of the political process; but legal means will be an important, indeed essential, supplement to the political process.[7]

(b) *The positive and negative nature of public law*

The assertion of a basic theoretical starting point is, however, only the first stage in devising a strategy for reform. We need to consider, next, what is meant by public law. It is essential to recognise that public law has both positive and negative features.

The positive side of public law relates to what may be described as the "substantive" or "power-conferring" aspects of public law. It is the substantive rules of public law that, *inter alia*, prescribe the government's powers to dispense largesse (*e.g.* the provision of welfare benefits or the granting of licences), to impose and collect taxation, to regulate a whole variety of aspects of industrial life and, more generally, the private sector of the economy, to establish and run nationalised enterprises, to maintain law and order, to defend the realm, and so on.

The negative side of public law consists of the procedural rules which relate to "review" or "power-control" or more generally "accountability." It is this branch of public law that defines the procedures and jurisdictional bases that may be used by the citizen or other groups[8] to call officials to account, or otherwise to attempt to influence the decision-taking process. This branch of "public law" operates not only in the courts on which many public lawyers concentrate, but in other contexts as well: tribunals, inquiries, ombudsmen, conciliation agencies, and other more or less formal complaints procedures.[9] In addition, this branch of public law also defines the remedies that may be available to those who are aggrieved, in one way or another, by the decisions of public authorities. By contrast with substantive public law, much of the "review" branch of public law has

[7] A most elegant analysis of the issue of "control" is by A. Dunsire "Administrative Law and Control on Government" (1984) 24 *Malaya Law Review*, 79–119.

[8] Including, of course, other governmental agencies: see P. McAuslan, "Inter-agency disputes and the politicisation of administrative law in England" (Unpublished paper for Conference on Comparative Administration and Law, 1984).

[9] The point is stressed by Harlow and Rawlings, *op. cit.* note 4.

been developed by the judiciary without direct statutory intervention, though specific areas of the law on review (*e.g.* relating to tribunals and inquiries) do derive from statute.

The essential point in these possibly rather obvious remarks is that too many public lawyers—basing themselves on the Diceyan tradition—have focussed their attention more or less exclusively on the *negative* side of public law, but have failed to relate this to the *positive* side. The emphasis has been on control, without any explicit consideration of what it is intended should be controlled. This has given much writing on public law a rather charming fairy-tale quality in which principles of law are asserted, but totally divorced from any social or political reality. It must now be recognised that public law should be seen "in the round," for if there is no awareness or recognition of the positive side, discussion of the negative side will be of limited value.

(c) *The many facets of public law*

The next point which needs emphasis, and which develops out of the last section, is that public law has many facets. These are evidenced in a number of ways:

(i) *The range of powers exercised by the organs of government.* Government exercises a wide variety of *types* of public power. It is absurd to regard, say, the powers of the state to defend the realm in the same way as, say, the powers of the state to grant welfare benefits, or to provide a system of education. The range of powers exercised by the state suggests, clearly, that a single means of attempting to ensure accountability would be misplaced; if there is a plurality of powers, equally there must be a plurality in the means of accountability.

(ii) *The range of organs of state which exercise public power.* A wide variety of agencies has been granted jurisdiction to exercise public law powers. They include central government, local authorities, nationalised industries, quangos of various kinds, and other public or quasi-public bodies.[10] In addition, bodies formally in the private sector, are increasingly subject to regulatory principles found in areas of public law. Again, it is important that the variety of exercisers of public power be recognised since the appropriate means of accountability or control are likely to vary sharply as between, for example, elected and non-elected agencies, centralised and localised bodies, public and private enterprises.

(iii) *The range of sources of public law.* Traditional legal theory

---

[10] See, on this issue, P. Craig, *Administrative Law* (Sweet & Maxwell, 1983) Chap. 1.

suggests that the substantive rules of public law must be found exclusively in formal rules of law—statutes, statutory instruments, cases, European law. It is becoming increasingly recognised that such a view is inadequate. For long, an important, though relatively neglected, source of substantive public law has been the royal prerogative. More recently there has been a rapid increase in the range of non-statutory rules, codes of guidance, discretionary codes, ministerial directives, agency rules, and the like, which are not regarded as "law" within a traditional jurisprudential framework, but which are nonetheless "rules" with substantive effect and in relation to which the theory and practice of public law must take account.[11]

(iv) *The range of methods of accountability.* There are few writers on public law who would now argue that the courts are to be seen as the *exclusive* focus for the operation of the "power-controlling" rules of public law—account is taken by most authors of tribunals, inquiries, ombudsmen and other methods of accountability. However the balance in the literature is often misplaced. Too many authors still write as though they assume that the *primary* focus of study must be on the courts where it is felt that the "real action" takes place.[12] Legal practitioners will often have an exclusively "court-focussed" view of the forums for pursuing questions of accountability. Such a distortion may derive partly from their legal education; partly, and more importantly perhaps, it will have arisen from the fact that work which focusses on or leads towards hearings in *court* is the work for which lawyers are usually paid, whereas work directed towards other forums of accountability tends to be ill-rewarded, or not paid for at all. Although the courts may be, in some senses, the most authoritative forum, they are by no means the exclusive forum and their relatively high-profile must not divert attention from other lower-profile forums.

If we accept that the scope of public methods of accountability must be seen as extending beyond the courts, a further question arises of where these extensions should stop. For example, some lawyers, often referred to as public interest lawyers,[13] would argue that it is appropriate for lawyers to operate, as lawyers, in any forum for negotiation with or challenge to government, including what have traditionally been regarded as exclusively political channels. This development

---

[11] See, *e.g.* R.E. Megarry "Administrative Quasi-Legislation" (1944) 60 L.Q.R. 125. This question is implicit in much of the analysis by Harlow & Rawlings, *op. cit.* note. 4.

[12] The recently published study by Harlow and Rawlings, *op. cit.* provides an important corrective for those who adopt such a view.

[13] For an introduction to the notion of public interest law, see my "Public Interest Law" (1979) *Legal Action Group Bulletin* 225.

must be borne in mind when we consider the proper scope of public law today, and in particular the means of accountability.

II. *Is the British System of Public Law Adequate?*

Having identified a number of general issues that need to be borne in mind when attempting to analyse public law, I turn, in this section, to the more basic question of whether the present state of British public law is adequate for the current needs of that society. This discussion will focus in particular on the "negative" side of public law, relating to methods of accountability.

Some may feel that this question does not even need to be raised; that there are already adequate legal checks on the operation of government.[14] After all, it can be said that the courts have developed principles of administrative law whereby judicial review of administrative action is possible. Allegations of maladministration can be placed before a variety of ombudsmen. There are apparently endless varieties of tribunal and inquiry which have jurisdiction to review specific categories of administrative decision. Even M.P.s may get questions asked in Parliament, or intervene behind the scenes to review administrative decisions or check on the accuracy of information held.

To be sure, a first glance might suggest that there is a formidable array of procedures. Yet it is clear that many do not regard this collection of procedures as an adequate framework for the legal control of government. In recent years many writers[15] have analysed the essential features of our administrative law and found it inadequate for modern conditions. And such criticism has not been confined to the work of academic scholars.[16]

What kinds of inadequacy have been identified? It is not possible here to offer a catalogue of all the complaints that have been laid at the

---

[14] Certainly a number of writers on administrative law imply that, so long as the courts remain active and aware of their role in controlling the administration, all should be well: see, *e.g.* H.W.R. Wade, *Administrative Law* (5th ed., 1982), Chap. 1.

[15] See, *e.g.* Prosser, *op. cit.*: M. Loughlin, "Procedural Fairness: A Study of the Crisis in Administrative Law Theory" (1978) 28 *Univ. of Toronto Law Journal* 215; R.B. Stewart, "The Reformation of American Administrative Law" 88 Harvard L.Rev. 1669 (1975); P. McAuslan "Administrative Law and Administrative Theory: The Dismal Performance of Administrative Lawyers" 9 *Cambrian Law Rev.* 40 (1978).

[16] See, for example, the work of the Justice—All Souls Conference on Administrative Law; Interim Report, April 1981. It had been hoped to include in this chapter an analysis of their final report. Regrettably it was not available at the time of writing. See however, A.E. Boyle "Reforming Administrative Law" (1984) *Public Law* 521.

door of British public law; but some of the most important may be identified as follows:

(i) Too many of the methods, theoretically provided by the legal system, for calling the executive to account are hedged around with uncertainty or unnecessary complexity. For example, the parliamentary or local councillor "filters" to the exercise by the central and local government ombudsmen of their jurisdiction over allegations of maladministration are now seen by many as a quite unnecessary complexity, which merely has the effect of reducing the access of the public to these means of redress.[17] A similar kind of criticism is made in relation to many aspects of court procedure; for example the basis on which standing to sue will be recognised,[18] or the circumstances in which the courts will assert jurisdiction[19] over differing kinds of administrative action are widely regarded as being so unclear that they too act as a deterrent to those who may seek to use the courts.

(ii) Criticism has frequently been voiced over the inadequacies of the remedies that may be obtained whether in the courts, or in other contexts, in particular the ombudsmen.[20]

(iii) Inadequate legal assistance is available in many cases where, in principle, it should be provided, for example because the legal aid scheme does not extend to most tribunals.[21]

In addition to these rather specific criticisms about the present methods of establishing the accountability of public officials to the rule of law, three rather more fundamental criticisms may be made:

(a) Perhaps most important of all, the attitude of successive British governments to the question of official secrets, and the failure to allow the public greater freedom of information about what goes on in the public domain has made it extremely difficult for all but the lucky or the most determined to call the government, at either central or local level, to account for its actions.[22]

(b) There is a whole range of public bodies that exercise a wide

---

[17] See, *e.g.* Justice, *Our Fettered Ombudsmen* (Justice, 1977); Cohen, "The Parliamentary Commissioner and the 'M.P.' Filter" (1972) *Public Law* 32.

[18] See the analysis in Craig, *op. cit.* above, note 10.

[19] See, generally, S.A. de Smith, *Judicial Review of Administrative Action* (4th ed., by J.M. Evans, Sweet & Maxwell, 1980).

[20] Consider, for example, discussion of the applicability of common law principles of compensation in the context of public law disputes: P. Craig, "Compensation in Public Law" (1980) 96 L.Q.R. 413; C. Harlow, *Compensation and Government Torts* (Sweet & Maxwell, 1982).

[21] There is an extensive literature on this point: see, *e.g.* M. Zander, *Legal Services for the Community* (Temple Smith, 1978), Chap. 1.

[22] See, *e.g.* the discussion in D.G.T. Williams, *Not in the Public Interest* (Hutchinson, 1965).

variety of public law powers that are subject to only limited or barely effective means of accountability.

(c) There is no single body or agency charged with the role of analysing the substantive rules of public law, to see whether they should be subject to additional forms of or forums for accountability, and if so, suggesting what these forms of accountability should take.

In short, although there exists in Britain a variety of legal means of calling the executive branch of government to account, it cannot be described as a coherent system, but rather an unco-ordinated hotchpotch. The next question to be posed, therefore, is whether a more co-ordinated structure could be created, and, are there lessons from overseas which might help in this endeavour?

III. *Lessons from Overseas: The Australian Model*

If it be accepted that we still have a need in this country for a principled body of administrative law, aimed at the legal control of state power, or, more precisely, rendering the exercise of state power more accountable in law, the question now to be addressed is whether we might be assisted in devising such a body of law by learning from experience abroad.

It is already the case that the eyes of some commentators have turned to the United States.[23] However, for a variety of reasons, developments in the United States are often regarded with deep suspicion here. In particular, although there are obvious attractions in examining legal developments in another English-language, common law jurisdiction, apparent similarities between our two cultures may well distract attention from the fact that, whatever its origins, the American legal system has developed a very different *character* from the British. Nowhere is this more true than in the context of the development of administrative law.[24] In any event, the emphasis in American administrative law on the use of adversary legal procedures as the primary legal tool for control of public power has recently begun to come under increasing attack.[25] It is thus rather less use as a comparative model than might at first appear.[26]

[23] See, *e.g.* B. Schwarz and H.W.R. Wade, *Legal Control of Government: Administrative Law in Britain and the United States* (Oxford U.P., 1972).

[24] See R.B. Stewart "Reform of American Administrative Law: The Academic Agenda vs. the Political Agenda" (Unpublished paper for Conference on Comparative Administration and Law, 1984).

[25] See, *e.g.* R.B. Stewart, *op. cit.* above, note 24, and note 15; also S. Breyer, *Regulation and its Reform* (Harvard U.P., 1982).

[26] For a general discussion of these issues see O. Kahn-Freund, "Comparative Law as an Academic Subject" (1966) 82 L.Q.R. 40; "On Uses and Misuses of Comparative Law" (1974) 37 M.L.R. 1. It is appreciated that this dismissal of the American experience will be regarded as far too cavalier by some readers. It must be excused by the exigencies of space.

Nonetheless, and notwithstanding the dangers of the comparative approach, I wish in the next section of this paper to draw attention to a series of developments that have occurred during the last 15–20 years in Australia which seem to me to be of major significance, but which have not attracted adequate attention in Britain.

(a) *The "New Administrative Law" in Australia*

The creation of what is now known as the "new administrative law"[27] in Australia can be said to have begun in 1965,[28] when Mr. Justice Else-Mitchell, then a judge in the Supreme Court of New South Wales, discussed the work of the (British) Franks Committee on Tribunals and Inquiries, and called for reform of administrative review procedures.[29] This inspired the Statute Law Revision Committee in the State of Victoria to prepare a report on Appeals for Administrative Decisions and an Office of Ombudsman. (This ultimately led to the Victorian Administrative Law Act 1978.) More importantly, for the purposes of this chapter there was established, in 1968 at the Federal level, a committee, known as the Commonwealth Administrative Review Committee under the chairmanship of Mr. Justice Kerr[30] whose primary purpose was to analyse what should be the administrative law jurisdiction of a new Federal Court, the creation of which had been urged earlier in the 1960s by the then Attorney-General Sir Garfield Barwick. However the Committee's terms of reference also allowed for the possibility of analysing, rather more deeply, fundamental issues as to whether existing procedures for obtaining review of administrative decisions were adequate; and whether the grounds for review were adequate.

Although all three members of the Kerr Committee were lawyers,[31] they determined to take a broad view of their task (influenced, to some

---

27 See J. Goldring, "The Foundations of the 'New Administrative Law' in Australia" (1981) 40 Aust. J. Pub. Admin. 79–102. Much of the following section is based on this account. See also his "Public Law and Accountability of Government," paper presented to Australian Universities Law Schools Association, 1981; a revised version was prepared in 1983, *cf*: B. Jinks, "The New Administrative Law: Some questions and assumptions" (1982) Aust. J. Pub. Admin. 209.

28 M. Kirby, "Reform and the bureaucracy" in *Reform the Law* (Oxford U.P., 1983), Chap. 6, p. 104.

29 "The Place of the Administrative Tribunal in 1965." Paper presented to the Commonwealth and Empire Law Conference, Sydney, 1965.

30 He later became Governor-General and was involved in the controversial decision to sack the Labour Prime Minister, Gough Whitlam, in 1975.

31 Besides Kerr, they were Prof. H. Whitmore, then Australia's leading academic public lawyer, but who also had considerable practical experience in the New South Wales' public service; and Mr. A.F. Mason, Q.C., later replaced by Mr. L.T. Elliott, Q.C., both Solicitors-General of Australia.

extent, by developments such as the Tribunals and Inquiries Act 1958, in the United Kingdom, and by other developments in the states of Australia). Their recommendations—published in 1971—fell under six broad but inter-related headings:

  (i) A *General Administrative Tribunal* should be established to review specified categories of administrative decision on questions both of law and of fact; the Committee argued that the Tribunal should also have power to substitute its own decisions for those of the original decision-maker;

  (ii) An *Administrative Review Council* should be set up. This was intended to supervise and co-ordinate the means of review, and advise on whether particular classes of administrative decision should be subject to review;

  (iii) An *Ombudsman*, or General Counsel for Grievances should be created, empowered to investigate maladministration;

  (iv) A *New Court* should be established to hear administrative cases under a simplified procedure for judicial review; the grounds for review were to be clarified and legislative obstacles to review were to be removed;

  (v) A legislative *Code of Procedure* for administrative tribunals was to be passed; and finally

  (vi) Greater *Public Access* should be given to government information, to allow a wider range of opportunities for challenges to governmental action.

It can thus be seen that the members of the committee had looked at developments that had occurred on a piecemeal, ad hoc basis in other countries, but had drawn them together and developed them, and laid down a strategic programme for the creation of a comprehensive administrative justice system, designed to make the Federal administration in Australia more accountable. Instead of the topsy-turvy system of individual tribunals that had developed in the United Kingdom, the Kerr proposal was for a single nationwide administrative tribunal, chaired by a judge, to promote standards of decision-taking generally across a wide spectrum of the (federal) administration. The Administrative Review Council would, unlike the British Council on Tribunals, not simply comment on existing and proposed tribunal and inquiry procedures, but would also generally oversee the federal administration and advise on those areas of administrative decision-taking that ought to be appealable to the Tribunal. The General Counsel for Grievances (Ombudsman) was to investigate *all* alleged instances of maladministration, not simply those over which no other remedy could be sought, and not only those referred by Members of Parliament. He would also be able to investigate on his own initiative;

he would not necessarily have to await a complaint from a member of the public. He would also be able to advise on appeal rights and even, it was recommended, represent individuals before the administrative tribunal in special cases.

These recommendations were not immediately enacted into law. Apart from anything else there was a considerable shock, horror reaction from the public service, who clearly had an interest in attempting to delay the implementation of the report's proposals. In the short term their opposition was successful for, instead of legislative action, a further committee was established, on administrative discretion. This was also a three man committee, this time chaired by Sir Henry Bland (a senior public servant), but which again included Professor Whitmore. It presented two reports, an *interim* one and a *final* one, in 1973.

The *interim* report focussed on the proposals of the Kerr Committee in relation to the Ombudsman/General Counsel for Grievances. Bland was concerned to keep the jurisdiction of the Counsel under control, and to try to ensure that policy making (as opposed to administration) was not subject to the Counsel's control. Bland's Committee thought the ombudsman should have a power to refuse to hear complaints; they recommended that he have no power to publish reports on his own initiative, but that all his reports should be referred to the relevant minister. And they sought to exclude large areas of administration from his jurisdiction. In short, the Bland Committee took a much more cautious approach than Kerr had done.

The *final* report of the Bland Committee was on the vexed question of administrative discretion, and the extent to which such discretion should/could be subject to review. Again, the tenor of the Bland Committee's report was more cautious than that of the Kerr Committee, although it did not dissent from the principle, clearly advanced by Kerr, that review on the merits in all fields of administration should be permitted, except in so far as it was totally impractical to allow such review.

(b) *Implementation of the new scheme*

Despite the delays that resulted from the appointment of the Bland Committee, legislation implementing the bulk of the Kerr Committee's proposals has now been forthcoming. It is worthy of note that, on balance, the more radical stance of the Kerr Committee's report has been preferred as the basis for legislation to that of the more cautious Bland Committee.

(i) *Administrative Appeals Tribunal Act 1975*. This legislation has a slightly misleading title since it created both the general Administrative

Appeal Tribunal (A.A.T.), and the Administrative Review Council (A.R.C.). Both bodies came into existence and operation in 1976.

The primary task of the A.A.T. is to act as a review body in relation to those categories of administrative decision over which it has been given jurisdiction. (It can only operate in relation to the *federal* administration, not state administrations). Review involves not only the question of whether the original decision was correctly taken, but also a determination, based on the material before the A.A.T., of what is the "correct and preferable" decision.[32]

In some areas, the A.A.T. constitutes a first-tier of appeal from the administration; in other areas (*e.g.* Social Security) it constitutes a second-line of appeal from pre-existing appeal Tribunals. The areas on which the Tribunal has jurisdiction are defined in a Schedule to the parent legislation, which was based, at least initially, on recommendations made by the Bland Committee, rather than (as the Kerr Committee intended), those of the Administrative Review Council.[33] Its jurisdiction has, however, been expanded in a rather ad hoc way, in response to recommendations from the A.R.C.

The A.A.T. is, at present, divided into three divisions (again the result of a recommendation of the Bland Committee) namely, medical appeals, valuation and compensation, and general administrative. (Further divisions may be created, but this has not yet happened.) Thus there is an element of specialisation for medical and valuation issues; otherwise the Tribunal has a broad jurisdiction.

The members of the Tribunal vary considerably in status from "Presidential members" who are judges or qualified lawyers, to "non-presidential members," who are, usually lay persons but with special knowledge or skills. It is possible for a Tribunal to be constituted entirely of non-presidential members.

Notwithstanding the apparent lack of specialist ability to deal with appeals arising in different areas of government, what happens in practice is that when a new area of jurisdiction is opened up, presidential members play an active part. They acquire a feel for the issues that are likely to be raised in the particular area. However once the bulk of the *legal* issues has been resolved, and (hopefully) the decisions, which the A.A.T. is called on to make, have become rather more routinised,

---

[32] See *Drake* v. *Minister for Immigration and Ethnic Affairs* (1979) 2 A.L.D. 60.
[33] See L.J. Curtis "Some Reflections on the Administrative Appeals Tribunal" in *The Workings of the Administrative Appeals Tribunal* (J. Goldring ed, 1979, Canberra Services in Administrative Studies: Seminar Proceedings 4; Canberra College of Advanced Education (mimeo)) at p. 6. Also A.N. Hall & R.K. Todd "Administrative Review before the Administrative Appeals Tribunal: A Fresh Approach to Dispute Resolution?" (1981) 12 *Federal Law Review* 71, 95.

the presidential members tend to be moved on to supervise the development of a new area of jurisdiction.[34]

There has been some doubt as to whether, constitutionally, the Tribunal should be regarded as a *judicial* body, as opposed to an *administrative* body. Certainly from a procedural point of view it has developed a very formal, judicial style of operation—too much so in some critics' view.[35] In part, this is a consequence of the fact that many of the details of its procedure are spelled out in the parent legislation.

One of the significant features of the work of the A.A.T. to date, certainly as compared to the highly fragmented forums for administrative appeal existing in Britain, is that the members of the A.A.T. have developed a clear and conscious awareness of the *general* purpose of their role, namely that they are in being to provide means for accountability and to act as a check and balance to the exercise of state power; they have not simply developed specialist skills in relation to specialist areas of law, as seems by comparison, to have happened in this country.[36] Members of the A.A.T. have, from the outset of their work, adopted a highly "independent" approach, and have frequently criticised the content of legislation, or the work of departmental officials or departmental policies in quite outspoken terms.[37]

(ii) *Administrative Review Council (A.R.C.).*[38] This was also established in 1976, very much on the lines recommended by the Kerr Committee. It is, basically, empowered to establish a constant supervision of administrative procedures and review procedures. It consists of the President of the A.A.T., the (Commonwealth) Ombudsman, the chairman of the (Federal) Law Reform Commission, and up to ten

[34] This certainly seemed to happen after the A.A.T. was given jursidiction over social security matters in 1980: see M. Partington "The Impact of the Administrative Appeals Tribunal on Social Security" (Monash Universiy, Continuing Legal Education, 1983). This specific impression was also supported by observations made to me by Mr. Robert Todd, Senior Member of the A.A.T. in discussions held in Sydney in June 1983.

[35] A point made strongly in the context of Social Security appeals by T. Carney, "Social Security Reviews and Appeals in Australia" (1982) 1 Aust. J. Law and Soc. 32.

[36] For example, when reading Sir Robert Micklethwait's lectures, *The National Insurance Commissioners* (Stevens, 1976), one gets a strong sense of the desire of the commissioners to ensure that particular decisions appealed to them are correct in law; one gets very little sense that the commissioners perceive themselves as having a broader task of ensuring the accountability of social security officials.

[37] See M. Partington, *op. cit.* above, note 34.

[38] The work of the A.R.C. is discussed in J. Griffiths, *Australian Administrative Law: Institutions, Reforms and Impact* (Unpublished paper presented to Australian Studies Centre, October 1984); Dr. Griffiths is Director of Research of the A.R.C. See also their quarterly bulletin *Admin. Review* obtainable from the A.R.C., G.P.O. Box 9955, Canberra, 2601.

others. Its staff includes a research strength, with four full-time research staff, as well as clerical and administrative staff. Annual reports are produced. It thus has a much more positive role to play than the British Councils on Tribunals, and its importance in the structure of federal administrative law is considerably higher than that of the Council on Tribunals.

For example, the A.R.C. monitors the operations and procedures of *all* review agencies, not only the A.A.T. and other review tribunals, but also the Ombudsman and review by the courts. It has issued reports on the work of specialist tribunals (*e.g.* Social Security Appeals Tribunals and the Taxation Boards of Review), which have examined whether they should continue to exist or be replaced by the A.A.T. Further, and equally importantly, it has been exploring the extent to which categories of official decision, which are currently unreviewable in any forum, should be brought within the A.A.T. (See, for example, its current work on immigration decisions.)

The A.R.C. has also been examining wider issues: for example the Council is currently examining the impact that the "new administrative law" has had on government; looking at problems of overlap between the A.A.T.'s jurisdiction and that of the Ombudsman; considering costs before administrative tribunals; and the immunities of statutory authorities.

(iii) *Ombudsman.* The Ombudsman Act was enacted in 1976, and the Ombudsman himself was appointed to office the following year— again very much on the lines advocated by the Kerr Committee. It is clear, from his annual reports, that there is substantial demand for his services (*cf.* the limited use of the Ombudsman in Britain). There is no "M.P. Filter" in Australia; indeed, as Kerr recommended, he is entitled to initiate investigations on his own motion. There is a broad jurisdiction (over federal administrative matters) attached to the office, which was expanded in 1983 to include actions (other than disciplinary proceedings and the grant of honours and awards) taken by a Department or prescribed authority in respect of a person's service in the Defence force.

(iv) *Judicial Review in the Courts.* The whole basis for proceedings for judicial review in the courts was reduced to a single Act of Parliament in 1977; the Administrative Decisions (Judicial Review) Act 1977. It came into force on October 1, 1980.

The Act, first, codifies the grounds on which judicial review may be sought (in the Federal Court of Australia[39]) in a way which either

---

[39] The Federal Court was set up in 1976 under the Federal Court of Australia Act 1976; see, generally, J. Crawford, *Australian Courts of Law* (Oxford U.P., 1982), Chap. 8.

restates or expands the scope of review as developed in the common law. Secondly, it introduces a relatively simple procedure for seeking an order in the court. Thirdly, the Act defines the classes of decisions "of an administrative character" which are susceptible to judicial review (and sets out a long list of exclusions).[40] It also provides a most important statutory right to obtain a statement of reasons for any decision of an administrative character that could be subject to judicial review, even though no proceedings have been started or even con-templated.[41] Reasons must be sought within 28 days of the decision being taken, and must be provided within 28 days of the request. (There are some exceptions, relating to national security and Cabinet deliberations.)[42] 1,800 requests for reasons were made in 1983; 180 applications for orders for review were made in 1983. The figures were both substantially up on those for 1982.[43]

The remedies available are very like those existing in Britain (prohibition, mandamus, certiorari, etc.). And similar problems of standing (who is a "person aggrieved") exist, though Australian jurisprudence on standing is somewhat more liberal than that in the United Kingdom. However, once proceedings have been started, there is a further procedure which enables "persons interested" in the proceedings to be joined to those proceedings.

Initially, there was some difficulty over the meaning of "decision" of an "administrative character." But the Federal Court has taken a broad view of this concept.[44] As a consequence certain categories of decision (*e.g.* personnel management decisions within the public sec-tor, and committal proceedings) have been adjudged within the scope of judicial review which were originally thought to be outside it. The Full Court of the Federal Court has, it appears, deliberately taken a broad view of the Act's ambit so as to bring as wide a range of Federal decision-taking within its ambit as possible.

(v) *Freedom of Information Legislation.* This was enacted in 1982, after further committees had discussed the issue, and it came into force on December 1, 1982. This gives extensive rights to individuals to check the accuracy of information held about them, as well as to others (*e.g.* investigative journalists) interested in digging out official informa-tion for media coverage. If information is shown to be faulty, the

---

[40] See Administrative Decisions (Judicial Review) Act 1977, Sched. 1. The range of exclusions is currently under review by the A.R.C.

[41] *Cf.* the *much* more limited right to a statement of reasons for tribunal decisions only provided in English Law by the Tribunals and Inquiries Act 1971, s.12.

[42] See, further, Administrative Decisions (Judicial Review) Act 1977, Sched. 2.

[43] Figures from Griffiths, *op. cit.* above, note 38.

[44] See *Lamb* v. *Moss* (1983) 49 A.L.R. 533; *Chittick* v. *Ackland* (1984) 53 A.L.R. 143.

person concerned has the right to request amendment of the information. And, all (federal) government agencies are required under the F.O.I. Act to publish information about their activities and powers, the categories of documents in their possession, and any internal manuals and guide books.

Exempt from these provisions are *inter alia*: most Cabinet documents; documents affecting national security; internal working documents; documents relating to law enforcement and public safety; documents affecting personal privacy; documents subject to legal professional privilege or obtained in confidence; and documents relating to business affairs and the national economy.

Figures for the first full year of operation of the legislation show that nearly 20,000 requests were made, spread over 152 agencies. 1105 requests were refused, of which 500 were reviewed internally, 27 were subject of complaint to the Ombudsman and 168 were referred to the A.A.T. The vast majority of requests related to access to personal files of applicants. There was a relatively small number of "commercial user" applications. Charges may be levied for handling of requests of information, but these are not sought where it would cause financial hardship or where a document relates to the applicant's personal affairs. Charges were levied in under 4 per cent. of all requests.[45]

In short, the only measure not legislated, to date, is the proposal for a general administrative code of practice. However it could be argued that this was the least important element in the Kerr Committee's proposals.

IV. *Conclusions*

It will be apparent that from the foregoing description, and bearing in mind the general considerations sketched out in the first two parts of this paper, that the Australian experience does have lessons for us in Britain. What it indicates is that it is *politically* possible for a relatively well structured and coherent body of public law to be created, in a country with a political environment and culture not totally dissimilar to the British, which does not bring Government to a halt by imposing over-bearing administrative burdens, but which, by a variety of channels, does afford greater accountability and, to an extent participation, for the citizens of that country over matters on which the state exerts its decision-taking powers. It is very important to stress the point that, although enacted at different times and coming into effect at different times, the legislative changes that have occurred in Australia are part

---

[45] Figures from Griffiths, *op. cit.* above, note 38.

of an integrated package based, in essence, on the work of the Kerr Committee.

By comparison, discussion in the United Kingdom has been fragmented and disjointed focussing almost exclusively on single issues.[46] The current Justice—All Souls review, although looking at a range of issues has failed (at least in its Interim Report) to take a comprehensive look at any of the range of theoretical questions sketched above. The one earlier proposal, which might have led to a more careful analysis of the issues, that the Law Commissioners should take a broad overall look at our public law, was vetoed by the Lord Chancellor of the day; it is hightime this decision was reversed.[47]

It is not the purpose of this paper to explore the reasons why there has been no successful attempt to create a structured programme of public law reform in Britain. The following suggestions are offered as steps towards an understanding of this lamentable failure in public policy creation:

(a) The Diceyan view of public law which proved so influential is no doubt part of the reason. This has lead to a very narrow and unsatisfactory analysis of the relationship between the law and the executive. The arguments of the late Professor Robson for long went unheeded. Now however the increasing acceptance of the inaccuracy of Dicey's analysis, combined with a burgeoning literature that makes it clear how inadequate traditional perspectives on public law are, suggest[48] that there may be more general changes in attitudes amongst both lawyers and others about the nature of our public law, and the importance of developing realistic concepts of public law.

(b) Related to the above, one can point to the intellectual insularity of public lawyers. With notable exceptions, academic public lawyers have worked from a surprisingly narrow base. They have largely failed to trace the links between propositions of law and broader issues of political theory and political reality which one might have expected would have informed their work.

(c) No doubt much of the reason lies in the extremely sophisticated

---

[46] See, for example, the list of developments set out above, note 2.

[47] It has been suggested that to refer this matter to the Law Commission would not be appropriate. But, it is understood that the immediate past chairman of the Law Commission, Mr. Justice Gibson, was anxious to resurrect the matter in the Commission's programme.

[48] In particular the recent work by H.W. Arthurs, "Rethinking Administrative Law: A Slightly Dicey Business" (1979) 17 Osgoode Hall L.J. 1; "Jonah and the Whale: The Appearance, Disappearance and Re-appearance of Administrative Law" (1980) 30 *Univ. of Toronto Law J.* 225; and other papers cited above, notes 3 and 15.

ability of officials in the public service in protecting their vested interests by arguing that any substantial changes in public law would hinder the government machine, cause extra expense, add to the burden of officials, increase inefficiency and so on.

(d) More speculatively, there may be something in the collective psychology of the British that results in a too easy acceptance of the decisions of those in "authority" and a general feeling that to encourage challenges to that authority would be undesirable, even in some ways improper. Whether or not such an attitude actually exists among the public at large, it undoubtedly suits those who operate the government machine to assume that it does.

(e) Feelings that it is hard to challenge authority may now be enhanced by the trend towards "expert" bureaucracies, whose members have access to a whole range of information that is denied to the ordinary citizen, a problem which makes challenges of official action by the citizen so difficult. Such images of "expertness" are likely to become increasingly apparent now that we are so firmly launched into the era of technological revolution.

(f) A further reason why there has been a lack of success in creating a strategy for public law reform may be the fact that lawyers in the civil service in Britain are regarded, on the whole, as rather narrow technocrats; persons with legal training and thus, possibly, an awareness of the possible merits in greater legal means of accountability over government have not on the whole been in a position to make their voice heard in the public service in the United Kingdom. This is in contrast to their counterparts in Australia, where it seems that there are many more legally-trained administrator public servants.[49]

Despite these, and other possible explanations why there has been no comprehensive examination of the public law system in the United Kingdom, it would seem as though there could be political advantage in these ideas for all the political parties. The Conservatives would, presumably, welcome the creation of mechanisms to keep bureaucrats on their toes and control the extent of their powers. (This was certainly the case with Malcolm Frazer's Liberal (Conservative) party in Australia.) The Labour party has always been keen to seek to defend the rights of individuals against the powerful agencies of the state, which it has itself created. The Liberals would equally want to defend the right of individuals to call the executive to account. And the S.D.P.

---

[49] On this point see the recent lecture by L. Blom-Cooper "Lawyers and Public Administrators: Separate and Unequal" (1984) *Public Law* 215.

has issued a number of policy documents relating to matters discussed in this paper.[50]

Before becoming too carried away with the Australian initiatives, however, at least two caveats must be entered.

First, for all its novelty and attraction, the new system of administrative law in Australia is only a first step towards the creation of what may be considered as a modern system of public law. It addresses only the procedural "power-controlling" aspects of public law, not, directly, the substantive or "power-conferring" aspects. Were the "power-controlling" aspects of public law to be considered more closely in conjunction with its "power-conferring" aspects, there might be a more careful matching of the appropriate means of accountability with the type of issue or decision over which such accountability was being asserted. The failure, to date, to create a code of good administrative practice might then be seen to be more important. There might be developed more flexible or more effective rules regarding the basic duties of public servants, the circumstances in which there should be public liability, more developed principles regarding remedies, and so on. Many of the specific problems of public law that have been identified in the current literature relevant to the United Kingdom remain unresolved, even under the reformed Australian scheme.

Secondly, it has to be recognised that the Australian system *does* impose extra burdens; it *does* cost money; it *does* increase the opportunities for public officials to be rebuked. But, first indications are that the direct costs are not as heavy as sceptics had suggested that they would be, prior to the introduction of the new system. And, in any event, the political argument may be reasserted that, despite the cost, the new system has created the beginnings of a more mature relationship between the public and the executive arm of government; it enhances the control that people feel they have over their lives, and should thus be supported.

Despite these reservations, the development of the "new administrative law" in Australia does provide a base model for the argument that theory and practicality at least to a degree can be merged and thus be utilised as the basis for a more comprehensive reform strategy in the United Kingdom as well. As indicated above, although there is a range of means of accountability in Britain, it is in important respects incoherent and unco-ordinated. Although it is hard to imagine that a single, over-arching, administrative tribunal, on Australian lines could be created in Britain, nevertheless, there may be

---

[50] See, *e.g.* Social Democratic Lawyers' Association, *Government Law and Justice* (S.D.L.A., 1984); and *Taming Leviathan: Towards Fairer Administration* (S.D.P., 1983). See A.J. Boyle, *op. cit.* note 16.

room for greater co-ordination and rationalisation than is currently recognised.[51] Furthermore, the lack of a principled structure for administrative law means that there are no official means for reviewing the range and types of governmental power that is exercised to see whether the forums of accountability in relation to those powers are adequate.[52] Even though it may be symbolic, it is to be hoped that the centenary of the publication of Dicey's classic work, and the publication of this volume, may provide a further impetus to a debate that has been sterile for far too long.

---

[51] For example, the recent amalgamation of National Insurance Local Appeal Tribunals and Supplementary Benefits Appeals Tribunals into a single Social Security Appeal Tribunal under the direction of a President (Health and Social Services and Social Security Adjudications Act 1983) may yet come to be seen as the first step towards the creation of an integrated social welfare tribunal: *cf.* J. Fulbrook, *et. al. Tribunals: A Social Court?* (Fabian Society, 1973).

[52] This lack of principle can be illustrated rather clearly in the context of two recent legislative developments. It is clearly arguable that the kinds of decision which local authorities are required to take under the Housing (Homeless Persons) Act 1977 are ones which warrant review mechanisms. Many issues of fact and law may be involved. Yet the Act contains no structure for redress other than the use which may be be made of the ordinary courts or local political pressures. Again, the review procedures developed for the Housing Benefits scheme do not seem appropriate in relation to the nature of the issues upon which they have to adjudicate: (see, for a preliminary analysis, M. Partington, H. Bolderson and K. Smith, *Housing Benefits Review Boards: a Preliminary Analysis* (Brunel University, 1984).) Accountability in the area of the nationalised industries may be regarded as even more problematic.

INDEX